SPORT CYBERPSYCHOLOGY

Sport Cyberpsychology is the first book devoted to assessing the influence of technology on human interaction, behaviour and mental health in a sport context, gathering research on the use of technology and the Internet by athletes, coaches and sport science support staff.

The book identifies the potential impact of technology on athletes' mental preparation for competition, as well as the role of technology in improving performance. It explores the use of technology by athletes and sport organisations for social interaction, while also considering the 'darker' side of athletes' Internet use.

It covers topics including:

- the role of GPS, gaming and virtual reality in training and injury recovery
- the use of social media by athletes and sport organisations
- the psychology of self-presentation and brand management, as well as issues of online privacy
- the use of technology by other elite groups, such as military and medical personnel, and non-elite sportspeople
- cyberbullying and online harassment of athletes
- online gambling and athletes' mental health in relation to their online activities
- virtual learning environments and the educational opportunities the online world can offer athletes

Accessibly written, with a companion website featuring lecture slides, reading lists, video links and suggested social media accounts, *Sport Cyberpsychology* offers a complete resource for students and instructors alike. It is important reading for any students of sport psychology, sport coaching or sport media, as well as coaches, athletes and sport science support staff.

Olivia A. Hurley is Lecturer in Psychology and Sport Psychology at the Institute of Art, Design + Technology (IADT), Dún Laoghaire, Ireland, and works as a Visiting Assistant Professor in University College Dublin (UCD), Ireland. She is a Chartered Psychologist with the Psychological Society of Ireland (PSI), and a consultant Sport Psychologist with the Sport Ireland Institute. Olivia holds a BSc (Hons) in Psychology, an MSc and a PhD in Sport Psychology from University College Dublin (UCD).

SPORT CYBERPSYCHOLOGY

Olivia A. Hurley

Thanks for your support!
Best wishes,
Olivia
x

Routledge
Taylor & Francis Group

LONDON AND NEW YORK

First published 2018
by Routledge
2 Park Square, Milton Park, Abingdon, Oxon OX14 4RN

and by Routledge
711 Third Avenue, New York, NY 10017

Routledge is an imprint of the Taylor & Francis Group, an informa business

British Library Cataloguing-in-Publication Data
A catalogue record for this book is available from the British Library

Library of Congress Cataloging-in-Publication Data
A catalog record for this book has been requested

ISBN: 978-0-415-78944-8 (hbk)
ISBN: 978-0-415-78945-5 (pbk)
ISBN: 978-1-315-22276-9 (ebk)

Typeset in Bembo
by Apex CoVantage, LLC

Visit the companion website: www.routledge.com/cw/hurley

MIX
Paper from
responsible sources
FSC   FSC™ C013985
www.fsc.org

Printed in the United Kingdom
by Henry Ling Limited

To Mum and Dad, Trish, Dave and Lee
'My Team'

To Granny and Grandad Bolton, to Anto, TJ and Jim
'My Angels'

And, finally, to Matt
'My Guardian Angel', who would have been first in line to get
Sport Cyberpsychology
(We will forever be dancing to 'Pretty Woman' in my head;
I continue to miss you every single day).

CONTENTS

PART III
Sport personnel in the online world   **103**

FOREWORD

Recent years have witnessed increasing popular and scholarly interest in sport psychology or the scientific study of the performance, mental processes and well-being of people who are involved in sport. Within this discipline, cutting edge research investigates how athletes use, and interact psychologically with, technology such as computers, mobile phones, virtual reality devices and gaming consoles. Against this background, it is a great privilege to introduce Olivia Hurley's important book on sport cyberpsychology – an emerging field that explores how sport performers and coaches interact with technology in sport settings. Adopting a theory-to-practice orientation, Olivia skilfully investigates the nature, implications and application of a range of fascinating issues in this field. For example, among the questions that she addresses are the following: Why is it important to study sport in cyberpsychology? What types of technology are commonly used in sport? How does technology affect an athlete's mental preparation? Can virtual reality devices enhance athletic preparation and performance? Can technological innovations (e.g., Skype, FaceTime, webinars) enhance sport psychology consulting? What are the advantages and disadvantages of athletes' engagement with social media? How do sport teams, coaches and organisations use online platforms in their day-to-day activities? What are the most effective strategies to counteract cyberbullying? Finally, can certain types of online behaviour impair an athlete's mental health? In order to enhance discussion of these questions, Olivia includes a number of impressive pedagogical features in her book, such as precise learning objectives, a helpful glossary, case studies and lots of practical exercises. Written in a clear and accessible style, and covering the latest research findings, *Sport Cyberpsychology* is an excellent introduction to a burgeoning field that lies at the interface between sport psychology and cyberpsychology.

Aidan Moran FPsSI, AFBPsS, Reg Psychol, C. Psychol., FAPS
Professor of Cognitive Psychology
University College Dublin

PREFACE

Aims of the book

The purpose of this textbook is to introduce the reader to this new and influential area of study within the discipline of sport psychology, namely that of cyberpsychology within the sport environment.

Athletes, coaches, sport psychologists and other sport scientists, technologists and data analysts are now some of the most prevalent users of technology within their roles, as they strive to perform or assist those they work with to perform to their potential best, often within high-pressure environments. Such individuals specifically use technology to: (i) analyse and assess performances, (ii) assist them in their physical and mental preparation, (iii) help their recovery from injury and/or illness and (iv) interact with spectators, supporters and the media online. The influence of such technology use on sport performances is potentially vast, yet no textbook appears to have gathered together available research findings and information on such topics in order to communicate them to their many interested parties. Therefore, the main aim of this textbook is to provide a solution to this issue and to help bridge the knowledge gap between the sport psychology and cyberpsychology worlds.

The key themes of this text centre around the use of technology by athletes and their surrounding networks of support individuals (e.g., their coaches, physiotherapists, movement analysts, psychologists and medics): (i) to improve their performances, (ii) to communicate with each other and (iii) to identify the potential dangers and risks associated with the use of such technology – mainly the Internet and social media – for athletes' performances, relationships with others and their overall mental health and well-being. No textbook to date appears to have attempted to address such issues in this integrated way, thus highlighting the unique contribution of this textbook to the literature on sport psychology, cyberpsychology, sport science and technology. This text includes some content relevant to other elite groups (e.g., dancers, military, medical personnel) and non-elite populations (e.g., exercisers/hobbyists) in order to appeal to a wide sport and performance audience. This text also uses some of the technology discussed within its chapters to supplement its content. For example, online resources for instructors and students who use this text as a core or supplementary textbook within their programme are available. PowerPoint materials, online article and journal resources, video links and relevant Twitter accounts are available/are suggested, along with some discussion/essay based questions and Multiple Choice Questions. These additional online materials complement the sport cyberpsychology theme of the text.

Structure of the book

This book is organised into four sections. This structure is considered appropriate, as it allows the reader to be introduced to the relevant topics first, before progressing to more detailed sections which address specific psychology and technology issues relevant first for the athletes, followed by their consultants and then for the wider sport network surrounding them (i.e., their coaches, clubs and organisations). The first section (Chapters 1 and 2) introduces the reader to the key disciplines and new technologies available within sport environments. The second section (Chapters 3 to 5) identifies the uses and impact of technology on athletes preparing for their sport. For example, it details the use of global positioning system (GPS), gaming devices and virtual reality (VR) technologies to help athletes train and complete in their sport. It also addresses the use of new technologies by other elite non-sport groups (e.g., the military, the arts and medical personnel). The third section (Chapters 6 to 8) then specifically explores athletes' and sport organisations' uses of technologies for social interaction online. Athletes, support team personnel and team organisations extensively use social media platforms such as Twitter, Facebook, YouTube and Instagram to communicate, recruit and promote themselves. The psychology of self-presentation, brand management and privacy issues surrounding such individual and group interactions online are discussed in this section. The final, fourth section of the book (Chapters 9 and 10) considers the darker side of sport cyberpsychology. These two chapters address the risks associated with athletes' use of social media, and the Internet in general. Cyberbullying, online harassment, problematic gambling and gaming, as related to athletes, are explored within these final two chapters.

This text also uses a number of key features to engage the reader's attention. Each chapter includes a case study at the start of the chapter to stimulate some thinking in relation to the topics being presented in that chapter and to provide readers with real-life examples to which they can apply a theory they are studying, for example. Definitions of relevant terms are provided at the start of each chapter also, in a mini glossary. Each chapter also concludes with a number of open-ended questions designed to promote discussion among students studying this new area of sport cyberpsychology. Lecturers and academic staff can make use of such questions in their classes in order to help their students engage with the content of this textbook. Each chapter also ends with a practical exercise, which will hopefully encourage some applied activities related to the content of the chapter.

ACKNOWLEDGEMENTS

This book would not have been possible without the help and support of a number of individuals. I would first like to thank my long-time mentor and 'academic dad', Professor Aidan Moran (UCD), for agreeing to write the foreword for this, my first solo book. Aidan, your constant encouragement and support have enabled me to reach this place in my career today. So many opportunities have come my way because of you, so thank you! I would also like to thank some specific colleagues in IADT, Dr Irene Connolly and Dr Grainne Kirwan, who helped me to believe I was ready to take on this first solo book project – your work ethic is a model for all in our field of Psychology. To Dr Annie Doona, our IADT President and Dr Andrew Power, our IADT Registrar – thank you both for always recognising my passion for my discipline of sport psychology and for helping me to achieve some of my greatest career goals to date. Your leadership is inspiring.

I would like to thank my editors at Routledge, Will Bailey and Rebecca Connor, and my copy editor, Holly Smithson at Apex CoVantage. Thank you all for your kind words and patience with me, when I needed it most! Thank you for placing your faith in me and for your willingness to take on this project. I will always be grateful for your help in bringing this passion project to life. Thank you also to Inpho Photography and Ruth Barry in IADT for providing me with a number of great images for *Sport Cyberpsychology*.

To my extended family, the Boltons: Maureen, Leo, Margaret, Claire and Jenny (and all the kiddies, including my godson Adam); to the Hurleys, especially Kay, 'Big' Cathal and 'Little' Cathal; to my brother-in-law Paul(ie) Cronin; and to my many cousins – thank you all for your unfailing love and support in my career and life to date – it is something I never take for granted.

To my dear friends, Margaret (Mags) O'Halloran, Deirdre (De) Gallagher, Breda Kiely, Paula Mee, Cliona Flood, John Fagan and Joan Cahill, as well as all of the McGuirk family and Kay Nolan. Thank you for always being there, for great chats and messages of support constantly, via all kinds of media, during this past year especially as I worked on this passion project. I am so lucky to have such great friends in my life, whom I consider to be really a part of my extended family too.

Thank you to all of the staff of IADT, especially my academic colleagues (and top of that list: Dr Andrew Errity and Mr Stefan Paz Berrios) and the wonderful caretaking staff, as well as all of my IADT psychology students and graduates. Thank you also to my academic friends in University College Dublin, the University of Limerick and the Royal College of Surgeons in Ireland, as well as all my pals in David Lloyd Club, Riverview and on Facebook too. Your constant interest in my work and my sport-inspired life is much appreciated. It helps to keep me motivated on a daily basis.

And, finally, to 'my team', Mum, Dad, Trish, Dave and Lee. No words can express my love for you five people. You are my heroes, the ones I know I can turn to at any time, who are always there, always willing to listen, to laugh, to support, to hug, to help, to guide and to love me unconditionally. I am so lucky to have you all in my life. I am so proud to be your daughter/sister. You all inspire me every day. I am the person I am, achieving my life goals, because of you. You are my oxygen, the air beneath my wings – I can only 'fly', because you are all there, beneath me, holding me up.

ABBREVIATIONS

AASP	Association for Applied Sport Psychology
ABC	American Broadcasting Company
APA	American Psychological Association
AR	Augmented Reality
BBC	British Broadcasting Corporation
BPS	British Psychological Society
FA	Football Association
FAI	Football Association of Ireland
GAA	Gaelic Athletic Association
GB	Great Britain
IRFU	Irish Rugby Football Union
IT	Information Technology
JETS	Jockeys Education and Training Scheme
MUFC	Manchester United Football Club
PR	Public Relations
PSI	Psychological Society of Ireland
QE	Quiet Eye
RPI	Rugby Players Ireland
USA	United States of America
USADA	United States Anti-Doping Agency
USSR	Union of Soviet Socialist Republics
VR	Virtual Reality
WADA	World Anti-Doping Agency
WiFi	Wireless

PART I

Introducing sport
cyberpsychology

1

WHAT IS SPORT CYBERPSYCHOLOGY?

CASE STUDY 1

Patricia is an accredited sport psychologist working with an elite group of young golfers aged between 18 and 24 years. Patricia is preparing a session for these young golfers, to discuss their uses of technology as part of their training and competition routines for their sport. Patricia hopes this session will increase these players' awareness of the role technology plays in both their sport and non-sport lives. Patricia will direct some of the discussion with these young golfers toward topics related to the potential psychological impact that various types of new technology within golf may have on these golfers' performances.

(i) What new technologies could be important for Patricia to discuss during this session with these young golfers?

(ii) Identify some of the psychological issues that may arise for these golfers, as they discuss this topic on the impact of new technologies used as part of their preparations for their sport of golf?

(iii) How could Patricia ethically use the information the players share during this session to develop guidelines for other athletes in other sports she works in, on how they too might effectively manage their use of technology within and indeed outside of their sport environment so that it could facilitate rather than debilitate their performances?

1.1 Overview

This chapter introduces the disciplines of sport psychology and cyberpsychology to the reader. It explains, in brief, the historical pathways of both disciplines. It also presents a rationale for considering this new, combined area of sport cyberpsychology study that brings sport psychology and cyberpsychology together under one heading, in order to create an exciting area of research and applied focus for sport psychologists and cyberpsychologists alike.

1.2 Learning objectives

1   To introduce this new discipline of sport cyberpsychology
2   To identify and define key terms related to sport cyberpsychology
3   To provide brief histories of sport psychology and cyberpsychology
4   To highlight some key developments within these disciplines of sport psychology and cyberpsychology that have led to interest in sport cyberpsychology being considered as a new, worthy area of theoretical and practical psychological study in the future

1.3 Definitions of relevant terms

Cyberpsychology

The branch of psychology that examines how people interact with each other when using technology. It includes an examination of how technology developers might be able to create the best possible technologies in order to meet the needs and demands of their users (known as Human Computer Interaction, or HCI). How technology influences the behaviours and mental states of its users is also of interest to cyberpsychologists.

Exercise psychology

The study of mental processes and behaviours within exercise and health settings.

Green exercise

The study of how exercise activities completed outdoors, within natural environments, may benefit the health and well-being of participants.

Performance psychology

The study of psychological principles applied to the performances of individuals not typically referred to as athletes, but whose performances also include demanding physical and cognitive elements. Such performers include dancers, medical personnel (e.g., surgeons), members of the military and defence forces (e.g., police force and army personnel) as well as other emergency service specialists, such as firefighters and rescue workers.

Sport cyberpsychology

The proposed new study of human interaction with technologies, including the Internet, mobile phones, games consoles and virtual reality devices, specifically within sport settings. This area of study could include consideration of the impact, both positively and negatively, of technological advances, on the mental states of athletes using these technologies within their sport environments.

Sport psychology

The area of psychology which examines the principles of psychology within sport settings. Psychology is often defined as a study of mental processes. Within sport psychology, the mental processes of athletes typically are studied in order to determine how they may impact on these athletes' performances within their sport.

1.4 A short introduction to sport psychology and cyberpsychology

Sport psychology can be considered the discipline of psychology which applies psychological theories, and methods, in order to understand the performances and mental processes of individuals involved in sport participation (Moran, 2012; Moran & Toner, 2017). Sport psychology has been described as one of the most rapidly growing areas of psychological investigation, with the potential to significantly impact a large number of individuals (Attrill, 2015). Cyberpsychology may be considered perhaps the only other sub-discipline of psychology that has had a greater impact on the daily lives of individuals within the past 20 years (Attrill, 2015). These two points alone could explain the recent spark of interest within the psychological community, and indeed, within the general public at large, in these two exciting and influential areas of psychological investigation, but in combination, rather than in isolation. A logical question to follow from such interest could then be: what should the focus of *sport cyberpsychology*, as a new discipline, be? This question will be explored, and hopefully answered, within the ten chapters of this new textbook, *Sport Cyberpsychology*.

1.4.1 Sport cyberpsychology – a working definition

Based upon the definitions of sport psychology and cyberpsychology at the beginning of this chapter, sport cyberpsychology could be considered the study of human interaction with technologies, including the Internet, mobile phones, games consoles and virtual reality, within sport settings. In recent years many athletes, their coaches and their support personnel (such as their physiotherapists and strength and conditioning personnel) have introduced an array of new technologies into the athletic environment, in order help improve the training and competition performances of their elite participants. It would be fair to say that such technological developments have resulted in many anecdotal, and some empirical (although somewhat lacking), reports of positive effects being recorded as a result of such technology use, both on the training methods and performance outcomes of many athletes. However, an awareness that these technologies may also result in, or have the potential to affect, the individuals using them in negative ways too should also prevail. As Dr Brenda Wiederhold stated,

> Technology, as opined by Carl Jung, is neutral. It is how we use that tech-
> nology that determines whether it will be positive or negative. On the
> positive side, we now see technology offering new opportunities for sci-
> entific research to be conducted more efficiently, social isolation relieved
> by networking tools and healthcare transitioned into the home and office.
> On the negative side, we see Internet gaming addiction, cyberbullying and
> cybercrime.
>
> *(cited in the Foreword of* An Introduction to Cyberpsychology
> *by Connolly, Palmer, Barton, & Kirwan, 2016)*

The various impacts of new technologies on the mental states of elite athletes, and indeed on all of the sport participants using them (i.e., novice and recreational athletes/exercisers), have remained largely unexplored from an empirical position. Searches for relevant research findings in peer-reviewed journals and texts exam-ining such issues uncovered this lack of consideration on the part of psychology researchers regarding these topics during the writing of this textbook, *Sport Cyber-psychology*. As a result, the potential positive, and negative, psychological effects of technology use within the world of sport will be the main focus of the material explored within the chapters of this new textbook.

However, in order to fully understand how sport psychology and cyberpsy-chology may come together to create this new and exciting area of psychological study, a necessary start is perhaps to give the reader an understanding of these two separate fields of psychology (sport psychology and cyberpsychology) in isolation first. From that position, an appreciation for how these two areas might then unite under a combined heading of new academic exploration may become apparent.

1.4.2 What is sport psychology?

Sport psychology, as defined at the beginning of this chapter, is generally regarded as the study of mental process and behaviours of individuals within sport set-tings. Included in those 'individuals' are coaches, managers, support personnel and spectators/fans, as well as the athletes themselves (Moran, 2012; Moran & Toner, 2017). A related area of psychology, namely *exercise psychology*, can be considered the examination of such mental processes and behaviours among non-elite, novice and recreational participants, who take part in physical, and sport, activities for predominantly health-related benefits. Research studies in such exercise contexts often focus on the impact of exercise on the physical and psychological well-being of the participants. One current 'hot' topic of study within exercise psychology is that of *green exercise*. This term refers to the activity of exercising within natural environments (for example, by the sea or in parks) and the impact of such exercise on participants' physical and mental health (for a review of this area of psychologi-cal study, see Donnelly et al., 2016, and GoGreenEx, 2017). Another area of study linked to sport and exercise psychology is *performance psychology*. This area will now be explained as it relates in some ways to content presented in some of the later chapters of this text.

1.4.3 What is performance psychology?

Performance psychology, as previously stated, has been linked in recent times to the areas of psychological study, sport and exercise psychology. This trend has led to a number of newly formed postgraduate programmes being established at various academic institutions (for example, at the University of Limerick in Ireland). Such third-level study has enabled students of psychology to study all three related disciplines of sport, exercise and performance psychology in greater depth within the one course. One justification for the bringing together of these three separate sub-disciplines of psychology has been their common theme of studying behaviours within elite and/or physically demanding performance settings. Kavussanu (2017), the new editor of the APA's peer-reviewed journal, *Sport, Exercise and Performance Psychology* (SEPP), wrote a recent review of the journal's accomplishments in contributing to academic research within psychology, while also outlining some areas for greater research consideration across these three disciplines. In this review, Kavussanu (2017) expressed a desire to see more research studies carried out within the performance psychology area specifically.

Performance psychology, as described by Martin (2012), is the examination of human performance across a wide spectrum of performance arenas, including the performing arts (i.e., dancers, artists and actors), the military or 'defense forces', and those from the medical profession, such as surgeons and doctors. Many of these performers are often asked to work or 'perform' within elite, life-saving, high-pressure environments. Such environments involve a necessity for high performance, with fine psychomotor skills and abilities required in order for positive outcomes to be derived (similar to the performance environments that athletes also partake in for their sport disciplines; Kavussanu, 2017; Martin, 2012). While this text on sport cyberpsychology briefly refers to these other populations of 'performers' (for example, within Chapter 4, which explores the use of virtual reality (VR) technology within such elite settings), performance cyberpsychology will not be the main focus of the material included because, as Kavussanu (2017) alluded to, there remains a need to increase the specific research offerings within this area. As such, it was considered too difficult, and too large an undertaking at the outset, for this text to focus on presenting material from both the sport and performance psychology research area while also considering it from the perspective of the cyber world. Therefore, the title for this text, of *Sport Cyberpsychology*, was considered more appropriate in this case. With that in mind, the main areas of study within sport psychology, first, as a stand-alone discipline, are presented next.

1.5 What is studied within sport psychology?

Having presented a definition of sport psychology as an area of academic and applied study, the question of what specifically is studied within sport psychology is a valid follow-on question. A number of popular topics of interest to sport psychologists in their research, and applied work, with athletes and others within the sport setting (such as coaches and spectators) are outlined in the following sections. Topics such as mental fitness, mental skills training and various applied mental strategies are highlighted, before a brief explanation of the history of the discipline of sport psychology is presented.

1.5.1 Mental fitness and mental skills training

Mental fitness may be defined as the way in which individuals use their mental resources and skills in order to advance, or overcome challenges they face, thus enabling them to thrive within their environments. This definition implies four principles: (i) that fitness is a positive term, without connotations of illness; (ii) that mental fitness can be understood by the wider community in a similar way to that of physical fitness; (iii) that mental fitness is, in some ways, measurable; and (iv) that mental fitness can be improved upon, again in a similar way to how physical fitness can be improved, using through various training procedures (Robinson, Oades, & Caputi, 2014).

A number of mental skills have been associated with this term of 'mental fitness'. They are often the focus of much of the applied work engaged in by many sport psychologists, in order to train the individuals they work with in how to improve their mental skills. This is perhaps why the term *mental skills training* has become popular for use within such contexts (Sharp, Woodcock, Holland, Cumming, & Duda, 2013). These mental skills are often considered to include skills such as concentration skills and coping or control skills, for example (Holland, Woodcock, Cumming, & Duda, 2010). These mental skills will now be explained.

1.5.2 Concentration

Individuals who may question if concentration is really a 'skill' might consider the following scenarios: Have you ever been engaged in the task of reading a book, only to find that you have been looking at the same sentence on the page for a few seconds and yet your thoughts have been directed elsewhere? Have you ever walked into a room to retrieve an item, only to find that when you reached the room you had forgotten what it was you went into the room to retrieve in the first place? If you have ever experienced either, or indeed both, of these scenarios in your daily life, then you have experienced what is referred to within cognitive psychology (which is the study of mental processes; see Moran & Toner, 2017, and Neisser, 1967) as a 'cognitive failure'. This 'failure' is sometimes more commonly referred to in everyday language as having 'lost your concentration'. In reality, concentration is never really 'lost', rather it may become *misdirected*, and thankfully, various strategies can be used to enable it to be 'found', or directed appropriately onto the task at hand once again (Moran & Toner, 2017).

For athletes, being able to maintain their focus or attention (both of which are applied here to mean the same thing as concentration, as cited earlier), on a task they are completing at any one moment in time in their sport, is very important.

Such focus is required in order for them to achieve the peak performances within their sport they typically strive for (Durand-Busch, Salmela, & Green-Demers, 2001; Northcroft, 2009). Ironically, athletes' concentration, or focus, is more likely to become misdirected during times of high pressure or stress (Ingle, 2008; Newman, 2015; Staph, 2011). Such times often typify the competition and even the training environments of such athletes. Therefore, it is little surprise to hear that seeking out ways to improve their concentration may often be one of the most popular reasons why athletes seek out the services of a sport psychologist in the first place (Moran & Toner, 2017).

1.5.3 Coping

Another mental skill considered important for athletes to master is that of being able to cope with the often stressful situations they find themselves in when taking part in their sport. Athletes often report feeling nervous or anxious before they compete in important sport events, and for some athletes, such nerves can be debilitating to their performances (e.g., USA gymnast, Alicia Sacramore, cited in Ingle, 2008). Interestingly, other athletes appear to be able to 'relabel' such nerves in a positive way in order for them to facilitate their performances (e.g., British tennis player, Andy Murray, cited in Mitchell, 2010; also see Mahoney & Avener, 1977). Having some mental strategies to call upon in order to control, or help athletes reinterpret, their feelings of nervousness, so that they can then perform to their potential, is again the basis of much of the research and applied work many sport psychologists engage in with their athletes (Moore, Wilson, Vine, Coussens, & Freeman, 2013). Strategies such as relaxation techniques and self-talk management (or thought-control techniques) are often advocated by sport psychology practitioners in order to help athletes cope with the various situations they face during important and demanding events within their sport setting. Although the empirical evidence regarding the effectiveness of such strategies is somewhat mixed (see Moran & Toner, 2017, for an in-depth review of these strategies), anecdotal reports from athletes do appear to support their use of such strategies in aiding their performances (Sharp et al., 2013), therefore, a number of the mental strategies reported to be of practical benefit to athletes are discussed in the following section.

1.6 Mental strategies used by athletes

As previously remarked, sport psychologists often, based on available positive empirical research evidence, suggest a number of mental strategies for their athlete clients to use in order to assist these athletes in their quest to improve their concentration and coping skills (Moran & Toner, 2017). These strategies often include goal setting, self-talk management, relaxation techniques, mental imagery, routines and simulation training, as well as newer strategies currently being explored to determine their effectiveness, such as resilience training (Fletcher & Sarkar, 2012; Sarkar &

Fletcher, 2013) and brain-training techniques (Hardy, Nelson, Thomason, & Sternberg, 2015). Technological advances now influence how athletes apply these strategies. For example, many web applications (commonly referred to as 'apps') are now available to athletes, to facilitate the recording and tracking of their goals. Apps may also assist athletes with relaxation and mental imagery exercises, while also enabling them to receive frequent reminders of their positive self-talk phrases, for example. The details of such apps, used to help athletes practice and apply the various mental strategies cited above, are discussed in more detail in Chapters 3 and 4 of this text. For now, an explanation of each of these applied mental strategies, as advocated by many applied sport psychologists, and the athletes they work with, is provided, starting with goal setting.

1.6.1 Goal setting

Goal setting involves the setting of targets, in order to achieve an aim or an objective (Locke, Shaw, Saari, & Latham, 1981). The effectiveness of goal setting, as a technique that can improve performance, has been studied across many different performance domains, including organisational or workplace settings (Locke & Latham, 1985). Such target or goal setting is thought to encourage and enable individuals, such as athletes participating in sport, to focus on tasks they are completing at specific points in time. Such goal setting appears to help athletes to remain *present*, or to be *task-focused*, rather than focusing on past or future events. Focusing on past or future events can result in athletes making costly sport performance errors in their skill execution in the *present* time (e.g., Irish athlete, Sonia O'Sullivan, cited in Curtis, 2000). One famous case of costly 'future thinking' by an athlete (such thinking could also be regarded as an internal or mental distractor; see Moran & Toner, 2017) is that of the golfer, Doug Sanders, who famously missed a putt of less than 3 feet. Had his putt been successful, Sanders would have won the 1970 British Open Championship. After the event, Sanders reported that as he was taking the putt, he was thinking "which section of the crowd I was going to bow to!" (cited in Gilleece, 1996). This error in his thought process, away from the task of the actual putt and onto the future task of bowing to the crowd, resulted in Sanders not only missing out on the opportunity to win his first major golf prize, but also losing approximately £10 million in prize money and endorsement contracts. Therefore, the goal of staying *task-focused* is one many athletes strive to achieve.

The ways in which athletes set such goals often follow some simple acronyms, such as the SMART principle of goal setting (Bull, Albinson, & Shambrook, 1996). This principle outlines how the goals that athletes set should be Specific, Measurable, Action-based, Realistic and Time-phased in order for them to be effective (Bull et al., 1996). Other variations of this SMART principle include the SCAMP principle, where the acronym represents how athletes' goals should be Specific, Challenging, Agreed, Measureable and Personal (see Kremer & Moran, 2013, for details of this goal-setting principle). Of course, goal setting is not the only mental strategy athletes may use to help them achieve optimal or outstanding sport performances. Another popular strategy is that of self-talk management.

1.6.2 Self-talk management

Self-talk management refers to the mental strategy of athletes managing, or controlling, their 'inner voice' – that conversation they have inside their own heads. This 'conversation' relates to their thought processes and often involves them using trigger words to direct their thinking onto specific actions, or skills, relevant to their sport performances (Kremer & Moran, 2013). When an individual's self talk is positive or instructional, it has the power to facilitate performance, according to those who use the technique such as golfer Rory McIlroy, who reported using trigger words to help him achieve his success at the 2014 Open Golf Championship (Corrigan, 2014). Tennis player, Serena Williams (Figure 1.1), also advocates this strategy, as she was seen reading key words from cue cards during breaks in play in her match against her sister, Venus, at the 2002 Wimbledon Tennis Championship (Williams, 2002).

An athlete's negative self talk, however, can have a debilitating impact on performance; therefore, athletes often try to avoid such thoughts (Day, 2015). Learning how to control their inner voice is one way an athlete may achieve greater mental fitness and more consistency in reaching their sport goals. However, 'nerves' may disrupt their thought processes, so having some relaxation strategies, to help them remain calm in high-pressure situations they experience within their sport, is also advocated.

1.6.3 Relaxation techniques

The *relaxation techniques* athletes often use include Progressive Muscular Relaxation (PMR) and deep, or diaphragmatic, breathing. These two relaxation techniques have been shown to be somewhat effective in facilitating the sport performances of athletes, by helping them to remain calm when they are experiencing feelings of pressure within their sport setting (Kelly, 1998; Williams, 2010). Many mobile phone apps claim to assist their users in the practice of such relaxation techniques. These apps, and their claims, will be reviewed as part of the content presented in Chapters 3 and 4 of this text.

1.6.4 Mental imagery

Mental imagery has been defined as "an internal representation that gives rise to the experience of perception in the absence of the appropriate sensory input" (Wraga & Kosslyn, 2002, p. 466), or as Moran (2012) stated "seeing with the mind's eye" (p. 168). Athletes across many different team and individual sports, such as swimming (Phelps, 2008) and soccer (Wayne Rooney, cited in Watson, 2012), widely

FIGURE 1.1 USA tennis player, Serena Williams, uses trigger words to help her perform well in her sport

Source: Courtesy of Pexels.

report using metal imagery in order to facilitate their performances (see MacIntyre et al., 2013, for an expert statement on the use of mental imagery in sport, exercise and rehabilitation contexts). Again, many apps have been designed to assist users in the use of this mental technique and again are the focus of some discussion later in this text (see Chapters 3 and 4).

1.6.5 Routines

Establishing routines can be an effective way for athletes to manage their training and competition schedules. Such routines have also been reported as effective concentration and coping strategies for athletes to use just before they complete certain sport skills. Often referred to as *pre-performance routines* (PPRs), these routines commonly involve a series of actions and thoughts the athletes engage in before completing a skill, for example, taking a penalty kick in sports such as rugby or soccer (Moran & Toner, 2017; see Figure 1.2).

PPRs have been reported to help athletes focus on their sport skills, while also helping them avoid becoming distracted (by past or future thoughts, for example, as happened to golfer Doug Sanders) or from *choking* (a term which refers to athletes producing less than optimal performances, when subjected to intense stress – as is often the case for many athletes within elite sport settings; see Baumeister & Showers, 1986). Technological advances to improve the PPRs that athletes execute within their sport are discussed in greater detail in Chapter 4, where the uses of virtual reality (VR) technology for such performance benefits are explored.

1.6.6 Simulation training

Simulation training involves the creation of situations within an athlete's training environment that mimic, as closely as possible, the competition environment of the athlete. Such simulations appear to best prepare athletes when they involve as many of the sense organs as is possible (for example, the sights, sounds, tastes and smells of the environment, as well as the kinesthetic, or 'feel' elements, of the setting). Incorporating such elements is considered to help the simulation appear 'real' for the athlete. Although some athletes, and coaches, have advocated for the effectiveness of such simulated training methods (Casey, 2011; US golfer Jordon Spieth's coach Cameron McCormick, cited in Hoggard, 2015), others, such as former Munster, Ireland, and Lions rugby player, Ronan O'Gara, have commented that it is very difficult to recreate the competition setting using such simulation environments in training (cited in Fanning, 2002). The jury remains 'out' regarding this issue, however, the possibility of a *transfer effect* taking place is worthy of more investigation in order to determine why many coaches and athletes, who employ such training, report some performance benefits (see Moran & Toner, 2017). Technological advances have enabled such simulated environments to be made more 'real-like' using, for example, virtual and augmented reality devices and simulations (Hoffman et al., 2011). Such technological advances, that

FIGURE 1.2 Irish rugby player, Ian Madigan, going through his pre-kicking preparations before taking a penalty kick

Source: Courtesy of Inpho Photography, with thanks to Irish rugby player, Ian Madigan.

could provide evidence of empirically based improvements in athletes' performances using such simulated techniques, are discussed in greater detail in Chapter 4.

1.6.7 Resilience training

In addition to the preceding strategies of goal setting, self-talk management, mental imagery, PPRs and simulation training, a specific type of mental skills training, known as *resilience training*, is also becoming popular within sport and performance environments. Resilience is described broadly as the ability of individuals to overcome barriers and failures in order to achieve their goals (see Sarkar & Fletcher, 2013, 2017a, 2017b, for a more detailed review of this area of research). A number of characteristics of resilient athletes, such as Olympic champions who have achieved sport successes despite past disappointments, have been studied and identified (Fletcher & Sarkar, 2012). Given the rise in references to this concept within the sport psychology research literature recently, how it could also be applied using technological measurement tools is explored in Chapters 3 and 4 of this text.

On a final note in this section, the question of how sport psychologists could become somewhat more certain that the mental strategies they advocate, as previously described, for use by their client athletes in order to improve their mental skills and overall sport performances, may be answered by considering some new technological measurement advances. Often self-report measures and qualitative methods are used within sport psychology research studies to attempt to determine the effectiveness of such mental strategies and techniques (Evans & Hardy, 2002; Gucciardi, Gordon, & Dimmock, 2009; Sharp et al., 2013). However, two recent technological developments that may help researchers to potentially achieve more reliable and objective measures, for the uses and effectiveness of such mental strategies and techniques, are now presented.

1.7 Measuring mental skills and strategies using technology – an introduction

Some technological advances have begun to provide sport psychologists with some objective ways of measuring the mental skills and strategies previously outlined in brief, rather than relying solely on the self-report measurements or using qualitative, interviewing and focus group methodologies. *Eye-tracking* and *brain-training* technologies are two such examples of how technology is now being used in psychological research studies to more objectively reconcile athletes' measurable behaviours, such as their eye gaze and brain activity, when watching or completing various sport-related skills, with their overall sport performances in the real-world context.

Eye-tracking technology (for a review, see Duchowski, 2007) enables researchers to use specially fitted cameras on goggles worn by the athletes to 'track' their eye gazes or 'fixations', and then measure the time the athletes spend 'fixated' on certain stimuli presented to them related to their sport environments (Vickers, 2007). This eye-tracking technology has been used quite extensively within the cognitive sport psychology research domain to date, particularly in the study of expert–novice differences and concentration (Moore, Vine, Freeman, & Wilson, 2012; Wilson & Pearcy, 2009). Eye-tracking technology, and the specific research findings in relation to its use, is detailed further in Chapters 2 and 3 of this text.

Brain-training devices have also become popular as technologies used within sport environments to potentially enhance athletes' performances, while also providing potentially more objective measures of their mental skills. Brain-training devices claim to measure the brain activity of athletes during various sport tasks and, with practice, may help to increase the athletes' mental fitness levels (Hardy et al., 2015). However, recently, companies that created such gaming devices and made claims regarding their ability to prevent, for example, cognitive decline in various populations, have been the subject of costly legal cases. A number of these companies were fined for making false claims in their advertising regarding the effectiveness of their products (Gallegos, 2017). Specific research findings on the uses and potential effectiveness of such brain-training devices within sport settings (Coutts, 2016; Smith et al., 2015) are presented in Chapter 3.

Having explained, in brief, various mental skills and strategies frequently used by sport psychologists in their applied work with their athlete clients, an understanding of the context in which such strategies emerged for use by such sport-based practitioners could be of interest to the reader. As such, a brief historical journey, mapping out the emergence of the discipline of sport psychology as a worthy sub-discipline of study within psychology, is provided next.

1.8 A brief historical overview of sport psychology

A generally agreed 'start point' for the discipline of sport psychology, in an academic sense, dates back to 1897–98, when a researcher by the name of Norman Triplett completed a study with some cyclists to determine if social facilitation (that is, the potential advantage of having other people in the same environment as a person while he/she is attempting to complete a specific task) occurred within their training and competition environments. The results of Triplett's (1898) study indicated that the participant cyclists did indeed appear to exert more effort in their cycling task (to get from a point A to a point B as fast as possible) when they completed the task as part of a group, rather than when they completed the task alone as individual cyclists.

Following on from this start point by Triplett, over 30 years later, Colman Robert Griffiths is credited with setting up the first dedicated sport psychology laboratory at the University of Illinois in 1925. However, this facility did not survive the American Great Depression (1929–39). Griffith's laboratory was closed down in 1932 and sport psychology, as a formal area of academic study, did not substantially re-emerge until another 40 years later, in the 1960s, when a number of developments facilitated the reawakening of interest in this sub-discipline of psychology (Moran & Toner, 2017). The first noteworthy development to take place was the space race between the USA and the then Union of Soviet Socialist Republics (USSR; also sometimes shortened to the Soviet Union). The interest of some researchers became focused on how astronauts were being trained to cope with the challenges of travelling into space. Mental skills and mental fitness, as explained earlier, appeared to be very relevant in such environments (Moran, 2008). A second development of note, which occurred around that time, was the emergence of cognitive psychology, described previously (Neisser, 1967), as a sub-discipline of psychology, with key topics of interest to its researchers being memory, concentration, mental imagery and decision making, all of which lent themselves well to study within sport settings.

Following on from these significant developments, in 1965, the International Society of Sport Psychology (ISSP) was established. It held its first congress in Rome that same year. This congress ignited the founding of other similar societies such as the Fédération Européenne de Psychologie des Sport et des Activités Corporelles (FEPSAC) and the Association for the Advancement of Applied Sport

Psychology (AAASP; now known as the Association of Applied Sport Psychology (AASP); Moran & Toner, 2017). These events occurred during the 1970s and 1980s. One of the most significant publications within sport psychology emerged in 1986, namely, the first edition of the peer-reviewed and high-impact journal (still today), *The Sport Psychologist*. Along with it, the foundation of Division 47, the specialist division of sport psychology (which includes 'exercise' in its name today), within the American Psychological Association (APA), occurred. Throughout the 1990s and 2000s many other sport psychology journals were first published, along with the inclusion of exercise and performance psychology in the names of various societies already devoted to the study of sport psychology. In 2012, the APA's specialist Division 47 published the first issue of its journal titled *Sport, Exercise and Performance Psychology*. For a more detailed account of the history of sport psychology, see Green and Benjamin (2009); Moran and Toner (2017); and Schinke, McGannon, and Smith (2016).

Having provided a brief outline of the discipline, topics of interest and history of sport psychology, the next question one might pose is: How does cyberpsychology, as a sub-discipline of psychology, compare to sport psychology? A similar exploration of cyberpsychology is now provided in order to answer this question.

1.9 What is cyberpsychology?

Cyberpsychology, as mentioned earlier, could be considered one of the newest areas, or sub-disciplines of study within modern psychology, along with sport psychology (Attrill, 2015). It is considered to have emerged as a separate discipline of psychology due to the increase in technological developments seen in recent years.

Cyberpsychology is defined as the study of how humans interact with technology, including mobile phone devices, smart technologies and virtual reality, to name but a few examples (Kirwan, 2016). The first programme to specifically offer cyberpsychology as a distinct discipline of academic study appears to have been established at the Institute of Art, Design + Technology (IADT) in Dún Laoghaire in Dublin, Ireland, in 2007. This was followed by the establishment of other similar programmes at postgraduate level, for example in England (Nottingham Trent University and the University of Wolverhampton) and also at undergraduate level in the United States of America (for example, at Norfolk University in Virginia). The entertainment media has also capitalised on the increased interest in this area of study, as was evident by the creation of a new addition to the 'Crime Scene Investigation' (CSI) on the CBS Television Broadcasting Network franchise titled 'CSI Cyber'. This series of fictional crime investigations starred well-established television and movie actors as the main characters in the show (Andreeva, 2016). The series ran for two seasons before being concluded in 2016. With this move in creating such an entertainment offering, the television industry gave recognition to this increase in interest in cyberpsychology from the point of view of the general public, as well as from the point of view of psychology's own professional academics, interested in studying it from a more empirical perspective. An overview of the history of cyberpsychology (which is brief, considering how recent its establishment as a sub-discipline of psychology itself has been) is now provided.

1.10 A brief historical overview of cyberpsychology

Compared to sport psychology, cyberpsychology could be considered very much in its infancy, having only emerged as a sub-discipline of psychology within approximately the past 20 years and having only had its first dedicated MSc programme established at IADT, Dún Laoghaire, in 2009, as cited previously. Interest in this area of psychological study has, however, increased at a rapid pace since 1998, when the first dedicated journal in this area, titled *Cyberpsychology, Behaviour and Social Networking* (CYBER), was published (see Attrill, 2015, and Connolly et al., 2016, for a more detailed account of such developments). In 1998, social networks such as Facebook, Twitter and Snapchat had not yet been developed. However, the speed with which these new online communication platforms emerged, along with the creation of new technologies on which they and other tools now function (as well as the large number of individuals who now use these platforms on a daily basis), signifies the exceptional 'reach' and importance of this area of study within the main discipline of psychology. Psychology is, after all, often described as the study of human interaction and behaviour, and as such interactions and behaviours now take place very frequently in the online world (interactions such as 'chats', 'dates' and 'business and/or social meetings'), the study of their impact on those using them should be considered important.

It is no surprise then that some psychologists working within sport settings also consider the impact of the cyber world on their sport communities too, especially when one considers the rise in technology use within these sport, exercise and performance arenas, as outlined earlier in this chapter. Technology's potential to impact on the performances of the individuals within these sport environments may often generate interesting conversations and debates within such circles, but its empirical study has been lacking to date. So why it is justifiable and important to consider the world of sport and sport psychology in the content of cyberpsychology, which is, after all, the main focus of, and argument for, this textbook titled *Sport Cyberpsychology*?

1.11 Why is it important to study sport in the context of cyberpsychology?

One of the key applications of sport psychology principles, as already mentioned, is in the realm of performance enhancement for athletes. The role of technology in that area has increased substantially in recent years too. Teams, coaches, athletes and support staff are using such technological advances in order to attempt to provide objective, measurable outputs of performance within their sport arenas. Global Positioning System (GPS), VR devices and smart devices (i.e., mobile phones and computer tablets) are just some examples of the new technologies frequently used within the world of sport, and which are now considered as much a part of athletes' training and competition environments as are their clothing, footwear, sport equipment (e.g., balls, cones, bibs, kicking tees, clubs, hockey sticks and oars) and protective items (e.g., gum shields, shin guards, protective padding and helmets).

However, although the impact of these technological devices on physical sport performance outcomes have been somewhat measured, and are in many ways appealing because of these measurement outputs, their psychological impact related to the performances of athletes since their introduction has remained less clear, largely because they have gone unstudied. There is a distinct lack of empirically generated research findings in this area to date and, as such, a number of key questions remain, such as: Do these new technologies enhance the mental preparation and mental states of the athletes using them? Are these new technologies generally facilitating, or are they sometimes preventing athletes from reaching their true performance potentials? How best might such new technologies be used to act as facilitators of good performance, rather than becoming some of the reasons why athletes may produce below par performances, especially during their most important sport events? This text hopes to provide its readers with some information and available research findings in order to answer these important questions.

Perhaps a good place to start in order to lead readers into such information in the upcoming chapters is to conclude this chapter by identifying some of the key developments that have ignited the interest of some academics and researchers in carrying out studies in this new area of sport cyberpsychology.

1.12 Key developments evoking the emergence of sport cyberpsychology

In recent years, a number of milestones have been reached in conversations regarding the combined impact of psychology and technology on performances within sport settings. In 2015, in a chapter titled 'Social Media and Networking Behaviour' (Rooney, Connolly, Hurley, Kirwan, & Power, 2015), within a textbook titled *Cyberpsychology*, edited by Attrill (2015), some issues regarding athletes and their use of social media were explored. The discussion on this topic was based upon a small number of research studies that had been carried out up to then, in an attempt to address these issues, namely by Browning and Sanderson (2012) and Pegoraro (2010). Following on from this chapter published in *Cyberpsychology*, the following year, in 2016, the first apparent book chapter introducing the discipline of sport cyberpsychology was published (Hurley, 2016), again in one of the first textbooks to introduce and explore the discipline of cyberpsychology itself (Connolly et al., 2016). This chapter, titled 'Sport and Health Cyberpsychology', explored sport psychology and cyberpsychology issues in a combined way and attempted to ignite interest in the discussion surrounding the potential impact of the cyber world, and technology, on the sport performances of athletes, from a psychological point of view.

One peer-reviewed paper by Cotterill and Symes (2014), published in the journal *Sport and Exercise Psychology Review*, had also addressed some of the issues related specifically to the important impact of technology on the sport psychology consultancy process. In their paper, Cotterill and Symes (2014) discussed the potential impact of technological devices (for example, Skype and FaceTime) replacing traditional, face-to-face consulting practices between athletes and their sport psychologists. Cotterill and Symes (2014) outlined the practical benefits of such remote interactions, such as overcoming the barrier of the consultant and the athletes being in different countries or cities, as is often the case when athletes travel away to training camps and the sport psychologist does not travel. The dangers associated with such consulting practices, using new technologies, were also outlined in this paper in a commendable way. For example, boundary, security and confidentiality of information issues shared during such technologically enabled exchanges were discussed.

However, prior to the publication of the Hurley (2016) book chapter, and indeed since then, academic papers published in peer-reviewed journals from either sport psychology or cyberpsychology disciplines on issues related to the psychological impact of technology on athletes' sport performances have remained scarce, despite references to the cyber world in articles in mainstream media on athletes and sport (Hendry, 2014). In her Foreword for *An Introduction to Cyberpsychology* (Connolly et al., 2016, p. xix), Dr. Brenda Wiederhold also commented that "Many of the chapters in this publication could easily be expanded into complete books". This comment was one of the inspirations for the decision to take on the challenge of writing this text, aimed at commencing a discussion, and encouraging more research to be carried out in this potentially significant area of sport cyberpsychology.

Given these key developments and inspirations by colleagues, as cited earlier, which have helped to ignite interest in sport cyberpsychology as an area of exploration among sport psychologists and cyberpsychologists, it is hoped the following nine chapters of this text will further advance this discussion of how sport psychology related issues could, and perhaps should, be explored in depth while considering the digital, cyber world context.

1.13 Conclusion

This chapter introduced the disciplines of sport psychology and cyberpsychology, along with providing an historical overview of these areas of psychological study. A number of key developments in the areas of sport psychology and cyberpsychology were also highlighted. The chapter introduced some of the important applied areas of study in sport psychology, such as mental fitness and mental skills (i.e., concentration and coping skills) as well as the use of strategies such as goal setting, self-talk management, mental imagery, relaxation techniques, routines and simulation training, where new technologies have begun to exert their influence in relation to their application and measurement (via VR, eye tracking, brain training and apps). This chapter also aimed to provide reasons why this new discipline of sport cyberpsychology is worthy of consideration and study, by highlighting some key developments in recent years regarding writings in this area of sport psychology from within the content of the cyber world.

1.14 Open-ended discussion questions

1   How have developments in technology enabled this new area of sport cyberpsychology to emerge as a legitimate area of research interest for psychology academics, as well as applied practitioners working with athletes and performers today?
2   What might be some of the greatest challenges for sport cyberpsychology, as the worlds of sport, performance and technology continue to evolve and develop in the future?

1.15 Practical exercise

In pairs, have your students select a mental skill, as outlined in this chapter, such as the mental skill of concentration or coping. Ask these pairs of students to consider some mental strategies introduced in this chapter, such as goal setting and relaxation techniques which could be used to improve that mental skill for an athlete they are working with, specifically using technology as the vehicle with which to deliver, and work on this skill with the athlete.

References

Andreeva, N. (2016). *'CSI-Cyber' cancelled by CBS after 2 seasons to end the 'CSI' franchise.* Retrieved from http://deadline.com/2016/05/csi-cyber-canceled-2-seasons-cbs-1201754436/

Attrill, A. (Ed.). (2015). *Cyberpsychology.* Oxford, UK: Oxford University Press.

Baumeister, R.F., & Showers, C.J. (1986). A review of paradoxical performance effect choking under pressure in sports and mental tests. *European Journal of Social Psychology, 16,* 361–383.

Browning, B., & Sanderson, J. (2012). The positives and negatives of twitter: Exploring how student-athletes use Twitter and respond to critical tweets. *International Journal of Sport Communication, 5,* 503–521.

Bull, S.J., Albinson, J.G., & Shambrook, C.J. (1996). *The mental game plan.* Eastbourne, East Sussex: Sports Dynamics.

Casey, B. (2011). Power of the mind key to curing a team with a stutter. *The Irish Times* (Sport), 21 February, p. 5.

Connolly, I., Palmer, M., Barton, B., & Kirwan, G. (Eds.). (2016). *An introduction to cyberpsychology.* London: Routledge.

Corrigan, P. (2014). *The Open 2014: Rory McIlroy puts in majestic display to race clear and banish memories of recent 'Freaky Fridays'.* Retrieved from www.telegraph.co.uk/sport/golf/theopen/10977388/The-Open-2014-Rory-McIlroy-puts-in-majestic-display-to-race-clear-and-banish-memories-of-recent-Freaky-Fridays.html

Cotterill, S.T., & Symes, R. (2014). Integrating social media and new technologies into your practice as a sport psychology consultant. *Sport & Exercise Psychology Review, 10,* 55–64.

Coutts, A.J. (2016). Fatigue in football: It's not a brainless task! *Journal of Sports Sciences, 34,* 1296.

Curtis, R. (2000). Sydney 2000. *The Mirror,* 2 October, p. 29.

Day, J. (2015). *Jason Day: I can get used to winning majors.* Retrieved from www.golf.com/tour-and-news/jason-day-winning-majors-battling-vertigo-and-his-team

Donnelly, A.A., McIntyre, T.E., O'Sullivan, N., Warrington, G., Harrison, A.J., Igou, E.R., Jones, M., Gidlow, C., Brick, N., Lahart, I., Cloak, R., & Lane, A. (2016). Environmental influences on elite sport athletes well being: From gold, silver, and bronze to blue green and gold. *Frontiers in Psychology, 7,* 1167. doi: 10.3389/fpsyg.2016.01167

Duchowski, A.T. (2007). *Eye tracking methodology: Theory and practice* (2nd ed.). New York: Springer.

Durand-Busch, N., Salmela, J., & Green-Demers, I. (2001). The Ottawa Mental Skills Assessment Tool (OMSAT-3). *The Sport Psychologist, 15,* 1–9.

Evans, L., & Hardy, L. (2002). Injury rehabilitation: A goal setting intervention study. *Research Quarterly for Exercise and Sport, 73,* 310–319.

Fanning, D. (2002). Coping with a stress factor. *Sunday Independent* (Sport), 6 October, p. 6.

Fletcher, D., & Sarkar, M. (2012). A grounded theory of psychological resilience in Olympic champions. *Psychology of Sport and Exercise, 13,* 669–678.

Gallegos, J. (2017). *Brain training games don't really train brains, a new study suggests.* Retrieved from www.washingtonpost.com/news/to-your-health/wp/2017/07/10/brain-training-games-dont-really-train-brains-a-new-study-suggests/?tid=ss_tw&utm_term=.24219e35cc5e

Gilleece, D. (1996). *Breathe deeply and be happy with second.* The Irish Times, 27 September. Retrieved from www.irishtimes.com/sport/breathe-deep-and-be-happy-with-second-1.71529

GoGreenEx. (2017). *Going green for wellbeing: A case study approach to implementing green exercise.* Retrieved from www.gogreenex.org/psi-event-going-green-wellbeing-case-study-approach-implementing-green-exercise/

Green, C.D., & Benjamin, L.T., Jr. (2009). *Psychology gets in the game: Sport, mind and behaviour, 1880–1960.* Lincoln, NE: University of Nebraska Press.

Gucciardi, D.F., Gordon, S., & Dimmock, J.A. (2009). Development and preliminary validation of a mental toughness inventory for Australian football. *Psychology of Sport and Exercise, 10,* 201–209.

Hardy, J.L., Nelson, R.A., Thomason, M.E., & Sternberg, D.A. (2015). Enhancing cognitive abilities with comprehensive training: A large, online, randomized, active controlled trial. *PLoS One.* Retrieved from http://doi.org.10.1371/journal.pone.0134467

Hendry, E.R. (2014). *How technology is changing the way athletes train.* Retrieved from www.smithsonianmag.com/innovation/how-technology-is-changing-the-way-athletes-train-180949633/

Hoffman, H.G., Chambers, G.T., Meyers III, W.J., Arceneaux, L.L., Russell, W.J., Seibel, E.J., Richards, T.L., Sharar, S.R., & Patterson, D.R. (2011). Virtual reality as an adjunctive non-pharmacological analgesic for acute burn pain during medical conditions. *Annals of Behavioural Medicine, 41,* 183–191.

Hoggard, R. (2015). *Spieth practices, thrives under pressure.* Retrieved from www.golfchannel.com/news/rex-hoggard/spieth-practices-thrives-under-pressure/

Holland, M.J., Woodcock, C., Cumming, C., & Duda, J.L. (2010). Mental qualities and employed mental techniques of young elite team sport athletes. *Journal of Clinical Sport Psychology, 4,* 19–38.

Hurley, O. (2016). Sport and health cyberpsychology. In I. Connolly, M. Palmer, H. Barton, & G. Kirwan (Eds.), *An introduction to cyberpsychology* (pp. 167–180). London: Routledge.

Ingle, S. (2008). *Olympics: Tearful Sacromone misses gold but lands on front pages.* The Guardian. Retrieved from www.theguardian.com/sport/2008/aug/13/olympics2008.olympics gymnastics

Kavussanu, M. (2017). Sport, exercise and performance psychology: Past, present and future. *Sport, Exercise and Performance Psychology, 6,* 1–5.

Kelly, L. (1998). Watson's new mountain. *The Irish Independent,* 26 October, p. 9.

Kirwan, G. (2016). Introduction to cyberpsychology. In I. Connolly, M. Palmer, H. Barton, & G. Kirwan (Eds.), *An introduction to cyberpsychology* (pp. 3–14). London: Routledge.

Kremer, J., & Moran, A. (2013). *Pure sport: Practical sport psychology.* London, UK: Routledge-Taylor and Francis Group.

Locke, E.A., & Latham, G.P. (1985). The application of goal setting to sports. *Journal of Sport Psychology, 7,* 205–222.

Locke, E.A., Shaw, K.N., Saari, L.M., & Latham, G.P. (1981). Goal setting and task performance, 1969–1980. *Psychological Bulletin, 90,* 125–152.

MacIntyre, T., Moran, A., Collet, C., Guillot, A., Campbell, M., Matthews, J., Mahoney, C., & Lowther, J. (2013). *The BASES expert statement on the use of mental imagery in sport, exercise and rehabilitation contexts.* The Sport Scientist, 38. Retrieved from www.bases.org.uk/Use-of-Mental-Imagery-in-Sport-Exercise-and-Rehabilitation-Contexts

Mahoney, M.J., & Avener, M. (1977). Psychology of the elite athlete: An exploratory study. *Cognitive Therapy and Research, 1,* 135–141.

Martin, J. (2012). About sport, exercise and performance psychology. *Sport, Exercise & Performance Psychology, 1,* 1–2.

Mitchell, K. (2010). Hard regime in the gym helps Murray find his feet on clay. *The Guardian* (Sport), 29 April, p. 6.

Moore, L.J., Vine, S.J., Freeman, P., & Wilson, M.R. (2012). Quiet eye training promotes challenge appraisals and aids performance under elevated anxiety. *International Journal of Sport & Exercise Psychology, 11,* 169–183.

Moore, L.J., Wilson, M.R., Vine, S.J., Coussens, A.H., & Freeman, P. (2013). Champ or chump? Challenge and threat states during pressurized competition. *Journal of Sport & Exercise Psychology, 35,* 551–562.

Moran, A. (2008). *Sport and exercise psychology: A critical introduction.* London: Routledge.

Moran, A. (2012). *Sport and exercise psychology: A critical introduction.* London: Routledge.

Moran, A., & Toner, J. (2017). *A critical introduction to sport psychology.* London: Routledge.

Neisser, U. (1967). *Cognitive psychology.* New York: Appleton-Century-Crofts.

Newman, P. (2015). *Australian open 2015: Andy Murray left frustrated by repeated Novak Djokovic 'distractions' in final defeat.* Independent. Retrieved from www.independent.co.uk/sport/tennis/australian-open-2015-andy-murray-left-frustrated-by-repeated-novak-djokovic-distractions-in-final-10016824.html

Northcroft, J. (2009). They shall not pass. *The Sunday Times* (Sport), 8 February, pp. 12–13.

Pegoraro, A. (2010). Look who's talking: Athletes on Twitter: A case study. *International Journal of Sport Communication, 3,* 501–514.

Phelps, M. (2008). Perfect physique to rule to pool. *The Guardian* (Sport), 13 December, p. 10.

Robinson, P., Oades, L.G., & Caputi, P. (2014). Conceptualising and measuring mental fitness: A Delphi study. *International Journal of Wellbeing, 5*(1), 53–73. doi: 10.5502/ijw.v5i1.4

Rooney, B., Connolly, I., Hurley, O., Kirwan, G., & Power, A. (2015). Social media and networking behaviour. In A. Attrill (Ed.), *Cyberpsychology* (pp. 88–102). Oxford, UK: Oxford University Press.

Sarkar, M., & Fletcher, D. (2013). How should we measure psychological resilience in sport performers? *Measurement in Physical Education and Exercise Science, 17,* 264–280.

Sarkar, M., & Fletcher, D. (2017a). Adversity-related experiences are essential for Olympic success: Additional evidence and considerations. *Progress in Brain Research, 232*, 159–165.

Sarkar, M., & Fletcher, D. (2017b). How resilience training can enhance wellbeing and performance. In M.F. Crane (Ed.), *Managing for resilience: A practical guide for employee wellbeing and organizational performance* (pp. 227–237). London, UK: Routledge-Taylor and Francis Group.

Schinke, R.J., McGannon, K.R., & Smith, B. (Eds.). (2016). *Routledge international handbook of sport psychology.* London: Routledge.

Sharp, L.A., Woodcock, C., Holland, M.J.G., Cumming, J., & Duda, J.L. (2013). A qualitative evaluation of the effectiveness of a mental skills training program for youth athletes. *The Sport Psychologist, 27*, 219–232.

Smith, M.R., Coutts, A.J., Merlini, M., Deprez, D., Lenoir, M., & Marcora, S.M. (2015). Mental fatigue impairs soccer-specific physical and technical performance. *Medicine & Science in Sports & Exercise, 48*, 267–276. doi: 10.1249/MSS.0000000000000762

Staph, J. (2011). *Usain Bolt's key to explosive starts.* Retrieved from www.stack.com/a/usain-bolts-key-to-explosice-starts

Triplett, N. (1898). The dynamogenic factors in pacemaking and competition. *American Journal of Psychology, 9*, 507–533.

Vickers, J.N. (2007). *Perception, cognition and decision making: The quiet eye in action.* Champaign, IL: Human Kinetics.

Watson, J. (2012). *Rooney: I see myself in scoring goals the night before a game.* Goals.com. Retrieved from www.goals.com/en-gb/news/2896/premier-league/2012/05/17/3109404/rooney-i-see-myself-scoring-goals-the-night-before-a-game

Williams, J.M. (2010). Relaxation and energizing techniques for arousal. In J. Williams (Ed.), *Applied sport psychology: Personal growth to peak performance* (6th ed., pp. 247–266). New York: McGraw-Hill.

Williams, R. (2002). Sublime Serena celebrates the crucial difference. *The Guardian* (Sport), 8 July, p. 6.

Wilson, M.R., & Pearcy, R.C. (2009). Visuomotor control of straight and breaking golf putts. *Perceptual and Motor Skills, 109*, 555–562.

Wraga, M., & Kosslyn, S. (2002). Imagery. In L. Nadel (Ed.), *Encyclopedia of cognitive science* (Vol. 2, pp. 466–470). London: Nature Group.

2

TYPES OF TECHNOLOGY COMMONLY USED IN SPORT – AN INTRODUCTION

CASE STUDY 2

Dave is an elite 30-year-old boxer who is interested in using some recent technological advances in order to obtain objective measures of his performance outcomes in training. He has heard from a number of his athlete friends, who compete in other sports such as rugby, soccer and pentathlon, that various technologies they use in their training allow them to monitor their training outputs. Dave hopes that such additions to his training could improve his performances in boxing and help him to be successful in his next competitive match, which is in ten months' time.

(i) What technologies could Dave apply in his boxing environment to measure his performance gains?
(ii) What empirical evidence is available to determine if such technologies are effective in facilitating the performances of athletes such as Dave?
(iii) What words of caution should be voiced to Dave when using the new technologies suggested in answer to the first question?

2.1 Overview

This chapter explains some new pieces of technology, such as Global Positioning System (GPS) devices, smart devices (i.e., mobile phones and tablets with various applications downloaded onto them) and gaming devices, which have emerged in recent years to help athletes prepare for, complete in and recover from their sport performances. The chapter content also includes an outline of some uses of these technologies by individuals working within various sport environments in recent years (i.e., in elite sport and also in non-elite exercise settings). The uses of virtual reality (VR) devices, such as the Oculus Rift and HTC Vive, are introduced in this chapter. However, a more in-depth examination of the application and impact of such VR and augmented reality (AR) devices within sport settings is covered in greater depth in Chapter 4 (as it is an exciting area of potential research within this new sport cyberpsychology area). Some of the available research findings, documenting the specific impact of these new technologies on athletes' preparations and performances, are detailed in Chapter 3.

2.2 Learning objectives

1   To introduce the reader to some of the most common pieces of technology currently used within sport settings to help athletes prepare for, complete in and recover from their sport activities
2   To highlight some strengths and limitations of these performance-assisting technological devices
3   To highlight some exciting potential research suggestions in this area of sport technology that could form the basis for future psychological study

2.3 Definitions of relevant terms

AlterG antigravity (AGAG) treadmill

This treadmill was designed to allow the user to run while being supported, so that only some, or none, of the individual's own body weight is being used. Typically within sport settings, such treadmills are used by injured individuals who wish to continue to train in order to stay aerobically fit, while also not having to support all of their own body weight (thus protecting the injured body area – such as the back, knee, hip, ankle or other leg regions) (Hickie, 2014).

App (application)

This refers to a piece of software, or a device, that fulfils a specific function. It is typically downloaded from sources such as iTunes.

Augmented reality (AR)

This is a visual portrayal of virtual objects that are placed over real-world displays using technologies such as cameras and screens (i.e., green screens) (Kirwan, 2016).

Global Positioning System (GPS)

This is a satellite-supported system that allows the motion of individuals, or other objects (such as moving vehicles), to be measured. The velocity, speed and direction of the moving object can be recorded using GPS technologies. Many cars and fitness apps, for example, now feature GPS-monitoring technologies.

Pressure pads

Pressure pads contain sensors that measure the force of contact made with the pad, usually from a foot landing on it. These pads can be used to measure the strength of athletes' legs, their reaction times, or the distribution of their body weight when their feet make contact with the pads in a walking, running or jumping action, for example.

Smart devices

These are electronically based devices, such as mobile phones or small computer tablets that connect to wireless devices, such as Bluetooth (now in many cars) or WiFi. Smart devices allow users to interact with each of their digital devices individually or all together at the same time.

The cloud

This refers to a storage facility where an individual can access information and share it across all of their Internet-connected devices (e.g., their mobile phones, tablets, laptops etc.). The related term, *cloud storage*, refers to all of the information an individual wishes to store on the web, which typically, is available at some cost to the individual via hosting companies such as Google. Such cloud storage facilities allow individuals to access their data from anywhere in the world, once an Internet connection is available in that location.

USB (Universal Serial Bus) flash drive

This is a data storage device that has flash memory with an integrated USB interface. It is also commonly referred to as a USB key or a USB stick. A USB enables communication among different computer devices. Data stored on a USB key can be transferred from one computer device to another once a USB port or socket is available in the device.

Virtual reality (VR)

This refers to an artificial environment generated by a computer which allows the user to interact with a non-real world as if it were physically present. This technology involves the use of equipment, such as head-mounted goggles, and sensor activated hand-wear, such as gloves or a joystick.

2.4 New performance-enhancement technology – an introduction

The use of technology to help prepare athletes for their sport performances has increased substantially within recent years, thanks to the introduction of sophisticated equipment which reports to monitor and measure the impact of athletes' movements on their bodies. In a recent television documentary, Ulster and Ireland rugby player, Tommy Bowe, was shown using pieces of equipment and new technologies to assist in his recovery from some serious injuries (Independent Pictures, 2013). An *AlterG antigravity* (AGAG) treadmill and *pressure pads* were shown in this documentary. They are used to analyse the running and jumping techniques, respectively, of the player, as previously explained. Other well-known athletes have also commented on the influence of new technologies in their training environments. For example, now retired Manchester United football player, Ryan Giggs, stated in 2011 that,

> When I started, you would get treatment, have a bit of ice and go home. . . . But now, you are working a couple of days after being injured. The gravity-free treadmill is great, especially if you have an ankle injury or something similar because you don't apply downward pressure. . . . You just jump on to it, fasten the zips around you and then get in. It's like being on the Moon, apparently – it's running, but it makes you float. There is an underwater treadmill, where you can get your running action back quickly because, in the water, you can run as hard as you want. . . . There are cameras underneath the pool which monitor your foot pattern, to make sure that you're not limping. There's no escape!
>
> *(cited in Ogden, 2011)*

Another athlete, American Matt Scott, a four-time wheelchair basketball paralympian, stated

> It's (sensor technology) made a huge, huge difference in my training. . . . It's made me a stronger athlete, a stronger player. I'm far more knowledgeable of what I'm capable of in the gym. The real-time data allows me to know if I'm getting the best out of my workouts. It takes the guesswork out of it.
>
> *(cited in Fitzsimons, 2016)*

The use of new technologies to measure the force of collisions and tackles made within many sports, such as rugby and American football, has also become popular within elite team settings over the past seven or eight years. *Global Positioning System (GPS)* devices, for example, allow coaches to measure the work rates of their players during training and in matches (Hartwig, Naughton, & Searl, 2011). GPS devices have the potential to impact on the mental, as well as the physical states of the athletes. The data recorded by these GPS devices can be used to inform the athletes not only of their own, but also of their teammates', performance statistics. In an environment where competition for starting places in a team is often high, this means that GPS-monitored athletes cannot afford to have many 'off days' because reduced efforts in their performances are constantly monitored, and in many cases shared, within their sport environments (Figure 2.1). As MUFC retired soccer player Ryan Giggs said in 2011, "With all the stats that you get, you can't hide. . . . You can't duck out of training or not work hard because it's all monitored" (Ogden, 2011).

However, empirical research examining and documenting the impact of wearing these GPS devices, specifically on the mental states and well-being levels of such athletes, is very much lacking and is a potential avenue for future research

FIGURE 2.1   Irish rugby player, Robbie Henshaw, having his GPS device fitted in training

Source: Courtesy of Inpho Photography, with thanks to Irish rugby player, Robbie Henshaw, and the Irish Rugby Football Union.

in this sport cyberpsychology arena. However, before considering such future research directions, some of these new technologies commonly used within sport today will be outlined in the sections that follow.

2.4.1 The AlterG antigravity (AGAG) treadmill

The AlterG antigravity (AGAG) treadmill was originally designed by Robert Whalen in the 1990s. It was developed to improve the design flaws of previous treadmills used in space by astronauts to exercise in order to prevent bone density loss that typically occurs due to the lack of gravity in that atmosphere (Fecht, 2014). The AGAG treadmill cocoons the user in an airtight plastic container, or support, that extends upwards from the base of the treadmill, covering it and the lower part of the individual's body from the waist downwards. The top of this plastic chamber is positioned and held in place around the waist of the individual. The amount of gravity experienced by the individual running or walking on the AGAG can be increased or decreased depending on the amount of gravity desired. In space, astronauts programme the AGAG treadmill to *increase* the amount of gravity experienced so that they can run in a way that simulates them bearing their own full body weight, as if running or walking back on Earth. This is done by lowering the pressure within the chamber cocooned around the waist and lower part of the individual's body, which has the effect of pushing the individual downwards, thus simulating more weight being borne by the lower part of the individual's body (i.e., in the hips, legs, knees and ankle areas; AlterG, 2017).

In contrast, in sport settings for example, the AGAG treadmill is more often used to *reduce* the amount of gravity athletes experience, in order to reduce the degree of their body weight they must support while running or walking on the AGAG treadmill. This allows injured athletes to engage in cardiovascular, aerobic training in order to maintain their physical fitness while protecting their injured site, such as knee, ankle, hip, or back areas. This effect is similar to what athletes experience when they engage in aqua-aerobic training in a swimming pool, where their body weight is supported by the water (AlterG, 2017; Fecht, 2014; Figueroa, Manning, & Escamilla, 2011; Ogden, 2011).

When using the AGAG treadmill, the athlete dresses in a pair of specially designed tight bicycle-like shorts, with a skirt-like design attached to them. The edges of the 'skirt' have zipper-like teeth that are then attached to the corresponding zipper inside the plastic container of the AGAG treadmill. The AGAG treadmill then measures the weight of the individual and 'lifts' the athlete upwards, to allow a running or walking motion to occur, without the person experiencing the weight-bearing element of that action (Fecht, 2014; Ogden, 2011).

Many elite, sport training environments and rehabilitation centres, across all kinds of team and individual sport, have invested in these AGAG treadmills. The strengths or beneficial uses of the AGAG treadmill to help athletes or, indeed any injured individual, to rehabilitate from their injuries have been documented (Figueroa et al., 2011; McNeill et al., 2015; Ogden, 2011; Patil et al., 2013; Saxena & Granot, 2011). However, no equipment is without limitations, and these are outlined next.

First, the AGAG treadmill is expensive (AlterG, 2017). When it was initially made available for commercial purchase, it cost approximately $75,000. Today, while not as costly, the AGAG treadmill still retails at between $35,000 and $65,000 depending on the model and specific requirements of the purchaser. Second, it is possible that the AGAG treadmill could also have some inhibiting features, from a mental perspective. The treadmill is a large piece of equipment requiring a power source, which is typically located indoors, within a gym or rehabilitation facility. Therefore, the user does not have the option of training in an outdoor environment when using it. The psychological benefits of 'green exercise' have been well documented (Donnelly et al., 2016) and has become a 'hot' topic of investigation by sport and exercise psychologists in recent years (see GoGreenEx, 2017), especially with increased interest in the health and well-being benefits of different kinds of training and sport activities also occurring. Many researchers have advocated for the benefits of training outdoors in natural settings (i.e., in parks and by the sea), including improvements in mood states and cognitive functioning, along with reduced levels of reported stress, to name but a few positive outcomes (Donnelly et al., 2016).

However, despite these limitations regarding cost and location options of the AGAG treadmill, it continues to be popular for use in helping athletes to rehabilitate from injury and is likely to continue to be used by such individuals to assist them in their return to their pre-injury levels of mobility and fitness.

2.4.2 Pressure pads

As previously defined, pressure pads contain sensors capable of measuring the force with which contact is made with the pad, usually from a foot landing on it (Foot and Leg Clinic, 2016). These pads can be used to measure the strength of athletes' lower body regions, their reaction times and the distribution of their body weight when their feet makes contact with the pads during walking, running or jumping motions.

Pressure pads were originally devised as security devices to detect unauthorised entry into restricted locations or private properties (Arun Electronics, 2014). For example, many museums and medical/research facilities, where the contents of such properties could be attractive targets for burglary, are often protected by alarms and censored flooring containing such pressure pad technology. In sport, however, the application of such pressure pads has been mainly to help in the design of training programmes for athletes to strengthen areas of weakness within their bodies, such as the ankle, hip, back or leg areas. Pressure pads are also used to help in the design of corrective footwear for athletes (i.e., orthotics) and also for injury diagnostics, when the distribution of the athlete's weight when it makes contact with the ground is considered a reason why some specific lower limb injuries may be occurring in locations such ankle, knee, hip and back areas of an individual (Tekscan, n.d.). Orthotic footwear can be designed from pressure pad sensory-recorded data, generated from an athlete's foot making contact with the pad, to counteract or help solve any imbalance in the distribution of the athlete's weight, which can help to prevent future injuries from occurring in the individual. The limitations of pressure pads include, like most technology, that they can be costly and may also be susceptible to malfunction and/or inaccurate data being generated from them.

2.4.3 Global Positioning System (GPS)

GPS is one of the new and growing technologies used within sport settings. While some sport teams (e.g., rugby) have been using GPS data recorders for the past ten years with their athletes in training, and a short time later in real competitive matches too, it was only in February of 2015 that the International Football Association Board (IFAB) changed its rules to allow soccer players to wear GPS data-recording devices inside their jerseys during games (usually positioned in the back-neck area of the players' jerseys, between the shoulder blades of the players), provided such devices did not compromise the safety of the players (Figure 2.2). The data gathered was also not permitted to be made available to the coaches or managers of the teams in the technical area while the match was 'in play' (Fleming, 2015). This rule does not, however, prevent the recorded GPS data from being relayed to coaches, managers and players at the half-time break in matches, within the teams' changing rooms.

The Manchester United Football Club (MUFC) was one of the first premiership football clubs in England to introduce GPS technology into their training

FIGURE 2.2 A GPS device, shown in the back-neck area of a player's jersey

Source: Courtesy of Inpho Photography.

environments in 2010 (Ogden, 2011). However, many more teams, and sports, have since introduced these injury and performance monitoring systems, that use GPS tracking, in their settings too. One recent partnership was announced between the Ultimate Fighting Championship (UFC, 2017) and the technology company, Kitman Labs (which also offered similar sport performance monitoring services to the British and Irish Lions on their 2017 summer tour of New Zealand; Kitman Labs, 2017).

GPS technology works by using a satellite-based navigation system, which was initially placed into space 12,000 miles above the Earth by the US Department of Defense (DOD) in the 1980s for their own military use. This constantly moving 24-satellite system, known as NAVSTAR by the US DOD, was then later made available to all countries and individuals for general civilian use. The satellites move at a rate of approximately 7,000 miles per hour. It is an attractive piece of technology because it is free to use. It also operates using solar power, with power boosters attached to it to power it when there is a solar eclipse. The satellite system works 24 hours each day, every day, and is weatherproof. Many well-known global technology-based companies, such as Garmin, for example, apply this technology in their navigation systems (Garmin, 2017), placed in cars, that direct the driver on how to get to a specific destination or provide information on the location of a place or thing (Figure 2.3). These devices are commonly known as satellite navigators, or satnavs, for short.

As cited previously, sport technology companies, such as Kitman Labs, soon followed the technology companies like Garmin, in exploring the uses of GPS

FIGURE 2.3   A satnav device in a car

Source: Courtesy of Pexels.

within sport settings. They applied such GPS tracking specifically to gather data on the position and speed (velocity) of the athletes as they moved around for their sport. The goal of such applications of GPS is now often used to assess athletes' risks of injuries, as well as their overall performance outputs completed within their sport (Kitman Labs, 2017; Ogden, 2011). This GPS tracking data is useful for team management personnel, as well as the athletes themselves, because it provides information on measures such as an athlete's heart rate, force of collision (e.g., tackles), number of collisions made by and on individual players, time taken to return to a standing position following a collision, speed of running into a collision (acceleration or pace), position of the head when making a tackle (which can be a very important piece of information to have if technique adjustments need to be made in order to prevent concussion-related injuries in athletes, for example – and also given that concussion is a 'hot' topic within many collision sports, such as rugby and American football at present), change of direction when running and the length of an athlete's stride patterns.

So, what types of tracking devices are commonly used in sport? Within soccer in the Premier League in England, for example, the most commonly used performance tracking devices are provided mainly by two companies: Catapult Sport's OptimEye S5 and STATSports Viper (Fleming, 2015). These devices contain: (i) GPS tracking, as well as (ii) *accelerometers* (electronic device that measure speed in a particular direction, also known as velocity, as well as recording changes in that velocity (or acceleration – described as the change in velocity divided by the time that change takes by the moving object, i.e., by the athlete), (iii) *magnetometers* (devices used to measure magnetic fields) and (iv) *gyroscopes* (devices that provide data regarding the rotation of the athlete per second and in which direction – clockwise or anticlockwise – for example). *Heart rate monitors* are also part of the Viper technology.

One of the main limitations of GPS technology use in sport, as already outlined for other technologies, is that it can malfunction. Therefore, having the data backed up as well as other measures of athletic performance available are encouraged, in order to support and corroborate the data gathered from GPS devices. Video analysis is one such method and is detailed in the next section. However, given that video analysis measures are also technology reliant, the human ingredient, or contribution of human observation, by coaches, other support staff and team members, is an important performance indicator and should not be overlooked in favour of technology-only measurements. Also, a somewhat neglected research area regarding the use of such GPS monitoring in sport is the link between the physical and psychological performance of athletes using such GPS technology. Athletes may 'feel' they are working hard in training or in a match situation, for example, however, the GPS data provided to them, and their coaches or sport scientists measuring their actual physical performance outputs, may indicate otherwise. The technology means there is little opportunity for athletes to 'hide' from their performances, as the quote earlier in this chapter from MUFC retired player, Ryan Giggs, revealed (Ogden, 2011). However, notes of caution in using such GPS data to indicate the effort an athlete has applied when performing should also consider the athlete's mental state and well-being (this issue is explored in Chapter 3).

In summary, however, all of the GPS movement monitors can be used to help athletes, their coaches and their sport science support staff in a variety of ways, such as: (i) to help with decisions regarding an athlete's sport skills technique and if any adjustments need to be made for performance or safety-related reasons, (ii) to help determine if an athlete is showing signs of fatigue and (iii) to help determine if an athlete is injured and, on a related point, in need of substitution during a competitive match or event (Watterson, 2015).

2.4.4 Video analysis technology

Video analysis involves the gathering of 'real-time' video footage of a sport performance, for example in competition, and also in training in many cases too. Most elite teams now have one or more sport science qualified specialists whose job it is to formally record and analyse the athletes' performances in their sport. They then make ready for presentation such information, to the athletes individually and to the team as a whole, as well as the team's management members (e.g., their coaching staff), to view in team meetings. Such video-based data analysis is not long in existence. It was first introduced in many sports for broadcasting purposes on television (Fleming, 2015). However, elite teams and performers quickly realised the potential value of this data as an objective performance output for the actual performers, in order for them to improve their skill set, to establish areas in need of more practice, while also of relevance and interest to sport psychologists especially, to help the athletes set effective objective, measureable goals – considered a cornerstone of sport and performance psychology strategies for peak performance (see Chapter 1 for a brief review of the goal-setting literature in sport psychology to date; see Moran & Toner, 2017, for a recent critical review of goal setting as a strategy in sport settings also).

A number of studies have been published within the psychological literature regarding the impact of video-based feedback, with both positive and negative outcomes reported (Groom, 2012). These studies are outlined in Chapter 3. However, one key strength of such video analysis data includes that such footage is generally an unbiased, objective, real-time example of an athlete's sport performance and, as such, it is not subject to human memory inaccuracies or emotional influences of verbal feedback provided by coaches to their athletes as the only source of performance assessment, prior to the availability of such video footage.

However, video analysis also has limitations; for example, (i) it is often delayed feedback (only provided to athletes hours, or even days, after the data was recorded) and (ii) it only gives athletes an external perspective, or view, of their performances (it does not provide an internal, 'through the athletes' eyes' perspective, in the same way that internal mental imagery may do for athletes; see Chapter 1, MacIntyre et al., 2013 and Moran & Toner, 2017, for more information on mental imagery use by athletes). Based on the previously cited limitations of video analysis, one interesting question that could be posed is: Does the delayed nature of the feedback provided to athletes from video analysis, for example, impact on an athlete's mental state in any significant way? Empirical research on this issue appears unavailable at present and is a possible direction for future study in this area. Also, one recently developed technology used by sport and cognitive psychologists, that attempts to more objectively measure mental practice and imagery use by athletes, as referred to earlier, is eye-tracking technology. This technology is explained next.

2.4.5 Eye-tracking technology

Eye tracking heralded the beginning of research on the movements of the eyes, and the insights such movements might give regarding the relationship between what people 'look' at and what they 'see'. Sport settings are one arena where such research has been focused in the hope of finding ways to measure what athletes are focused on when they are performing in their sport. Eye-tracking equipment involves athletes wearing specially designed goggles, mounted with cameras, which capture an athlete's eye movements and eye fixations as they complete skills in their sport, for example, returning a serve in tennis, or dribbling a ball in soccer. A number of eye-tracking devices have been developed, such as the Applied

Science Laboratories' (ASL) 5000 SU eye-tracking system and the Tobii system (see Duchowski, 2007, and Moran & Toner, 2017, for more details).

The benefit of eye-tracking technology is that it provides objective data regarding where, and on what, athletes' eyes focus when presented with various visual stimuli within their sport arena. Some limitations of eye-tracking equipment include that, like all of the types of technology previously cited, it may be subject to incorrect calibration and misreadings. Also, it cannot be guaranteed that what a person is 'looking' at matches directly what the person reports 'seeing' (which may be regarded as an indication of what the individual is concentrating on; see Duchowski, 2007, and Moran & Toner, 2017, for more details).

2.4.6 Smart devices

Most athletes and their support staff now use smart devices, such as mobile phones and small computer tablets, to video, record and store information related to an athlete's performance. Of interest to psychologists perhaps, is also the requirement for many elite athletes now to complete daily well-being measures, using such smart devices (i.e., their mobile phones or computer tablets). While such electronic records are useful, in some cases athletes do not store this information securely, that is, using the *cloud*, for example. Therefore, if something happens to these devices, there is a danger that all of this information may be lost, which is potentially distressing for the athlete, before even considering the privacy and ethical issues that could arise (Cotterill & Symes, 2014), especially if such data is then passed on, for example, to media personnel or other competitors. (One example of such a security breach of athletes' data was the hacking of the World Anti-Doping Agency (WADA) and the United States Anti-Doping Agency's emails by the cyber group known as Fancy Bears; see Ingle, 2016).

Smart devices also need to have their batteries charged, like all forms of technology, in order to function properly. This is one more thing athletes need to consider if using such devices within their training environments. As many sport settings for athletes take place outdoors, without battery sockets available for charging such devices, athletes often need to purchase wireless operating chargers for such devices as a back-up option for using the devices within their training environments. In the past, athletes may have kept written (paper/pencil-based) copies of the information now stored on many technological devices. They often used diaries, for example. Such records may still be advisable for athletes, as well as another electronically stored version of the data created perhaps on a password-protected device such as a USB key, in addition to the information stored on the athlete's smart device. These can all act as forms of backup of the athlete's sensitive and important personal medical, sport and training-related data.

2.4.7 Computer games

The popularity of computer games has risen enormously in recent years (Goh, Ang, & Tan, 2008), and, as such, a number of companies have developed products to help athletes prepare mentally and physically for their sport using such gaming devices. Some gaming companies have developed products that mimic the environments of major sport events such as the recent FIFA World Cup, the Rugby World Cup and Formula One motor racing, for example. Research on the benefits of individuals playing such video games for their sport events, has produced mixed results (Boot, Blakely, & Simons, 2011). Some studies on this topic have shown benefits for performance from playing video games, such as improvements in decision-making skills (Nelson & Strachan, 2009), reaction times (Ramsey, Tangermann, Haufe, & Blankertz, 2009), mental imagery skills and spatial awareness (Spence & Feng, 2010). Other studies, however, have found no significant benefits, or indeed have reported some potential adverse effects on sport performances from playing such video games, if they do not 'tap' into the relevant 'real-time' physical skills that athletes must perform in order to be successful in their sport (Wollersheim et al., 2010). This gaming technology research is discussed in more detail in Chapter 3.

2.4.8 Wearable technologies

In elite sport, where winning margins can be fractions of a second, these margins are being explored by sport scientists in the industry of *wearable technology* (Figure 2.4). Athletes have sought out these devices in order to improve their sport skills and performances. Such interest has seen sales in GPS wearable devices vastly increase in recent years. As mentioned earlier, companies like Kitman Labs have

FIGURE 2.4 A wearable smart watch

Source: Courtesy of Pexels.

created such technologies and now supply their products to some of the top global sport teams (e.g., the British and Irish Lions Rugby Tour in 2017; see Chapter 3 also). Other wearable technologies have been developed especially for exercise or physical activity tracking and for sleep monitoring, for example.

Unfortunately, many of the digital devices that claim to monitor sleep have not been tested accurately or rigorously for both their reliability and validity (Bassett, Rowlands, & Trost, 2012; Evenson, Goto, & Furberg, 2015; Halson, Peake, & Sullivan, 2016; Kooiman et al., 2015). Unrealistic expectations can also be a factor when it comes to behaviours such as sleep, with the 'perfect night's sleep' not feasible or attainable for many athletes at different times of their training, competition and rest periods, due to many factors (Halson et al., 2016). Indeed, it is possible that some individuals who use sleep monitors actually become so focused on their data outputs that they actually 'lose' sleep because of them.

Athletes should always be mindful of the underlying motivations of companies who devise such wearable technology, that is, to make money or profits. To illustrate this point, in 2016 wearable technologies were reported to be a $6 billion industry (Duking, Hotho, Holmberg, Fuss, & Sperlick, 2016), with growth in this market expected to reach $34 billion by 2020 (Lamkin, 2017). Therefore, athlete users of these devices should not be naïve regarding the sometimes overzealous or somewhat inaccurate claims of performance enhancement that such devices may legally offer the athletes who use them (Halson et al., 2016). Athlete endorsements of these devices should also be viewed with some caution or scepticism. These athletes are being paid to endorse such devices and that motivation alone can have an influence on what they report about the products (see Hambrick & Mahoney, 2011, and Chapter 6 for more information on athletes and their online/technology brand relationships).

Some athletes have actually written of the benefits of removing all new technological devices (or 'gadgets') from their training and just returning to pre-technology, data-recording days where only the distance, time taken and perceived effort were recorded using a simple stopwatch (Stulberg, 2017). Research support for such actions has also been noted, with Brick, Campbell, Metcalfe, Mair, and MacIntyre (2016), for example, reporting some benefits from not using metrics to monitor running pace. Instead, these researchers had their participants focus on staying relaxed and attending to the actual act of running. Brick et al. (2016) reported gains of up to 10% on participants' performance times in their research study. They commented that relying on technology to monitor times and distances covered, rather than focusing on the 'feel' of the task, could lead to unhelpful stress on athletes and a feeling of pressure to speed up, which may be counterproductive for some athletes' performances.

2.5 Conclusion, including future directions for research

This chapter has attempted to inform the reader about some of the recent technologies introduced into sport settings, specifically to monitor and attempt to improve athletes' performances, as well as to help them rehabilitate following injury, for example.

Halson et al. (2016) proposed a number of guidelines regarding wearable and performance-enhancing technologies. In the context of the technologies used in sport settings and introduced in this chapter, some of the same notes of caution could be applied: (i) the technology or device should, first, do no harm to the user, in this case, the athlete; (ii) the athlete should always question the claims regarding the reliability and validity of the technology/device and ask to see the scientific, peer-reviewed evidence supporting the performance gains as documented by the manufacturers; (iii) if empirical data is not available, it should be gathered as the athlete uses the device/piece of technology, in order to determine its effectiveness (however, if this is done after the device has been purchased, it may be a costly post-purchase exercise, especially if the device is later found to be ineffective when compared to the manufacturers' claims of specific performance enhancements and (iv) athletes (and their support/coaching staff) should assess the potential usefulness of the technology being introduced, compared to the risk of information overload and potential stress or anxiety that wearing such technology could cause (Brick et al., 2016; Halson et al., 2016; these issues are explored in more depth in later chapters in this text also). There is a danger that athletes could become over-vigilant of their physical skill execution and become distracted from just performing in their sport when using any of the technologies outlined in this chapter. A danger of 'choking' could also exist for such athletes (see Moran, 2012, for a review of choking, as related to sport contexts).

Some interesting avenues for research could arise from such technological advances too in sport. For example, based on the cited limitations of video analysis, one interesting question could be posed. Does the typically delayed nature of the feedback provided to athletes from video analysis (which can be a day or two of a delay after the performance itself, for example), impact on the athletes' mental states in any significant way? Empirical research in this area appears unavailable at present and is a possible direction for future studies.

To conclude, the goal of this chapter was to introduce the reader to some of the most common pieces of technology currently used within sport settings to help athletes prepare for, complete in and recover from their sport activities. It also aimed to highlight some strengths and limitations of these performance-assisting technological devices, as well as provide some words of warning regarding the general application of such technologies by athletes within sport settings (Halson et al., 2016). Chapter 3 details some of the sport-specific research findings regarding the positive and negative performance outcomes of athletes using some of these previously cited technologies, from a mainly psychological perspective.

2.6 Open-ended discussion questions

1   Why might athletes find the use of some new technologies in their training and competition settings especially attractive in an attempt to improve their sport performances?

2   Should sport-governing bodies consider the possible unfair advantage access to new technologies has for some performers? Is there an argument for banning certain kinds of technologies from being used in sport settings if they, like some prohibited drugs in sport, create an unfair playing field for all performers?

3   Are other technologies being used for performance enhancement purposes that are not included in this chapter? If so, what are they?

2.7 Practical exercise

Contact an athlete you know and ask him/her to keep a diary for one week, recording all of his/her uses of various technologies within his/her training and competition environment. Ask the athlete to consider some suggestions for how he/she could achieve the same training goals if he/she did not have access to these technologies due to a technical failure of all of the technological devices currently being used.

References

AlterG. (2017). *Alter-G anti-gravity treadmill*. Retrieved from www.alterg.com/

Arun Electronics. (2014). *Pressure mat/pad switches*. Retrieved from www.arun-electronics.co.uk/pressure_mat.htm

Bassett, D.R., Rowlands, A., & Trost, S.G. (2012). Calibration and validation of wearable monitors. *Medicine & Science in Sports & Exercise, 44*, S32–S38. doi: 10.1249/MSS.0b013e3182399cf7

Boot, W.R., Blakely, D.P., & Simons, D.J. (2011). Do action video games improve perception and cognition? *Frontiers in Psychology, 2*, 226. doi: 10.3389/fpsyg.2011.00226

Brick, N.E., Campbell, M.J., Metcalfe, R.S., Mair, J.L., & MacIntyre, T.E. (2016). Altering pace control and pace regulation: Attentional focus effects during running. *Medicine & Science in Sports & Exercise, 48*, 879–886. doi: 10.1249/MSS.0000000000000843

Cotterill, S.T., & Symes, R. (2014). Integrating social media and new technologies into your practice as a sport psychology consultant. *Sport & Exercise Psychology Review, 10*, 55–64.

Donnelly, A.A., MacIntyre, T.E., O'Sullivan, N., Warrington, G., Harrison, A.J., Igou, E.R., Jones, M., Gidlow, C., Brick, N., Lahart, I., Cloak, R., & Lane, A.M. (2016). Environmental influences on elite sport athletes well being: From gold, silver, and bronze to blue green and gold. *Frontiers in Psychology, 7*, 1167. doi: 10.3389/fpsyg.2016.01167

Duchowski, A.T. (2007). *Eye tracking methodology: Theory and practice* (2nd ed.). New York: Springer.

Duking, P., Hotho, A., Holmberg, H.C., Fuss, F.K., & Sperlick, B. (2016). Comparison of non-invasive individual monitoring of the training and health of athletes with commercially available wearable technologies. *Frontiers in Physiology, 7*, 71. Retrieved from https://doi.org/10.3389/fphys.2016.00071

Evenson, K.R., Goto, M.M., & Furberg, R.D. (2015). Systematic review of the validity and reliability of consumer-wearable activity trackers. *International Journal of Behavioural Nutrition & Physical Activity, 18*(12), 159. doi: 10.1186/s12966-015-0314-1

Fecht, S. (2014). How does the anti-gravity treadmill work? *Mental Floss*. Retrieved from http://mentalfloss.com/article/57102/how-does-anti-gravity-treadmill-work

Figueroa, M.A., Manning, J., & Escamilla, P. (2011). Physiological responses to the Alter-G anti-gravity treadmill. *International Journal of Applied Science and Technology, 1,* 92–97.

Fitzsimons, M. (2016). *Go for the gold: How tech is transforming Olympic training.* Retrieved from www.techradar.com/news/world-of-tech/go-for-the-gold-how-technology-helped-athletes-on-the-road-to-rio-1326022

Fleming, N. (2015). *How science is fine tuning our elite footballers.* Retrieved from www.the guardian.com/football/2015/aug/02/science-fine-tuning-elite-footballers

Foot and Leg Clinic. (2016). *Benefits of pressure plate analysis.* Retrieved from http://thefoot andlegclinic.co.uk/pressure-plate-analysis-benefits/

Garmin. (2017). *About GPS.* Retrieved from www8.garmin.com/aboutGPS/

GoGreenEx. (2017). *Going green for wellbeing: A case study approach to implementing green exercise.* Retrieved from www.gogreenex.org/psi-event-going-green-wellbeing-case-study-approach-implementing-green-exercise/

Goh, G.D., Ang, R.P., & Tan, H.C. (2008). Strategies for designing effective psychotherapeutic gaming interventions for children and adolescents. *Computers in Human Behaviour, 24,* 2217–2235.

Groom, N.R. (2012). *Towards an understanding of the use of video-based performance analysis in the coaching process.* Retrieved from https://dspace.lboro.ac.uk/dspace-jspui/bitstream/2134/13020/4/Thesis-2012-Groom.pdf

Halson, S.L., Peake, J.M., & Sullivan, J.P. (2016). Wearable technology for athletes: Information overload and pseudoscience. *International Journal of Sports Physiology and Performance, 11,* 705–706.

Hambrick, M.E., & Mahoney, T.Q. (2011). It's incredible – trust me. Exploring the role of celebrity athletes as marketers in online social networks. *International Journal of Sport Management & Marketing, 10,* 161–179. doi: 10.1504/IJSMM.2011.044794

Hartwig, T.B., Naughton, G., & Searl, J. (2011). Motion analyses of adolescent rugby union players: A comparison of training and game demands. *Journal of Strength and Conditioning Research, 25,* 966–972.

Hickie, G. (2014). Lineout coach. *Learn from the pros: Leinster use of technology in rugby.* Retrieved from www.lineoutcoach.com/2014/07/28/learn-from-the-pros-leinsters-use-of-technology-in-rugby/

Independent Pictures. (2013). *Tommy Bowe's Bodycheck.* Retrieved from www.youtube.com/watch?v=PhN4td07S4A&feature=youtu.be

Ingle, S. (2016). *Fancy Bears hack again with attack on senior anti-doping officials.* Retrieved from www.theguardian.com/sport/2016/nov/25/fancy-bears-hack-again-with-attack-on-senior-anti-doping-officials

Kirwan, G. (2016). Psychological applications of virtual reality. In I. Connolly, M. Palmer, H. Barton, & G. Kirwan (Eds.), *An introduction to cyberpsychology* (pp. 271–285). London: Routledge.

Kitman Labs. (2017). *British and Irish lions go on tour with Kitman Labs.* Retrieved from www.kitmanlabs.com/press-releases/&idx=397&limit=27236#!

Kooiman, T.J.M., Dontje, M.L., Sprenger, S.R., Krijnen, W.P., van der Schans, C.P., & de Groot, M. (2015). Reliability and validity of ten consumer activity monitors. *BMC Sports Science, Medicine & Rehabilitation, 7,* 24–35.

Lamkin, P. (2017). *Wearable tech market to be worth $34 billion by 2020.* Retrieved from https://www.forbes.com/sites/paullamkin/2016/02/17/wearable-tech-market-to-be-worth-34-billion-by-2020/#33c26a9e3cb5.

MacIntyre, T., Moran, A., Collet, C., Guillot, A., Campbell, M., Matthews, J., Mahoney, C., & Lowther, J. (2013). *The BASES expert statement on the use of mental imagery in sport, exercise and rehabilitation contexts.* The Sport Scientist, 38. Retrieved from www.bases. org.uk/Use-of-Mental-Imagery-in-Sport-Exercise-and-Rehabilitation-Contexts

McNeill, D.K.P., de Heer, H.D., Bounds, R.G., & Coast, J.R. (2015). Accuracy of unloading with the anti-gravity treadmill. *Journal of Strength and Conditioning, 29,* 863–868.

Moran, A. (2012). *Sport and exercise psychology: A critical introduction.* London: Routledge.

Moran, A., & Toner, J. (2017). *A critical introduction to sport psychology.* London: Routledge.

Nelson, R.A., & Strachan, I. (2009). Action and puzzle video games prime different speed/accuracy tradeoffs. *Perception, 38,* 1678–1687.

Ogden, M. (2011). *United's appliance of science.* Retrieved from www.independent.ie/sport/soccer/uniteds-appliance-of-science-26616385.html

Patil, S., Steklov, N., Bugbee, W.D., Goldberg, T., Colwell, C.W., & D'Lima, D.D. (2013). Anti-gravity treadmills are effective in reducing knee force. *Journal of Orthopaedic Research, 31,* 672–679.

Ramsey, L., Tangermann, M., Haufe, S., & Blankertz, B. (2009). *Practising fast decision BCI using a 'goalkeeper' paradigm.* Poster presentation at the Eighteenth Annual Computational Neuroscience Meeting, on 18–23 July, Berlin: Germany.

Saxena, A., & Granot, A. (2011). Use of an anti-gravity treadmill in the rehabilitation of the operated Achilles tendon: A pilot study. *The Journal of Foot and Ankle Surgery, 50,* 558–561.

Spence, I., & Feng, J. (2010). Video games and spatial recognition. *Review of General Psychology, 14,* 92–104.

Stulberg, S. (2017). *Want to run fast? Listen to your gut.* Outside: Science of performance. Retrieved from www.outsideonline.com/2151696/the-art-of-training-by-feel

Tekscan. (n.d.). *Pressure mapping, force measurement and tactile sensors.* Retrieved from www.tekscan.com/test-measurement

Ultimate Fighting Competition (UFC). (2017). *UFC and Kitman Labs launch innovative sports science program.* Retrieved from www.ufc.com/news/UFC-Kitman-Labs-Launch-Innovative-Sports-Science-Program

Watterson, J. (2015). *Rugby looks to science for better players.* The Irish Times. Retrieved from www.irishtimes.com/sport/rugby/rugby-looks-to-science-for-better-players-1.2156366

Wollersheim, D., Merkes, M., Shields, N., Liamputtong, P., Wallis, L., Reynolds, F., & Koh, L. (2010). Physical and psychosocial effects of Wii video game use among older women. *International Journal of Emerging Technologies and Society, 8,* 85–98.

PART II

Exploring the use of technology to prepare athletes for their sport

3

ATHLETIC PERFORMANCE

The impact of technology on the mental preparation of elite athletes

CASE STUDY 3

Adam is an elite 28-year-old rugby player on a well-known rugby team. He has recently been recovering from left shoulder surgery, which was required due to an injury Adam suffered during a competitive rugby game. Adam is now physically ready to return to full contact training, as his medical specialists – his surgeon, doctor and physiotherapist – have all confirmed that his shoulder is fully healed. The shoulder-strengthening and mobility work Adam has been completing in the gym with his strength and conditioning coach for the past number of weeks have indicated his left shoulder is now at the same level of mobility and strength as it was before Adam sustained his injury. Adam's team uses GPS and video analysis technology to record and measure various aspects of their players' performances in training and in matches. The performance outputs from each individual player for each session are made available for all of the management team, the squad players and the sport science support team to view.

 (i) How might the GPS technology his team uses help Adam return to full fitness for his sport of rugby?
(ii) What notes of caution are advised for athletes, teams and coaches using such technology?
(iii) How might the availability of GPS and video technology data to all of Adam's teammates and support staff be of assistance, but could also potentially harm Adam, as he works towards a return to his pre-injury levels of fitness and performance for rugby?

3.1 Overview

This chapter expands on the information presented in Chapter 2, where an explanation of some new pieces of technology (i.e., Global Positioning System (GPS) devices, video analysis technology, smart mobile devices and gaming devices) created in recent years to help athletes prepare both physically and mentally for their sport performances were described. This chapter presents some theoretical perspectives, as well as some empirical research findings regarding the uses of these technologies by athletes in their preparations for their sport. Specific focus is placed on these technologies' potential impact on athletes' mental states. The application and implications of virtual reality (VR) devices, such as the Oculus Rift and HTC Vive, within numerous elite and non-elite performance arenas will be presented in Chapter 4, as such VR applications are considered an extensive area for potential future research within the sport cyberpsychology domain.

3.2 Learning objectives

1 To explain some key terms presented in this chapter
2 To highlight research findings currently available regarding the potential impact of some of the devices introduced in Chapter 2 on the preparations of athletes
3 To suggest some exciting future research directions for these applied technologies in the area of sport cyberpsychology

3.3 Definitions of relevant terms

Achievement goal theory (also known as goal orientation theory; Nicholls, 1984)

This theory explains two types of motivation orientations in athletes, namely an *ego orientation* (where the athletes focus on displaying their abilities by performing better than their opponents) and a *task orientation* (where the athletes focus on performing to personal 'best' standards, often referred to in sport as PBs).

HawkEye

A technology-based system that detects if a point has been scored in Gaelic football and hurling. It uses four high-speed cameras, mounted on the upright goal posts, in order to detect if the ball has gone through the posts and a point can be correctly awarded. HawkEye can detect the match ball at 26 meters above the posts and 4 meters outside of the posts. It can make a decision regarding whether a point should be awarded within one second, so that this 'view' can then be watched as a replay on a large screen at a game venue by the officials, players and spectators alike.

Television Match Official (TMO)

The TMO is an individual positioned in a room, at a game venue of, typically, high profile rugby union matches, with a series of television screens that enable the individual to watch/replay a piece of the game from a number of different angles in order to make a correct decision – such as, if a try has actually been scored, or if any sanction should be taken against a player if there is a suspicion that foul play has been committed by the player). The TMO is typically called upon by the main match referee to help with such decisions when the referee's own view of the play or incident has been obscured in some way (i.e., by other players' body positions) in real-time during the game.

The Quiet Eye (QE)

This term describes the length of time that passes between the last fixation of a skilled performer's gaze on a specific target and the start of the targeted skill to be executed commencing.

3.4 Introduction

As already commented in Chapters 1 and 2, in this digital age, the interaction between technology and psychology, especially when considering the physical and mental preparation of athletes for their sport cannot be ignored. Sport science professionals charged with preparing athletes for competition are now working closely with team and individual athletes, coaches, as well as technology professionals, in order to create devices that report to measure and assist in enhancing the performances of athletes in their sport, and indeed others working in areas where motor skill execution is of great importance to performance outcomes too, such as in medical surgery procedures. Chris Kluwe, sport biomechanics expert and lead scientist for ESPN's *Sport Science* show, noted that,

> Every generation, we feel like we've reached that pinnacle where we've run the fastest 40 time we're going to run, or we've gone the fastest through the downhill we're ever going to go, or this technology is perfect, or technology can't get any better. But then we always go past it.
>
> *(cited in Loria, 2015)*

To help achieve such feats, GPS technology, eye-tracking equipment, video motion analysis and smart mobile devices (i.e., smartphones and tablets), as well as AGAG treadmills and pressure pads, for example, which were explained in Chapter 2, have been integrated into the routine assessment and training or rehabilitation environments of many elite athletes. For example, Ian Madigan, former Leinster and Bordeaux rugby player, now playing with Bristol Rugby in the UK, speaking about his coaches (Pat Lamb, Bristol Rugby head coach, and Joe Schmidt, Irish Men's Rugby team head coach) on their use of video analysis technology in their training environment, referred to such technology, saying,

> Pat (Lamb)'s attention to detail is incredible. We use the *[airborne] drone* in training. Pat must watch the training footage at least 30 times because it seems as if he is man-marking everyone and [seeing] which guys are working hard

and which guys aren't. Who's out of position. Who's getting off the ground quickly. . . . I remember when Joe (Schmidt) came in, the *video analysis* guys were worked off their feet because Joe wanted to measure so many different things for every player. Pat is no different.

(cited in The Hard Yards, 2017)

While the developers of these devices may claim they provide benefits for athletes in their sport performances and training outputs, searches for empirical, evidence-based findings on the psychological impacts of these devices were much less fruitful and, therefore, give rise to some concerns regarding the widespread use of these devices in sport settings. Much of the evidence available from coaches and athletes using these devices and commenting on their impact, especially from a psychological perspective, appear largely anecdotal in nature. This chapter presents some of the available research findings generated to date on the advantages and disadvantages of using such technologies in the training environments of athletes, from a largely psychological perspective. Suggestions for future research projects by sport psychologists and cyberpsychologists, working together, to uncover the specific impacts of such technologies within sport and performance arenas are suggested at the end of this chapter.

3.5 Research findings on the impact of GPS devices

Many team sports performing at an elite level now employ some form of GPS monitoring of the players' performances in training and also in competition. As mentioned in Chapter 2, such performance-monitoring systems provide objective information to coaches, sport scientists and the athletes themselves on a range of performance outputs, such as heart rate, force of tackles (i.e., 'hits') made, number of collisions (tackles – made by and on players), time taken to return to a standing position following a collision, speed of running into a tackle (acceleration/pace), position of an athlete's head in collision sports (important in concussion-related research and monitoring protocols), change of direction when running and the length of an athlete's stride patterns. All of these movement monitors can help coaches and an athlete's support staff to decide if, for example, certain players are fatiguing or may be injured. Such information can then help in the decision-making process regarding player substitutions (Watterson, 2015). According to Dellaserra, Gao, and Ransdell (2013), two types of GPS networks are available today, namely differential and non-differential, with the latter being more favoured for use in sport settings in recent times because they are often smaller and less costly (Townshend, Worringham, & Stewart, 2008). They are, however, sometimes considered less accurate on measures such as speed, and require more research in sport settings in order to ensure their measurements are valid (Adrados, Girard, Gendner, & Janeau, 2002).

Dellaserra et al. (2013) provided an in-depth review of the use of integrated technology (typically including accelerometers, GPS and heart rate monitors) in team sport and made some commendable suggestions for future research such as finding ways to incorporate technology in sport in order to test for the effects of supplements and hormones on athletes' performances. They also suggested more research in the area of wearable technology (see Halson, 2016, for a review of wearable technology for athletes). However, Dellaserra et al.'s (2013) review of the use of integrated technology in team sport did not address the issue of potential psychological impacts the use of such technologies on the athletes being monitored may have.

For sport psychologists, the link between the physical and mental performances of athletes whose performances are being tracked using GPS technology is an interesting one. For example, some athletes may report 'feeling' they are exerting their best efforts in training or in match situations. However, their GPS data might not indicate this, yet it provides them and their coaches with what are often considered the best indicators of that effort. A number of subjective self-report measures and methods have been created to also capture the athletes' ratings of their perceived exertion (known as RPE) in training and in competition settings. Such measures have included athletes keeping diaries, where they record their RPEs, as well as specific psychological self-report measures such as Borg's RPE measurement tool (Borg, 1998), the session RPE (sREP; Foster, 1998), the Recovery-Stress Questionnaire for Athletes (Kellmann & Kallus, 2001, 2016), the Acute Recovery and Stress Scale and the shortened version of it, called the Short Recovery and Stress Scale (Kellmann, Kölling, & Hitzschke, 2016); see Saw, Kellmann, Main, & Gastin, 2017, for a detailed overview of the characteristics of, and guidelines for use of, these various athlete psychological monitoring instruments, when applied in sport environments. Such psychological measures do provide helpful feedback regarding an athlete's perceived efforts, as well as being commendable measures for assisting in decisions regarding any potential overtraining by athletes. These measures are also more cost-effective and faster to obtain than some other, perhaps more objective, physiological and blood marker tests, which can take days or even weeks to complete (Bourdon et al., 2017).

But one important consideration for psychologists and other sport science professionals using these popular GPS technologies is that, from a psychological perspective, the impact of this technology remains unavailable or is in its infancy at best at present. As mentioned in Chapter 2, one possible reason for the favoured use of such technologically driven, objective, GPS tracking measures is that they provide little in the way of 'hiding' for the athletes they monitor. As such, having these objective data measurements to indicate the applied work efforts of athletes when partaking in their sport could result in positive changes in the athletes' motivation levels. Perhaps they increase their efforts in both training and in competition because such measurements are being recorded (as some anecdotal comments from athletes and their coaches, as well as some support staff, attest to – see Ian Madigan's quote at the start of this chapter, for example, and Perry, 2015).

Another advantage, and protective aspect, of GPS technology is that it allows coaches to receive 'live' information from their data analysts 'in-game', so that some warning signs for a player, perhaps reaching a point of fatigue as indicated by the amount of ground covered in a game decreasing for that player, is tracked and relayed to the coaches. The coaches can then make an informed decision to substitute the player as a result of this available information (Kitman Labs, 2017). However, are there other reasons why a player's movement and 'effort' may decrease during a game that is unrelated to his/her physical fatigue levels increasing or an injury having been sustained? A possible answer to this question is presented next.

Despite this GPS data available to coaches to help them in their important decision-making processes in sport, many of them still admit to relying on their subconscious, gut feeling to make their final decisions regarding selection and substitutions during or before games, irrespective of the GPS data they have received from their analysts (Collins, Collins, & Carson, 2016). Given that athletes often cite fairness in coaching decisions as an issue of importance, it is interesting to read that many coaches may still choose to disregard the objective data available to them in favour of other less tangible opinions and feelings they may have about a particular athlete at a specific point in time (Bradbury & Forsyth, 2012). If such coaches cannot justify their decisions to substitute players using the objective outputs, such as GPS data, what impact could this have on their players' future efforts for the team? This point relates back to the question posed earlier regarding fatigue being the only reason for a decrease in the performance efforts by athletes during training or competition settings. Perhaps it is not – perhaps an athlete's motivation to work hard for the team is impacted upon by what could be perceived as a lack of fairness or the lack of a logical explanation regarding the coach's or manager's decisions, often related to team selections and/or player substitutions.

Sport psychologists interested in team cohesion factors have identified and studied the phenomenon of 'social loafing' within team sport for many years (Moran & Toner, 2017). From such research it has been concluded it is possible that players who display decreased performance efforts are not actually physically or mentally fatigued, but rather their motivation levels to 'work hard' for their team, or indeed their coach/manager, can decrease instead due to unexplained or perceived unjustified player selection or substitution decisions by their coaches or managers (De Backer, Boen, Cuyper, Høigaard, & De Brock, 2014). GPS monitoring does not allow for such psychological reasons for reductions in athletes' efforts to be captured. Only detailed psychological assessment, in combination with GPS monitoring perhaps, could potentially uncover the real reasons why athletes display reduced performance efforts within their sport environments (De Backer et al., 2014).

As mentioned earlier, although definitely useful, GPS monitoring could also have some psychologically harmful effects for athletes. Ironically, these effects may have been the reasons the technology was introduced in the first place (i.e., to monitor overreaching or overtraining and burnout in athletes, as well as those at increased risk of physical injury and illness). Athletes may actually feel *more* pressure to work hard to 'up their stats' while wearing GPS monitors, when perhaps rest and recovery may actually be what they need. As Ryan Giggs, cited in Ogden (2011) and referred to in Chapter 2, said: "With all the stats that you get, you can't hide. . . . You can't duck out of training or not work hard because it's all monitored". Is it possible then that coaches and analysts, through the use of GPS technology, may be placing some athletes at risk of injury or burnout?

Many teams, as mentioned earlier, also publish the data gathered from their athletes wearing such GPS devices, so that all members of their training squads and support staff can see them (Dellaserra et al., 2013; Ogden, 2011). This action may act as a motivator for some athletes, such as athletes with greater 'ego-oriented' motivations for their performances. Such individuals may be more averse to finding themselves positioned at the bottom of a list of their teammates for various performance output measures recorded by their GPS monitors. However, such data outputs could be more useful for 'mastery-oriented' athletes because they typically set training and performance goals based on improving previous objective training efforts, or their existing personal bests (see an explanation of achievement goal theory (Nicholls, 1984) in Section 3.3; see Conroy & Hyde, 2014, for a review of mastery-oriented and ego-oriented performance goals). So, in summary, while publishing athletes' performance outputs may be beneficial within some team cultures, by assisting in, for example, the creation of higher performance standards within those team environments, in other cases, athletes in such settings may feel under immense pressure to train beyond their current capabilities and suffer injuries as a result of putting added pressure on their bodies. All sport personnel should be aware of these potential risks to the physical and mental health of their athletes when using these technologies and maintain a balanced approach to the importance of the data GPS monitors gather within such sport performance settings.

To conclude this section, the application of wearing GPS devices is in its infancy within competitive sport environments, given that it is only in the last seven or eight years that many teams have started to fully implement the use of such technology within their sport environments. There does still appear to be a lack of empirical research available to clearly illustrate their psychological impact, both positively and negatively, on the athletes using them. What is known is that GPS technology is not infallible. The higher the movement or 'change' in velocity of the athlete, for example, the lower the reliability of the GPS data (Akenhead, French, Thompson, & Hayes, 2014; Dellaserra et al., 2013; Varley, Fairweather, & Aughey, 2012). Indeed, Bourdon et al. (2017) clearly stated that "acceleration, deceleration and directional change data from GPS should be interpreted with caution" (p. S2-163). (For a more detailed review of GPS and IT validity and reliability, see Dellaserra et al., 2013, and Scott, Scott, & Kelly, 2016). The limitations of such GPS monitoring technology in sport needs to be communicated openly and widely to, and understood by, athletes and coaches alike, so that the data generated from these devices are only regarded as 'one' and not 'the' measure for evaluating an athlete's performance. But what about the impact of the other technological devices described in Chapter 2? The potential impact of video motion analysis technology within elite sport settings is presented next.

3.6 Research findings on the impact of video analysis technology

Video analysis, like GPS, is now used by a large number of sport teams and individual athletes to identify areas for improvement within their sport performances. It is a valuable tool in such settings because, similar to the GPS technology, it provides objective feedback to athletes and coaches on what aspects of a performance are being executed in a positive way and also what areas could benefit from some improvement. Video analysis can also, like GPS devices, be used to help prevent injuries in players. It can do this by identifying biomechanical flaws in an athlete's movement patterns. Ryan Giggs, former MUFC player, alluded to this in the quote at the start of Chapter 2 when he stated,

> There is an underwater treadmill, where you can get your running action back quickly because, in the water, you can run as hard as you want. . . . There are cameras underneath the pool which monitor your foot pattern, to make sure that you're not limping. There's no escape!
>
> *(cited in Ogden, 2011)*

Video motion data provides sport scientists with important information to help them advise athletes on how best to correct the sport skill execution anomalies that could, if left unchanged, lead to injuries in the athletes in the future.

Another advantage of video analysis technology is that it allows athletes to model their performance patterns, moves and tactics on those of the best athletes participating in their sport. Modelling such expert behaviours can enable athletes to improve their own performances (Boschker & Bakker, 2002; Boyer, Miltenberger, Batsche, & Fogel, 2009; SooHoo, Takemoto, & McCullagh, 2004). Video analysis data also allows athletes to study the performances of their potential opponents in order to devise strategies to overcome their opponents in future competitions (see Madigan, cited in his interview for The Hard Yards, 2017).

As discussed earlier for GPS technology, video analysis data could also have both positive and negative psychological outcomes for athletes. It can act as a motivator, similar to GPS data, to help athletes identify areas for improvement and then enable them to set training goals in order to improve those areas of their sport performances. Such strategies often help athletes to continue to increase their performance standards within their sport too (Williams, 2013). However, some athletes have also remarked on the psychological and social difficulties they experience when watching back over such video data of their performances, especially within large public team settings (FM104 Sport, 2014). Individual, privately given, one-to-one feedback is typically recommended for academics giving their students their course performance feedback (Reynolds, 2013). Such private feedback strategies in educational settings are recommended because they are thought to protect students from experiencing negative psychological outcomes, such as, if other members of their class group also hear the feedback and form negative opinions about the student as a result. Such feedback strategies are not typically applied within sport settings, especially team environments where the individual's performance often impacts on the overall team performance. As such, there appears to be a culture of athletes being encouraged to take responsibility for their individual performances and 'owning' them in the presence of their teammates (Kidman, 2005). Resilience training (as explained in Chapter 1) has become a popular strategy employed by sport psychologists to help combat and protect athletes from the potentially negative consequences that making mistakes can have on their psychological well-being (Fletcher & Sarkar, 2012; Sarkar & Fletcher, 2013, 2017a, 2017b). Perhaps such resilience training is a way to protect these athletes from any negative psychological consequence of such video analysis feedback also. Indeed, such resilience training could protect athletes against the impact of receiving negative GPS data readings also.

Another benefit of video analysis data, although not related to the athletes' performances, is its use in improving the performances of the officials umpiring sport events. Video analysis is now used to help referees make correct decisions, when, for example, their line of sight has been obscured during a real-time action in a sport event. Rugby union is one sport that has introduced such playback video analysis technology in order to help their officials in such situations. The Television Match Official (or TMO; defined at the start of this chapter) is now regarded as a member of the match officials whose job it is to communicate with the on-pitch umpire(s) when asked for assistance in order to make a correct decision regarding a specific piece of game play (for example, whether or not to award a try – i.e., asking if the ball has been grounded successfully – or if a piece of illegal play has taken place that warrants some kind of sanction against a player by the match officials). With an understanding that officials can make cognitive errors when placed in such high-intensity environments in sport (Neville, Balmer, & Williams, 2002), such technological supports have typically been welcomed within the sport world in general, and by the sport personnel using them, in certain situations, such as for try-line decisions in rugby union as cited previously (Santiago, 2009).

However, as with practically all such technology, video analysis has its critics and its limitations. For example, international rugby union referee, Nigel Owens from Wales, who is regarded as one of the best referees in the sport of rugby union recently stated that, in his opinion, there needs to be a 'rethink' of the role of the TMO in rugby. Owens stated that such technology use has led to an over-reliance on it to make decisions for match umpires and that the TMO's role has the potential to erode the spectators' and players' confidence in the umpire to make any correct decisions within a game (RTE Sport, 2016). Other journalists and commentators in rugby union have voiced similar concerns and criticisms regarding the use of the TMO (Kelly, 2016). However, given its reliability and ability to determine the outcomes of matches in some cases, such video technology is unlikely to be removed from sports where it has been introduced to ensure a greater degree of fairness and accuracy in the decision-making process, especially during high profile sport events.

Other sports have introduced similar technology to assist officials in making decisions when they too are unsure of what the correct decision should be (O'Connor, 2015). For example, within Gaelic games (e.g., Gaelic football and hurling in Ireland), HawkEye technology has followed the introduction of the TMO in rugby union. HawkEye has been introduced in major Gaelic games in the All Ireland Championship in order to help officials determine if a player has successfully scored a point. The technology helps the officials when they are not certain if the ball has or has not passed through the two upright posts in real-time, especially in the game of hurling when the ball can often move at speeds too quick for the human eye to track. Similar technology is used in tennis where the ball also travels at very quick speeds. In tennis, HawkEye is typically used to determine if the tennis ball has bounced inside or outside of a line on the tennis court, from a serve, for example (Newcomb, 2015).

3.7 Research findings on the impact of eye-tracking technology

Eye-tracking technology used in sport, as mentioned in Chapter 1 and explained in Chapter 2, enables researchers to 'track' an athletes' eye gazes or 'fixations', using specially fitted cameras on goggles worn by the athletes, in order to measure where and for how long the athletes are 'fixated upon' or 'looking at' certain stimuli within their sport environment.

This eye-tracking technology has been used extensively within the cognitive sport psychology domains, particularly in the study of expert-novice differences in individual sport, such as golf, and in team sport, such as basketball. Typically, it is used to analyse closed skills (a skill where another individual cannot interfere with the athlete as the skill is executed – such as putting in golf or taking a 'free-throw' in basketball) (Vickers, 1996, 2007). A specific type of visual patterned behaviour known was the 'quiet eye', or QE, was identified within such sport-based research studies. This pattern of longer eye gazing described the phenomenon that expert performers typically displayed when preparing to execute a targeted skill, like a golf putt. Expert performers who were recorded as gazing for longer periods of time before executing such skills were also found to be more successful in their skill efforts (Rienhoff, Fischer, Strauss, Baker, & Schorer, 2015). Reasons for such successful outcomes were proposed by Klosterman, Kredel, and Hossner (2014) as being due to other alternative movement variables being prevented and by Moore, Vine, Freeman, and Wilson (2012) as a way of encouraging an external focus of attention. This implies that training athletes to 'quieten their eye', or to fixate their visual gaze for a longer period of time on a specific aimed-for target prior to executing the skill could be an effective concentration strategy for the athletes to apply. Such training in QE has been carried out by a number of researchers, with some positive effects on sport skill performances being reported (Vine & Wilson, 2011; Vine, Moore, & Wilson, 2014). Such eye-tracking and QE training has also been shown to be somewhat effective in alleviating symptoms of anxiety in athletes (Causer, Holmes, & Williams, 2011; Vickers & Williams, 2007) and, as such, could enhance their performances as a result of applying these techniques.

3.8 Research findings on the impact of brain-training devices

Brain-training devices have also become popular technologies used within sport environments to potentially enhance some of the mental skills of athletes as detailed in Chapter 1 (namely, their concentration skills, for example). These devices claim to measure the brain activity of athletes during various sport tasks and, as such, help to increase the brain's mental fitness, or reduce what is commonly referred to as mental fatigue (Smith, Marcora, & Coutts, 2015). Team sports, soccer for example, have been identified as some of the most mentally demanding sports on their participant athletes' resources (Coutts, 2016). A tired brain is now thought to have as great an impact on an athlete's performance as a tired muscle or limb may have. Such mental fatigue was found to impair the performances of soccer players (Smith et al., 2016). Many sport scientists recognise that this fatigue exists and it is now common for caffeine supplements to be ingested prior to and during competitive sport contests by athletes attempting to ward off such fatigue. Since 2003, caffeine is no longer on the World Anti-Doping Agency's (WADA) list of prohibited substances. However, it remains on the watched, or monitored, list of substances which WADA uses to indicate products it is still studying in order to determine if they should be banned substances. Caffeine could be placed back on WADA's banned list in the near future, if some commentators are to be believed (Yeager & Lindsey, 2017).

Brain-training devices such as BRAINY have been designed in recent years (for the Google Glass augmented headset platform) and researchers have begun to explore the cognitive enhancement such devices may be able to offer generally to individuals in many performance environments, including sport (Swan, Kido, & Ruckenstein, 2014). However, the ability of such cognitive-training devices to actually improve cognitive performances have been called into question in recent times, with a study by Kable et al. (2017) refuting the claims that these devices have a positive effect on cognitive abilities such as decision making. A consistent criticism of these brain-training games is that if any improvements in test scores are seen the improvements may only be specific to that particular test, in essence that the improvement is a practice effect (Swan et al., 2014). More research is needed in this area in order to provide a clearer picture of what the benefits of such brain-training games actually are if they are to be advocated among populations interested in mental and brain fitness, such as athletes.

3.9 Research findings on the impact of computer games

As the popularity of computer games has risen in recent years (Goh, Ang, & Tan, 2008), so too has the number of companies developing game products to help athletes prepare mentally and physically for their sport. Products such as the bio-feedback technology tool, FlexComp Infiniti (Perry, Shaw, & Zaichkowsky, 2011), have been developed for such uses. The potential of such technology to help athletes control their emotions and assist their performances has been reported (Perry et al., 2011).

Game developers have also specifically created virtual worlds to help prepare athletes for their own specific sport competitions. For example, some gaming companies have developed products that mimic the environments of major sport events such as the recent FIFA World Cup, the Rugby World Cup and Formula One motor racing. However, specific research findings on the benefits of individuals playing video games in order to benefit mentally from them in their own sport events has produced mixed results (Boot, Blakely, & Simons, 2011). Some studies have reported benefits in athletes' performances from playing such video games, for example, improvements in their decision-making skills (Nelson & Strachan, 2009), their reaction times (Ramsey, Tangermann, Haufe, & Blankertz, 2009) as well as their mental imagery and spatial awareness skills (Spence & Feng, 2010).

Some athletes' on-field behaviours also appear to have been impacted upon in positive ways as a result of playing computer-generated games. For example, Alert Hockey (AH) was shown to be effective in reducing the aggressive behaviours of ice hockey players in their real play following time playing the AH computer game. The game rewarded 'safe' play, while still focusing on successful outcomes (Ciavarro, Dobson, & Goodman, 2008). AH also had injury-reduction pay-offs, as aggressive ice hockey players were more prone to experiencing concussions and these episodes of injury were noted as occurring less when the players displayed more desirable 'safe' plays during their real games. Ciavarro et al.'s research findings indicated the potential use for such video games in changing real-time game-play behaviours of athletes.

Other studies, however, have found no significant benefit, or indeed have actually reported some potential adverse effects of such video game playing on the sport performances of athletes, explained by some researchers as being due to such games not 'tapping into' the relevant 'real-time' physical skills that athletes must perform in order to be successful at executing specific skills within their own sport (Wollersheim et al., 2010).

Interestingly, some health and exercise applications (apps) designed for mobile devices, although not specifically designed for use by elite athletes, are nonetheless often popular among such populations perhaps because they offer mobility and ease of use (Hurley, 2016; Radovic et al., 2016). Many athletes have reported using mental health targeted apps specifically to prepare for their sport events. For example, Team GB diver, Tom Daley, commented on his use of a mindfulness app in his preparations for the Rio 2016 Summer Olympic Games. Tom stated that he engaged in mindfulness training and meditation using the app Headspace for 10 minutes every morning when he woke. He reported that this app was also used by many other Team GB athletes as part of their Rio Games preparations and that they too had reported mental benefits in using it for preparations for their sport (PA Sport, 2016).

Radovic et al. (2016) examined the use of a number of such mental health apps by young people seeking information about various mental health issues or looking for ways to alleviate symptoms of mental distress. The most frequent uses of such apps was for symptom alleviation (41%), followed by psychological-based education (18%) and self-diagnosis (10%). Radovic et al. identified the most common interventions recommended for use on these latest apps included low-level mindfulness interventions, as well as various relaxation and self-monitoring practices, all of which would could potentially benefit individuals suffering with mild symptoms of mental distress, but which are unlikely to impact on severe, clinical levels of depression or anxiety, for example. Such unsatisfactory outcomes for individuals in already distressed states should be a cautionary note, as they could add to the feelings of helplessness experienced by already vulnerable individuals, especially considering their over-expectancy of the potential effectiveness of such apps, based on the testimonials of non-comparable individuals, in very different mental states.

Another risk of using and relying on such apps in any elite sport or in health settings is that such apps are often designed by non-academic, unqualified individuals. Any advice regarding training regimes and physical or mental health advice offered on such apps should be combined with consultations with experts trained to provide advice in those areas to individuals in vulnerable mental health states.

3.10 Conclusion, including future directions for research

The aim of this chapter was to highlight the research findings currently available regarding the potential impact of some of the devices, introduced in Chapter 2, on the preparations of athletes. Some exciting future research directions for these applied technologies in the area of sport cyberpsychology are apparent from the review of the available research to date on these devices. Only by completing more extensive, empirically sound, longitudinal studies can the many questions raised in this chapter about the psychological benefits of such devices, as used by athletes for sport performance enhancement, be truly answered. Perhaps qualitative methodologies could be applied in order to gather athletes' personal views on such technologies? This research approach could help to determine if the use of GPS monitoring and video analysis, for example, within athletes' training and competitive environments have any repercussions for their mental preparation, as well as for their general health and well-being.

Also, some of the criticisms of mobile sport and exercise apps include their lack of empirical-based evidence regarding their apparent effectiveness. Much of the support for their effectiveness comes from anecdotal accounts such as user testimonials. Future researchers could consider designing more rigid, experimental-based studies in order to test the potential cognitive and performance-related effectiveness of these apps in a more robust way.

3.11 Open-ended discussion questions

1   How might resilience training, as applied within sport psychology, be used to protect athletes against any negative impact of technology-based feedback (i.e., video analysis) provided to them on their sport performances?
2   Other than practice effects, what potential flaws in the testing of brain-training devices could account for their cognitive enhancement false-positive results?

3.12 Practical exercise

In pairs, have your students carry out a fun role-play exercise between a 'coach' and one of his or her 'team players'. The player is arguing against the wearing of GPS devices for monitoring players' performances in training and matches. The coach is taking the opposite position, in favour of the team's players all wearing this monitoring technology. Both students must present empirically-based reasons in support of their differing positions as the coach/player. Whose argument is most convincing?

References

Adrados, C., Girard, I., Gendner, J.P., & Janeau, G. (2002). Global positioning system (GPS) location accuracy improvement due to selective availability removal. *Comptes Rendus Biologies, 325,* 165–170.

Akenhead, R., French, D., Thompson, K.D., & Hayes, P.R. (2014). The acceleration dependent validity and reliability of 10 Hz GPS. *Journal of Science and Medicine in Sport, 17,* 562–566.

Boot, W.R., Blakely, D.P., & Simons, D.J. (2011). Do action video games improve perception and cognition? *Frontiers in Psychology, 2,* 226. doi: 10.3389/fpsyg.2011.00226

Borg, G. (1998). *Borg's perceived exertion and pain ratings scales.* Champaign, IL: Human Kinetics.

Boschker, M.C.J., & Bakker, F.C. (2002). Inexperienced sport climbers might perceive and utilize new opportunities for action by merely observing a model. *Perceptual and Motor Skills, 95,* 3–9.

Bourdon, P.C., Cardinale, M., Murray, A., Gastin, P., Kellmann, M., Varley, M.C., Gabbett, T.J., Coutts, A.J., Burgess, D.J., Gregson, W., & Cable, N.T. (2017). Monitoring athlete training loads: Consensus statement. *International Journal of Sports Physiology and Performance, 12,* S2-161–S2-170.

Boyer, E., Miltenberger, R.G., Batsche, C. & Fogel, V. (2009). Video modeling by experts with video feedback to enhance gymnastics skills. *Journal of Applied Behaviour Analysis, 42,* 855–860.

Bradbury, T., & Forsyth, D. (2012). You're in, you're out: Selection practices of coaches. *Sport, Business & Management: An International Journal, 2*, 7–20.

Causer, J., Holmes, P.S., & Williams, A.M. (2011). Quiet eye training in a visuomotor control task. *Medicine and Science in Sports and Exercise, 43*, 1042–1049.

Ciavarro, C., Dobson, M., & Goodman, D. (2008). Implicit learning as a design strategy for learning games: Alert Hockey. *Computers in Human Behaviour, 24*, 2862–2872.

Collins, D., Collins, L., & Carson, H. (2016). 'If it feels right, do it': Intuitive decision making in a sample of high level sports coaches. *Frontiers in Psychology, 7*, 504. doi: 10.3389/fpsyg.2016.00504

Conroy, D.E., & Hyde, A.L. (2014). Achievement goal theory. In R.C. Ekland & G. Tenenbaum (Eds.), *Encyclopedia of sport and exercise psychology* (Vol. 1, pp. 1–5). London: Sage Publications.

Coutts, A.J. (2016). Fatigue in football: It's not a brainless task! *Journal of Sports Sciences, 34*, 1296.

De Backer, M., Boen, F., Cuyper, B. De, Høigaard, R., & De Brock, G. Van. (2014). A team fares well with a fair coach: Predictors of social loafing in interactive female sport teams. *Scandinavian Journal of Medicine & Science in Sports, 25*, 897–908.

Dellaserra, C., Gao, Y., & Ransdell, L. (2013). Use of integrated technology in team sports: A review of opportunities, challenges, and future directions for athletes. *Journal of Strength & Conditioning Research, 28*, 556–573. doi: 10.1519/JSC.0b013e3182a952fb

Fletcher, D., & Sarkar, M. (2012). A grounded theory of psychological resilience in Olympic champions. *Psychology of Sport and Exercise, 13*, 669–678.

FM104 Sport. (2014). *Healy says video session wasn't pretty.* Retrieved from www.fm104.ie/sport/healy-says-video-session-wasn-t-pretty/

Foster, C. (1998). Monitoring training in athletes with reference to overtraining syndrome. *Medicine & Science in Sport & Exercise, 30*, 1164–1168.

Goh, D.H., Ang, R.P., & Tan, H.C. (2008). Strategies for designing effective therapeutic gaming interventions for children and adolescents. *Computers in Human Behaviour, 24*, 2217–2235.

The Hard Yards. (2017). *Episode 25: Ian Madigan's time in France, ROG's pre-season and South Africa's pro14 teams.* Retrieved from https://soundcloud.com/thehardyardssportsjoe/ep-25-ian-madigans-time-in-france-rogs-pre-season-and-south-africas-pro14-team

Halson, S.L. (2016). Wearable technology for athletes: Information overload and pseudoscience? *International Journal of Sports Physiology and Performance, 11*, 705–706.

Hurley, O. (2016). Sport and health cyberpsychology. In I. Connolly, M. Palmer, H. Barton, & G. Kirwan (Eds.), *An introduction to cyberpsychology* (pp. 167–180). London: Routledge.

Kable, J.W., Caulfield, K.M., Falcone, M., McConnell, M., Bernardo, L., Parthasarathi, T., Cooper, N., Ashare, R., Audrain-McGovern, J., Hornik, R., Diefenbach, P., Lee, F.J., & Lerman, C. (2017). No effect of commercial cognitive training on neural activity during decision making. *Journal of Neuroscience, 10*, 2832–16. Retrieved from https://doi.org/10.1523/JNEUROSCI.2832-16.2017

Kellmann, M., & Kallus, K.W. (2001). *The recovery-stress questionnaire for athletes.* Champaign, IL: Human Kinetics.

Kellmann, M., & Kallus, K.W. (2016). Recovery-stress questionnaire for athletes. In K.W. Kallus & M. Kellmann (Eds.), *The recovery-stress questionnaires: User manual* (pp. 86–131). Frankfurt am Main, Germany: Pearson Assessment & Information.

Kellmann, M., Kölling, S., & Hitzschke, B. (2016). *The acute measure and short scale of recovery and stress for sports: Manual.* Köln, Germany: Sportverlag Strauß.

Kelly, D. (2016). *'The TMO undermined the referee': Five things we learned from Ireland's defeat to the All Blacks.* The Irish Independent. Retrieved from www.independent.ie/sport/

rugby/international-rugby/the-tmo-undermined-the-referee-five-things-we-learned-from-irelands-defeat-to-the-all-blacks-35229423.html

Kidman, L. (2005). *Athlete-centred coaching: Developing inspired and inspiring people*. New Zealand: Innovative Print Communications Ltd.

Kitman Labs. (2017). *British and Irish lions go on tour with Kitman Labs*. Retrieved from www.kitmanlabs.com/press-releases/&idx=397&limit=27236#!

Klosterman, A., Kredel, R., & Hossner, E.J. (2014). On the interaction of attentional focus and gaze: The quiet eye inhibits focus-related performance decrements. *Journal of Sport & Exercise Psychology, 36*, 392–400.

Loria, K. (2015). Science is creating super athletes – and making sports unrecognizable to previous generations. *Business Insider UK*. Retrieved from http://uk.businessinsider.com/how-science-and-technology-are-changing-sports-2015-8?r=US&IR=T

Moore, L.J., Vine, S.J., Freeman, P., & Wilson, M.R. (2012). Quiet eye training promotes challenge appraisals and aids performance under elevated anxiety. *International Journal of Sport & Exercise Psychology, 11*, 169–183.

Moran, A., & Toner, J. (2017). *A critical introduction to sport psychology*. London: Routledge.

Nelson, R.A., & Strachan, I. (2009). Action and puzzle video games prime different speed/accuracy tradeoffs. *Perception, 38*, 1678–1687.

Neville, A.M., Balmer, N.J., & Williams, M.A. (2002). The influence of crowd noise and experience upon refereeing decisions in football. *Psychology of Sport and Exercise, 3*, 261–272.

Newcomb, T. (2015). *The history of tennis umpiring: How Hawk-Eye changed the game*. Retrieved from www.si.com/tennis/2015/11/11/history-of-hawk-eye-tennis-umpiring

Nicholls, J.G. (1984). Achievement motivation: Conceptions of ability, subjective experience, task choice, and performance. *Psychological Review, 91*, 328–346.

O'Connor. (2015). *Why it's time to introduce a TMO at top-level GAA*. Retrieved from http://irishpost.co.uk/why-its-time-to-introduce-a-tmo-to-top-level-gaa/

Ogden, M. (2011). *United's appliance of science*. Retrieved from www.independent.ie/sport/soccer/uniteds-appliance-of-science-26616385.html

PA Sport. (2016). *Tom Daley preparing for Rio Olympics with meditation app*. Retrieved from www.espn.com/olympics/story/_/id/17149668/tom-daley-preparing-rio-olympics-using-headspace-meditation-app

Perry, C. (2015). *Breaking down the top 3 player performance tracking systems*. SportTechie. Retrieved from www.sporttechie.com/breaking-down-the-top-3-player-performance-tracking-systems/

Perry, F.D., Shaw, L., & Zaichkowsky, L. (2011). Biofeedback and neurofeedback in sports. *Biofeedback, 39*, 95–100.

Radovic, A., Vona, P.L., Santostefano, A.M., Ciaravino, S., Miller, E., & Stein, B.D. (2016). Smartphone applications for mental health. *Cyberpsychology, Behaviour and Social Networking, 19*(7), 465–470.

Ramsey, L., Tangermann, M., Haufe, S., & Blankertz, B. (2009). *Practising fast decision BCI using a 'goalkeeper' paradigm*. Poster presentation at the Eighteenth Annual Computational Neuroscience Meeting, on 18–23 July, Berlin: Germany.

Reynolds, L. (2013). *Giving student feedback: 20 tips to do it right*. Retrieved from www.opencolleges.edu.au/informed/features/giving-student-feedback/

Rienhoff, R., Fischer, L., Strauss, B., Baker, J., & Schorer, J. (2015). Focus of attention influences quiet-eye behavior: An exploratory investigation of different skill levels in female basketball players. *Sport, Exercise, and Performance Psychology, 4*, 62–74.

RTE Sport. (2016). *Referee Owens calls for a rethink on TMO decisions*. Retrieved from www.rte.ie/sport/rugby/2016/1115/832023-ref-owens-calls-for/

Santiago, K. (2009). *Technology versus officials: What are the problems and issues caused by introducing the goal line technology in football and how does this affect the referees?* Unpublished thesis, Cardiff Metropolitan University.

Sarkar, M., & Fletcher, D. (2013). How should we measure psychological resilience in sport performers? *Measurement in Physical Education and Exercise Science, 17*, 264–280.

Sarkar, M., & Fletcher, D. (2017a). Adversity-related experiences are essential for Olympic success: Additional evidence and considerations. *Progress in Brain Research, 232*, 159–165.

Sarkar, M., & Fletcher, D. (2017b). How resilience training can enhance wellbeing and performance. In M.F. Crane (Ed.), *Managing for resilience: A practical guide for employee wellbeing and organizational performance* (pp. 227–237). London, UK: Routledge-Taylor and Francis Group.

Saw, A.E., Kellmann, M., Main, L.C., & Gastin, P.B. (2017). Athlete self-report measures in research and practice: Considerations for the discerning reader and fastidious practitioner. *International Journal of Sports Physiology & Performance, 12*, S2-127–S2-135.

Scott, M.T., Scott, T.J., & Kelly, V.G. (2016). The validity and reliability of global positioning systems in team sport: A brief review. *Journal of Strength and Conditioning Research, 30*, 1470–1490.

Smith, M.R., Coutts, A.J., Merlini, M., Deprez, D., Lenoir, M., & Marcora, S.M. (2016). Mental fatigue impairs soccer-specific physical and technical performance. *Medicine & Science in Sports & Exercise, 48*, 267–276.

Smith, M.R., Marcora, S.M., & Coutts, A.J. (2015). Mental fatigue impairs intermittent running performance. *Medicine & Science in Sports & Exercise, 47*, 1682–1690.

SooHoo, S., Takemoto, K.Y., & McCullagh, P. (2004). A comparison of modeling and imagery on the performance of a motor skill. *Journal of Sport Behavior, 27*, 349–366.

Spence, I., & Feng, J. (2010). Video games and spatial cognition. *Review of General Psychology, 14*, 92–104.

Swan, M., Kido, T., & Ruckenstein, M. (2014). *BRAINY: Multi-modal brain training app for Google Glass: Cognitive enhancement, wearable computing and the Internet-of-things extended personnel data analytics.* Retrieved from www.melanieswan.com/documents/VLDB.pdf

Townshend, A.B., Worringham, C.J., & Stewart, I.B. (2008). Assessment of speed and position during human locomotion using nondifferential GPS. *Medicine & Science in Sport & Exercise, 40*, 124–132, 2008.

Varley, M.C., Fairweather, I.H., & Aughey, R.J. (2012). Validity and reliability of GPS for measuring instantaneous velocity during acceleration, deceleration and constant motion. *Journal of Sports Science, 30*, 121–127.

Vickers, J.N. (1996). Control of visual attention during the basketball free throw. *American Journal of Sports Medicine, 24*, S93–S97.

Vickers, J.N. (2007). *Perception, cognition and decision making: The quiet eye in action.* Champaign, IL: Human Kinetics.

Vickers, J.N., & Williams, A.M. (2007). Performing under pressure: The effects of physiological arousal, cognitive anxiety and gaze control in biathlon. *Journal of Motor Behaviour, 39*, 381–394.

Vine, S.J., Moore, L.J., & Wilson, M.R. (2014). Quiet eye training: The acquisition, refinement and resilient performance of targeting skills. *European Journal of Sport Science, 14*, S235–S242.

Vine, S.J., & Wilson, M.R. (2011). The influence of quiet eye training and pressure on attention and visuo-motor control. *Acta Psychologica, 136*, 340–346.

Watterson, J. (2015). *Rugby looks to science for better players.* The Irish Times. Retrieved from www.irishtimes.com/sport/rugbyrugby-looks-to-science-for-better-players-1.2156366

Williams, K. (2013). Goal setting in sport. In E.A. Locke & G.P. Latham (Eds.), *New developments in goal setting and task performance* (pp. 375–396). London: Routledge.

Wollersheim, D., Merkes, M., Shields, N., Liamputtong, P., Wallis, L., Reynolds, F., & Koh, L. (2010). Physical and psychosocial effects of Wii video game use among older women. *International Journal of Emergingw Technologies and Society, 8,* 85–98.

Yeager, S., & Lindsey, J. (2017). *Caffeine might be headed back to WADA's banned list.* Retrieved from www.bicycling.com/culture/pro-cycling/caffeine-might-be-headed-back-to-wadas-banned-list

4

ATHLETIC PERFORMANCE

The role of virtual reality

CASE STUDY 4

Deirdre is an elite 29-year-old canoeist preparing for an upcoming major championship in her sport of canoe slalom. Part of her recent preparations have included the introduction of virtual reality (VR) training sessions into her training programme. These sessions, prepared by her national team, have enabled Deirdre to use a head-mounted VR device to 'immerse' herself in a lifelike version of the courses she will race in her upcoming canoe slalom competitions. Canoe slalom is one of a small number of sports where the competitors cannot practice 'on' the competition course before actually carrying out their competition 'run'. In this type of situation, athletes often use mental imagery to help them prepare mentally for competition in advance of such events. Deirdre also uses this mental preparation strategy in her pre-competition routine and hopes VR training will add another beneficial element to her preparations for competing in canoe slalom.

(i)   What physical and mental benefits could the new VR training sessions have on Deirdre's performances in canoe slalom?

(ii) What potential limitations remain for such VR training in sport in general, and also in Deirdre's sport of canoe slalom?

(iii) What impact, if any, could Deirdre's age have on the introduction of such VR technology into her sport preparation at this stage of her career?

4.1 Overview

This chapter expands on the content introduced in Chapter 2 regarding virtual reality devices and their use within sport settings in order to: (i) motivate athletes; (ii) help athletes engage in physical and mental practice for their sport performances, especially within high-pressure situations and (iii) assist athletes in their rehabilitation from injury or illness. Virtual reality (VR) use to assist other elite and non-elite populations in their attempts to perform more effectively in their performance settings is discussed in the latter sections of this chapter.

VR devices used within entertainment and clinical/therapeutic environments to create phenomena such as *presence* and *immersion* has been the focus of much recent cyberpsychology research (see Kirwan, 2016, for a review of some of this VR research). However, the psychological application of VR specifically within sport and other elite performance environments to enhance, for example, motor skill learning in young athletes and performers, as well as the coping skills of such individuals at major competitions (e.g., the Rugby World Cup and the Olympic Games), remain exciting and relatively unexplored avenues of research for sport-focused cyberpsychologists (Hurley, 2016b). The future directions such research involving VR might take within these sport settings is outlined in the latter sections of this chapter.

4.2 Learning objectives

1   To identify and define key terms related to the domain of virtual reality
2   To explain the strengths and limitations of virtual reality devices for influencing the performances of elite individuals, as well as those engaged with such individuals within their environments (i.e., their coaches, analysts, medical personnel and match officials)
3   To highlight some exciting future research possibilities in this area of virtual reality for sport technologists, sport psychologists and sport analysts

4.3 Definitions of relevant terms

Augmented reality (AR)

This refers to the positioning of virtual objects over real-world scenes to create a visual representation. It is done using various screens (e.g., green screens) and cameras.

CAVE

This refers to a Cave Automatic Virtual Environment. It is a fully immersive virtual reality system (Kyan et al., 2015).

Head-mounted displays (HMDs)

These are the pieces of technology worn on the head of the VR user in order for that individual be able to move around the virtual world in a three-dimensional, more lifelike way.

HTC Vive

This refers to the virtual reality headset that was launched in 2016 to compete with the Oculus Rift (OR; see Oculus Rift below). It has a key advantage over the OR in that it allows the user to experience the virtual world from a vertical standing or moving position. This makes the HTC Vive experience more realistic, or believable, for the user (HTC Corporation, 2016). However, its setup is more complex than that of the OR and there is the added danger of the user possibly becoming entangled in the cables necessary for the HTC Vive to operate. Such dangers are not present for an OR user, who usually remains in a seated position when using the device.

Immersion

This term refers to the degree of sensory information a virtual experience or video game provides the user. It is considered an objective characteristic, in terms of its quality and quantity.

Oculus Rift (OR)

This refers to the specific virtual reality headset launched by the company Oculus VR in March of 2016 (Oculus VR, 2016). The headset allows users to engage in all types of virtual movement around a virtual world in a way they could not previously. The OR device is used, however, from a sitting position, unlike its HTC Vive competitor (previously discussed).

Presence

'Presence' refers to the feeling of being totally immersed in the virtual world, to the extent that it seems real to the individual engaged in it.

4.4 Introduction

VR technology allows users to enter into a three-dimensional, lifelike world, while remaining in their work environments, schools, health centres and, most relevant in the context of this chapter, their sport settings. Wiederhold (2016) recently presented a review of the lessons learned as VR enters into its third decade of existence and identified a number of areas where VR technology has helped to improve the lives of many individuals (such as patients in clinical settings and students in educational settings). Wiederhold (2016) also highlighted the increased numbers of individuals who now have access to VR technology through the availability of affordable HMDs, such as the Oculus Rift (Oculus VR, 2016) and HTC Vive (HTC Corporation, 2016). Wiederhold (2016) commented on the reduced price of such VR devices (currently retailing from approximately $400 to $1,000 depending on the model purchased) in helping this situation to arise for many individuals (see Figure 4.1).

FIGURE 4.1 An example of a head–mounted VR display device

Source: Courtesy of Pexels.

The environments in which VR can now be used have also extended beyond previous 'specialty' VR centres. Today, for example, many individuals can access VR options on their smart mobile devices (e.g., their smartphones and computer tablets) from within their own homes. Such individuals are also capable of using these options to enhance their own lives, by controlling them themselves, which often results in a sense of personal empowerment and control over their situations (Kirwan, 2016).

Today, the use of VR to support various therapies is also grounded in empirical evidence, given the past two decades of research in the area. This research evidence has also allowed for VR assessment tools for various conditions to be designed (see Kirwan, 2016, for a review of this specific area of research). Within sport, the potential benefits of VR helping athletes to excel have also been highlighted. For example, Simon Timson, Director of Performance at UK Sport said recently,

> The advantages of virtual training should not be underestimated in the pursuit of excellence. This adaptation of new technology allows us to digitally bottle [that] experience for elite athletes and help them perform at their best. Every extra benefit we can offer our athletes ahead of elite competition is significant, so this innovative application of 3D Video and Virtual Reality technology should provide an advantage in helping athletes familiarise themselves with new courses.
> *(cited in Griffiths, 2016)*

However, a number of questions remain regarding VR use within sport settings. These questions include: (i) Where is VR currently positioned as a beneficial preparation tool for athletes across different sports? (ii) How might VR technology be improved upon in the future to continue to assist such athletes, and those working with them, to perform at their best in their sport? This chapter explores these issues, presenting some of the most recent empirical research available in this VR area in the hope of answering these questions, while also suggesting some exciting possibilities where VR, and augmented reality (AR) also, may be used to even greater effect by athletes in the future.

4.5 Virtual reality as a preparation tool for athletes

The use of VR devices to enhance performance preparations, cognitive processes and motivation levels has been reported in a number of recent research studies, including elite performers, such as dancers (see Chan, Leung, Tang, & Komura, 2011). Within elite sport environments specifically, VR devices have been used in an attempt to understand the decision-making process athletes engage in when performing within their sport environments. Bideau et al. (2010) commented that

> Improving performances in sports requires a better understanding of the perception-action loop employed by athletes. Because of its inherent limitations, video playback doesn't permit this type of analysis. Interactive, immersive virtual reality can overcome these limitations and foster a better understanding of sports performances.
>
> *(p. 64)*

The limitations of video playback that Bideau et al. (2010) is referring to in this quote include: (i) the fixed viewpoint that is only available in video playback, given the position of the camera(s) when recording the play; (ii) the presentation of only the actions that did actually take place during that particular piece of sport play and (iii) the lack of stereoscopic (or depth) features in the displays presented to the athlete using only video playback (as discussed in Chapters 2 and 3). Indeed, using video playback technology alone has been reported to decrease the elite anticipation judgements of some athletes, namely, tennis players, over time, as reported in a study by Shim and Carlton (2006). The gradual judgement declines in the anticipation performance of these tennis players were due to a possible lack of 'presence' (that feeling of a situation being experienced as 'real') being experienced by the athletes in their study, which used video playback alone to present the information to the participants (Shim & Carlton, 2006).

VR technology allows for the three previously cited limitations of video playback, as outlined by Bideau et al. (2010), to be overcome by: (i) allowing many different types of 'play', or sport actions, to be presented to athletes; (ii) allowing the actions to occur in an interactive, immersive environment; and (iii) allowing the actions to be stereoscopic in nature (that is, making and presenting them to the athletes in a three-dimensional (3D) way, rather than only using the two-dimensional (2D) perspective, as is the case in video displays). All of these VR technology benefits can make the experience more real for the athletes using it.

This could result in its use being potentially more effective as a mental skills training aid for athletes in their sport environments rather than using video playback alone, as is the case in many sport settings at present. How might this occur? Well, VR technology may offer athletes an opportunity to work on one of their important cognitive sport skills, identified as important by Bideau et al. (2010), namely, their anticipatory skills. These skills are considered to be essential perceptual skills for athletes to fine-tune, especially when developing tactical ways to counteract the movements of opponents (see Davids, Williams, & Williams, 1999). Studies by Bideau et al. (2003) in handball, Craig, Berton, Fernandaz, and Bootsma (2006) in soccer and Brunnett, Rusdorf, and Lorenz (2006) in table tennis, have all reported some benefits of VR training in enhancing these anticipatory skills in athletes. Other mental skills, as discussed in Chapter 1, which may benefit from VR training are athletes' concentration and coping skills. These specific mental skills benefits from VR training are discussed in the following section.

4.5.1 Virtual reality and mental skills training

The use of mental strategies, such as mental imagery and mental practice to enhance the physical skill performances of athletes, has been well documented in many sports (Cotterill, 2015; Moran, 2012; Moran & Toner, 2017). Within the sport of rugby, for example, players have often referred to their use of such beneficial mental strategies prior to carrying out closed skills within their sport (e.g., kicking or penalty-taking skills; Sharp, Woodcock, Holland, Cummings, & Duda, 2013; Wilkinson, 2006). However, in times of pressure, when such athletes often experience heightened levels of anxiety, or 'nerves' (for example, during or before important matches), such mental rehearsal strategies, especially their mental imagery routines, may become disrupted. See Box 4.1 for an outline of the arousal–anxiety–performance theories proposed to explain such arousal and anxiety–related performance declines often seen in athletes in high pressure environments in their sport.

BOX 4.1   AROUSAL–ANXIETY–PERFORMANCE RELATIONSHIP THEORIES IN BRIEF

The anxiety–performance relationship has been extensively studied by sport psychologists, with established theories such as the *inverted U hypothesis* (Yerkes & Dodson, 1908), the *catastrophe theory* (Hardy, 1990, 1996; Hardy, Beeatie, & Woodman, 2007) and the *conscious processing hypothesis* (also known as the reinvestment hypothesis; Masters & Maxwell, 2008) dominating the literature in the area.

The *inverted U hypothesis* (Yerkes & Dodson, 1908) presents one potential understanding of the relationship between arousal and performance. It proposes that arousal levels, as they increase, often benefit athletic performance, up to an optimum point. After that point, continued increase in athletes' arousal levels results in declines in their performances. A related, but somewhat different theory, the *catastrophe theory* (Hardy, 1990) attempts to explains the decreases seen in athletic performances as not a gradual decline, as the inverted U hypothesis suggests, but rather as a dramatic (or catastrophic) steep drop in athletes' performances (sometimes described as choking) due to heightened levels of anxiety being experienced by the athletes at those times.

The *conscious processing hypothesis* (also referred to as the reinvestment hypothesis; Masters, 1992) explains the decreases seen in the athletic performances of anxious athletes as being due to these individuals, when they feel anxious, engaging in a process of 'investing' their conscious thinking to tasks they previously completed in an automatic way in their sport. Athletes' skills often break down, or are not completed as effectively when they apply such deliberate thinking to well-practiced and normally well-executed sport skills.

Anxiety is now considered a multidimensional construct, with different types of anxiety having been identified (e.g., somatic/cognitive anxiety and trait/state anxiety; see Moran, 2012, and Moran & Toner, 2017, for more details on these types of anxiety). Research studies have suggested that cognitive (i.e., thought-induced) anxiety may be more detrimental to sport performances than somatic anxiety (the body's response to anxiety-provoking situations e.g. sweating, increased heart rate, etc.; see Hardy, 1990, 1996, and Hardy et al., 2007, for a review of these situations and responses). This conclusion is supported by research studies evaluating somatic anxiety measurement tools, such as heart rate monitors and galvanic skin response measures. These devices often indicate the same types of data recordings for individuals who report being in a heightened state of anxiety, as for those individuals who claim to be in a heightened state of excitement about an event (Kremer & Moran, 2013).

In high–pressure and often anxiety–inducing situations, athletes' performances often decline. This may occur if a negative mental image of, for example, a penalty kick, replaces a desired positive outcome of the kick attempt in the mind of the athlete immediately prior to the skill being executed. VR training of such skills may offer athletes the opportunity to rehearse their closed skills, such as their penalty-kicking skills, prior to real match scenarios. In such VR settings, the virtual stimulus can be manipulated so that such players only 'see' the positive outcome of their kicking attempts through the VR headset. This could have the effect of, in a sense, re–wiring the image for the athlete back to a positive one in his or her mind, prior to taking to the field of play (at the start of a game or at the re-start, after the half-time break). Such recently 'seen' successful mental rehearsals of their skills could help the athletes to more successfully execute them in real play. Perhaps this is something to pilot test in the future in such sport environments?

4.5.2 Virtual reality and anxiety management

Given the detrimental impact that anxiety, specifically cognitive anxiety, may have on athletes' sport performances, the use of VR devices to help such athletes develop coping strategies to manage incidences of anxiety experienced within their sport environments is an exciting development. VR has been used successfully to desensitise individuals experiencing anxieties and fears in other similarly anxiety-provoking situations, such as when flying (fear of which is referred to as *aviophobia*) or those with insect phobias, for example *arachnophobia* (see Kirwan, 2016, for more details). Clinically diagnosed anxiety conditions, such as general anxiety disorder, panic attacks, obsessive compulsive disorder and post-traumatic stress disorder (PTSD) have also been successfully treated 'in vitro' using VR interventions (Kirwan, 2016). However, many of the studies reporting successes in such situations have also cited notes of caution, as the 'in vitro' carry-over effects seen in such studies using VR technology have been somewhat mixed, especially when the individual participants in some of these studies moved back into their 'real-life', in vivo, environments (Wiederhold & Wiederhold, 2014). Phobia-experiencing individuals may be willing to face a non-real fear in a virtual world (for example, participants in phobia-examining studies knew the stimuli they were exposed to were artificial). However, it is not uncommon for such participants to remain unwilling to face their fear-inducing stimuli when they return to the real-life contexts. In sport environments, Hurley, Moran, and Guerin (2007) reported that one of the specific fears many athletes report is the fear of re-injury, especially following extended periods of rehabilitation after experiencing a moderate to serious injury in their sport. VR sessions, as used in some phobia desensitisation studies, could be designed to help these returning-from-injury athletes to virtually experience their sport participation and then gradually help them to increase their confidence levels, in order to help them feel ready to return to their full range of movement and contact-training with their teammates and/or opponents, if such contact is part of their sport. This use of VR in such injury-protection and rehabilitation scenarios post injury or illness, is discussed in more depth in the following sections.

4.5.3 Virtual reality and injury protection

VR training may offer some protective feature for athletes by helping them to avoid certain injury situations. Pre-competition anxiety levels are often high for many, even experienced, elite athletes (Wilkinson, 2006). When in such states, these athletes may also be more susceptible to injury (Hurley, 2003). The reason for this may be because athletes in such heightened states of arousal and anxiety may be considered to be more distractible and one of the erroneous decisions they may make in such states is to engage in *more* practice of their physical sport skills than is optimal for good per-formance. Such actions could place them at risk of overreaching or overtraining and could lead to physical injury. In recent years, psychology and technology researchers have begun to explore ways athletes can rehearse their physical sport skills without placing their bodies under additional physical training strain, in order to protect them from the risk of such injuries, and also from general burnout. VR training could provide an exciting avenue to help such players 'practice' or 'experience' their sport skills, without engaging in any intense physical movements (Watson et al., 2011). VR training could offer an ideal environment in which athletes' physical and mental skills (as highlighted earlier), including their cognitive skills of decision making, problem solving, mental imagery and memory, as well as their coping skills (of arousal and anxiety control, for example), could be practiced in experimental-like, controlled field conditions and potentially be improved, but without any significant increases in the athletes' already high physical training load (Hurley, 2016a).

4.5.4 Virtual reality and pain management

Another positive use of virtual reality has been its application in helping individu-als to cope with the pain associated with injury. The psychology of pain, and its management, has been the focus of research for many psychologists, especially within the past 40 years, since Meldzack and Wall (1967) proposed the Gate Con-trol Theory of Pain to describe how pain is experienced in the body.

Meldzack and Wall's (1967) Gate Control Theory of Pain explains how, at many times in life when injuries occur, there is a delayed period of time before perception of the pain associated with the physical trauma to the body is actually experienced or perceived by the individual. This is especially common in sports where athletes often report having no recollection of, or experience of, intense pain that typically accom-panies the acquisition of bruises, or breaks and fractures of bones, during an injury episode. As a result, many athletes have continued performing in their sports despite having suffered, what would be regarded in many situations a serious injury. For example, Leinster Rugby player, Isa Nacewa, played the last few minutes of a league rugby match with a broken arm, while Liverpool's soccer player, Dietmar Hamann, played the 2005 Champions League final with a broken foot and Manchester City's goalkeeper, Bert Trautmann, played the final 15 minutes of the 1956 FA Cup final with a broken neck, after a challenge with an opposition player (Irish Examiner, 2008). One possible explanation for such feats in sport is that at the time of the injury, these athletes were intensely focused on other tasks associated with their sport participation. This focus at such times is thought to have a blocking effect of the pain of the injury, stopping it from coming into the individual's conscious awareness (i.e., the 'gate' remains closed off to the painful stimulus and it is not brought into the athlete's conscious awareness). When this blocking of the pain gateway ceases, as well as the adrenaline and endorphin levels of the athletes drop to pre-event levels, the individual may then start to feel, or experience, the pain of the injury (i.e., the 'gate' opens and the pain floods the individual's consciousness; Kirwan, 2016).

VR stimuli are thought to be effective by also blocking the individual from experiencing the painful stimuli from the injury. In some cases, VR has even been reported as an effective replacement for drug-based or pharmaceutical interventions in such cases (i.e., replacing painkillers/analgesic drugs). For example, some effective virtual worlds have been specifically designed to directly counter the sensations of certain kinds of pain. For burn patients, 'ice or snow worlds' have been designed to act as pain distractors for individuals who are required to endure painful procedures, such as bandage changing, as part of their treatment and recovery regimes (Hoffman et al., 2011). Such VR uses in sport-specific situations could also be used, for example, to distract athletes from the pain of injuries that occur 'on the pitch', and that may have to be treated without drug therapy (due to anti-doping rules perhaps, for example) in the athletes' medical facilities on-site during competitions or in training.

4.5.5 Virtual reality benefits post-injury

VR technology could also help injured athletes to maintain and enhance their physical and mental skill levels when they cannot engage in physical training sessions when injured (Figure 4.2). As the Rugby World Cup 2015 illustrated, injuries

FIGURE 4.2 Virtual reality is now being used in sport psychology research – for example, in applied performance enhancement, and rehabilitation, settings

Source: Courtesy of the Institute of Art, Design + Technology (IADT), Dún Laoghaire, with thanks to Lorraine Colman.

to some of the most experienced and high profile players deprived many countries of their top performers (Hurley, 2016a). Such incidences are an unfortunate, yet expected, part of a collision sport such as rugby (Hurley et al., 2007; Lewis, 2015; Neil, Mellalieu, & Roberts, 2016). Much is known about the physical consequences of such injuries, including the pain, surgery, restricted movement, and rehabilitation issues athletes in such positions face (Neil et al., 2016). The psychological impact of such injuries on the mental states of players has also been explored and documented (Neil et al., 2016; Hurley et al. 2007; Pearson & Jones, 1992).

VR has been used with some success with individuals who have suffered neurological episodes, such as strokes (Pessoa et al., 2014; also see: (i) Lloréns, Noé, Colomer, and Alcañiz's (2014) research findings regarding a VR telerehabilitation programme for balance recovery after stroke; (ii) Gamito et al.'s (2015) findings regarding a cognitive training programme for stroke patients via virtual reality-based 'serious' games; and (iii) Colomer, Lloréns, Noé, and Alcañiz's (2016) mixed reality-based intervention on arm, hand and finger function on chronic stroke). Lee, Kim, and Lee (2015a) reported posture and walking improvements in stroke patients following the use of VR dance training, in combination with cognitive task training. Lee, Lee, and Song (2015b) also utilised a VR dance regime to test its benefits on Parkinson's disease patients specifically with regard to their balance, daily life activities and clinically diagnosed depressive symptoms. The VR dance regime was shown to benefit the patients on all three of the factors tested in the study. Clinicians working with chronically ill and stroke patients, have stated the use of virtual reality to improve patient recovery is a positive development, but more time and research-based knowledge, along with more 'in-house' training for them as clinicians to use it effectively with their patients, is needed (Glegg et al., 2013). Such research findings are encouraging when arguing for the use of VR technology to help rehabilitate injured athletes also.

4.6 Limitations of virtual reality in elite sport settings

To date, the VR environments created for use in sport settings have been somewhat limited. For example, as mentioned in the explanation of the OR at the start of this chapter, this VR device can only be used in a stationary, usually sitting, position. Athletes in highly interactive sports have had to wait for technologists to develop VR platforms that mimic more accurately their real-life sport environments. The newly created HTC Vive (HTC Corporation, 2016) has emerged as a VR tool with the potential to meet this demand. A key strength of the HTC Vive, over the OR, as explained at the start of this chapter, is its position-tracking technology. This added element suggests it may be more suitable for use in sport settings. Another potentially suitable technology is the XSens MVN BIOMECH 3D Human Kinematics Motion and Performance Capture System (Starrs, Chohan, Fewtrell, Richards, & Selfe, 2012). A 'best position' may actually be to develop a blended combination of both types of technology. Future research studies could include an exploration of such technological blending in order to advance the potential benefits of VR technology in sport settings.

4.7 Virtual reality as a preparation tool for other elite performers

It is also important to point out that VR is not only a potentially useful device for preparing and training elite athletes for competition. It can also be employed by other elite performers, such as dancers, medical personnel and military personnel, to prepare them for their equally demanding performance environments. Some research study findings involving these individuals are the focus of the next section.

4.7.1 Dancers

As mentioned previously, dance environments have provided researchers with effective opportunities to develop and test the benefits of VR to enhance the performances of participants. Chan et al. (2011) developed a VR environment, based around the traditional principles already used in dance environments for dancers to learn new movements, namely, by: (i) watching the movements of their teachers and other elite dancers and then imitate their movements, as well as (ii) listening to the feedback provided to them on their dance movements, in many cases, by their teachers, but also possibly by their peers or dance partners. Chan et al. (2011) reported that their dance participants did find their VR dance tool useful when learning new dance moves and that it also motivated them to want to learn in their dance environment.

Other investigators also interested in this use of VR in dance environments included Kyan et al. (2015) who developed a ballet dance training device, specifically using MS Kinect and a CAVE VR environment. Kyan et al. (2015) reported that their dance participants, using their VR environment, were able to experience their performances and also evaluate them, in the same spatial contexts in which they were usually performed in 'real life'. This, Kyan et al. (2015) concluded, provided their dance participants with a unique and valuable opportunity to perform and improve their dance skills using VR training.

4.7.2 Military personnel

As mentioned earlier, other environments require elite performances, including serious 'life-preserving' settings, and may also, therefore, benefit from VR training opportunities (for example, within military and defence settings). VR has been used to effectively prepare such personnel, both physically and emotionally, for combat or when on peacekeeping duties in waring countries (Rizzo, Ford-Morie, Williams, Pair, & Galen-Buckwalter, 2005). Among the advantages of such VR training for such personnel are: (i) the cost-effectiveness of the training (as it reduces the cost of having to employ instructors to be present to physically train recruits), (ii) the reduced need to constantly train new recruits if such VR training is used to upskill current personnel and (iii) the ability to adapt such VR training to different areas of military speciality, such as the Navy, Army or Air Force, allowing for highly interactive, lifelike scenarios to be experienced by these different trainees. This, like for athletes using VR, affords them an opportunity to prepare mentally for the demands of such differing situations (Unimersiv, 2016). This preparation, is often referred to in sport psychology literature as a 'what if' strategy, where scenarios in sport are devised to help prepare athletes for situations they may face in their sport. See Box 4.2 for an explanation of this 'what if' preparation technique used by many sport psychologists to help prepare athletes for challenges they may face in their sport settings.

BOX 4.2   THE 'WHAT IF' STRATEGY USED FOR SPORT PREPARATION

A commonly employed mental preparation strategies advocated by sport psychologists is that of 'what if' planning (Kremer & Moran, 2013). This strategy involves sport psychologists, along with their client athletes, discussing a series of 'what if' scenarios that could potentially occur during a competition or important sport occasion, for example, the Olympic Games. The sport psychologist and the athlete then devise a plan to help the individual manage each situation envisaged, should it arise during that competition. VR offers an opportunity where such situations could be created, perhaps in a game-like scenario, to allow the individuals to engage in virtual role playing, in order to prepare for such situations, rather than what is currently relied upon, which is typically the use of some form of mental rehearsal by the athletes, imagining, in their 'mind's eye' (Kremer & Moran, 2013) the situation and their desired response to it. Alternatively, they simulate such situations in less 'real' environments to that of the competition setting, such as in the athlete's training centre or in the sport psychologist's office space, both of which are unlikely to be actual competition venues.

4.7.3 Medical personnel

The potential use of VR within medical settings has also been explored. Surgeons, for example, have become advocates of VR technology for their training, as well as mental practice, for example. They cannot practice their fine motor surgical skills on their living patients in many cases, therefore, these alternative training options are attractive for them (Arona et al., 2011). Given that many operations involve life-saving scenarios, surgeons require significant amounts of practice of their surgical skills, in order to complete them effectively in real-life and often high-pressure contexts. The Royal College of Surgeons in Ireland (RCSI) in the summer of 2016 launched the first VR simulator application (app) for training surgical personnel in how to treat a patient in an emergency department of a hospital following a road traffic accident (McDermott, 2016). Such VR-based apps have the potential to provide invaluable training opportunities for trainee doctors. They enable them to develop not only their physical motor skills in such situations but also their decision-making and coping skills in such high-pressure situations too (Oculus, 2016; RCSI, 2016).

As the preceding sections have uncovered, the potential uses and developments for VR technologies across a wide range of elite settings is vast. However, other non-elite populations may also benefits from their applications, as described in the following section.

4.8 Virtual reality as an exercise aid for non-elite populations

The introduction of physical exercise into video games became popular approximately ten years ago due, perhaps in part, to requests by medical and health professionals, as well as parents, for digital gaming companies and their technologist gaming experts to find ways to increase the movement component of their offerings (Gao, Chen, Pasco, & Pope, 2015). The technology industry, perhaps aware of the criticism they were receiving for apparently contributing to the increased levels of inactivity across many sections of the general population, as facilitated by technological advances, responded by developing video games that included exercise components in order for them to be played successfully.

The most popular commodity motion-sensing devices developed initially were the Nintendo Wii and the Wii Fit. They both used body motion as part of the mechanics of their games. Gaming technologists have continued to explore ways to increase the 'real feel' elements of the experience for individuals playing such games and, in turn, perhaps increase the motivation levels of such individuals to want to continue playing such games. By increasing the motion components of these games and making them more immersive and stereoscopic, some developers hoped they might also increase the motivation levels of the participants, both young and old, to then engage in greater levels of actual, real-life, physical activity when not playing these virtual, motion-added component games. For example, Finkelstein et al. (2011) developed the Astrojumper, an immersive VR game, aimed at motivating its users who played the game to then exercise more in real life following on from their positive gaming experiences. Finkelstein et al. (2011) wished to address the limitations of previous exergames, by including features that required players to move during their game-playing activity, rather than finding ways to successfully play such games while engaging in nearly no physical movement. This is what had happened when players discovered they could 'win' virtual tennis matches on the Nintendo Wii by simply moving their wrists while sitting on their couches, rather than standing up and swinging the virtual racket.

Finkelstein et al.'s (2011) Astrojumper game overcame the limitation of the Wii console by designing their game to sense players' motions in six different directions of force (DOF). The movements of the head, torso and limbs were able to be detected by the device. This allowed the game to incorporate activities such as dodging, ducking, jumping over and reaching for virtual stimuli to be presented to players as part of the game's required actions. The more immersive and realistic a game is, the more enjoyment it appears to generate for its players and the more motivated the players in Finkelstein et al.'s (2011) study were, too, to engage in more physical exercise activities after the virtual game-playing experience ended (Finkelstein et al., 2011). IJsselsteinijn, de Kort, Westerink, de Jager, and Bonants (2006) reported similar exercise enjoyment findings in their study when their participants had access to a virtual coach to motivate them to cycle on a stationary bike within their own homes. Finkelstein et al.'s (2011) results emphasised the point that exergames need to be fun and engaging for participants in order for them to obtain the greatest effects as exercise generators.

Pasco, Roure, Kermarrec, Pope, and Gao (2017) also tested the impact of a physically demanding video gaming device on participants' motivation levels to engage in physical activity, as well as on their actual physical activity levels. Specifically, Pasco et al. (2017) tested the Greedy Rabbit exergame developed by Vescape, to determine if it succeeded in its objective of promoting its players to engage in moderate-to-vigorous physical activity (MVPA). They examined the effects of this device using an exercise bike activity with the Greedy Rabbit exergame platform paired wirelessly using a Bluetooth device with the exercise bike, in order to measure the video game's effect on the participants' physical activity levels, as well as measuring their motivation levels and their situational interest (that is, the participants' degree of how appealing they reported the activity to be and how intriguing the participants reported elements of the activity were as it was being carried out). Pasco et al. (2017) reported that the exergame did promote similar levels of MVPA compared to a traditional biking exercise. However, they did suggest that games' developers aim to increase the level of game difficulty and increase the gameplay intensity in order for these games to potentially result in the more intense levels of MVPA that typically occur when healthy and active populations engage in traditional bike riding.

4.9 Conclusion, including future research directions for virtual reality within sport

This chapter sought to highlight how VR is currently used in sport settings, and also how it could be used in new and exciting ways for the future mental preparation benefits of elite athletes and other performers, as well as among non-elite exercise populations. Appealing applications of VR technology have included its use in helping athletes to maintain or improve some of their mental skills, such as their reaction times and spatial awareness skills, even when they are forced to be away from their sport (e.g., when they are injured or when they are suspended from playing due to rule violations).

But what lessons, to date, can be drawn from VR use across the performance settings just discussed? Wiederhold (2016) provided a useful list of lessons learned as the third decade of VR application commences. These lessons include: (i) more conditions are now being treated using VR technology and its limits seem to know no bounds (this would also appear to be true when considering some of the exciting avenues referred to in this chapter where VR could be used to enhance the performances of athletes and other elite performers, as well as promote more physical activity among the general non-elite populations); (ii) VR can be used as an assessment tool for various conditions; (iii) the use of VR is now evidence-based, with numerous studies being carried out to test its effectiveness across a variety of settings; and (iv) VR is no longer limited to specialised centres. Individuals may now use VR technology in the comfort of their own homes, or in the case of athletes and other elite performers, in their training, performance, or elite work settings. This is in part due to more affordable VR devices and equipment being available for purchase by such individuals, as well as the emergence of new VR apps that can be downloaded for use on mobile devices such as smartphones and tablets.

Wiederhold (2016) also commented that "All of us are riding the wave of technology development" (p. 578). New VR technology could perhaps be developed to enable athletes and elite performers to experience visual, auditory (and potentially olfactory) real-time simulations, delivered through the first person perspective, thus making them even more 'real-like'.

Some specific new directions for research in this area could include the creation of new virtual reality platforms, using the HTC Vive, and the XSens MVN BIOMECH 3D Human Kinematics Motion with Performance Capturing System, for example, as suggested in this chapter. Such technology could have multiple benefits for athletes, such as potentially: (i) enhancing their physical and mental skills, (ii) assisting their injury rehabilitation regimes, (iii) helping to monitor their competition and training loads and (iv) providing additional psychological- and performance-related data to what is already available, in order to determine the long-term consequences of injuries (such as concussions, for example). These are all exciting and worthy areas of exploration by individuals with the expertise and facilities to develop, and test, such technology use in a scientific way.

A further exciting goal of new VR environments could be to create separate immersive and interactive environments for the training of sport referees and officials, with the aim of helping them to also develop their mental skills for their specific sport roles, such as their decision-making, problem-solving and coping skills. They too experience high-pressure competition-like situations, similar to athletes, and therefore should not be forgotten when devising VR applications for performance enhancement uses within sport settings.

4.10 Open-ended discussion questions

1   What role can new virtual reality technologies play in helping athletes recover effectively from injury, and help them prepare for a best possible return to their pre-injury performance levels?
2   Discuss the advantages and disadvantages of various VR devices for helping athletes to prepare mentally for anxiety-provoking pressure situations within their sports.

3   What specific improvements in VR technologies would perhaps be welcomed additions to the training environments of athletes and other elite performers?

4.11 Practical exercise

Interview one athlete and one coach, asking them the following three questions:

1   What role, if any, would you like to see VR technology have on preparations for your sport over the next three years?
2   What role could VR technology have in training referees/officials within your sport in the next three years?
3   What role could VR technology fill in the future in helping athletes' rehabilitation post-injury? (The two individuals' responses to these questions could be used as a qualitative data analysis opportunity for students to practice. The themes identified from the interviewees' responses could be shared with a class group as part of an assignment or continuous assessment task in research methods also).

References

Arona, S., Aggarwal, R., Sirimanna, P., Moran, A., Grantcharov, T., Kneebone, R., Sevdalis, N., & Darzi, A. (2011). Mental practice enhances surgical technical skills. *Annals of Surgery, 253,* 265–270.

Bideau, B., Kulpa, R., Ménardais, S., & Fradet, L. (2003). Real handball goalkeepers versus virtual handball throwers. *Presence, Teleoperators and Virtual Environments, 12,* 411–421.

Bideau, B., Kulpa, R., Vignais, N., Brault, S., Multon, F., & Craig, C. (2010). Using virtual reality to analyse sports performance. *IEE Computer Graphics and Applications, 30,* 64–71.

Brunnett, G., Rusdorf, S., & Lorenz, M. (2006). V-Pong: An immersive table tennis simulation. *IEE Computer Graphics and Applications, 26,* 10–13.

Chan, J.C.P., Leung, H., Tang, J.K.T., & Komura, T. (2011). A virtual reality dance training system using motion capture technology. *IEEE Transactions on Learning Technologies, 4,* 187–195.

Colomer, C., Lloréns, R., Noé, E., & Alcañiz, M. (2016). Effect of a mixed reality-based intervention on arm, hand and finger function on chronic stroke. *Journal of NeuroEngineering and Rehabilitation, 13*(45). doi: 10.1186/s12984-016-0153-6

Cotterill, S. (2015). Preparing for performance: Strategies adopted across performance domains. *The Sport Psychologist, 29,* 158–170.

Craig, C.M., Berton, E., Fernandaz, E., & Bootsma, R.J. (2006). Judging where the ball will go: The case of curved free kicks in football. *Naturwissenschaften, 93,* 97–101.

Davids, K., Williams, A.M., & Williams, J.G. (1999). Anticipation and decision-making in sport. *Visual Perception and Action in Sport, 1,* 96–142.

Finkelstein, S., Nickel, A., Lipps, Z., Barnes, T., Wartell, Z., & Suma, E.A. (2011). Astrojumper: Motivating exercise with an immersive virtual reality exergame. *Presence, 20,* 78–92.

Gamito, P., Oliveira, J., Coelho, C., Morais, D., Lopes, P., Pacheco, J., Brito, B., Soares, F., Santos, N., & Barata, A.F. (2015). Cognitive training on stroke patients via virtual reality-based serious games. *Disability and Rehabilitation: An International, Multidisciplinary Journal,* 1–4. doi: 10.3109/09638288.2014.934925

Gao, Z., Chen, S., Pasco, D., & Pope, Z. (2015). A meta-analysis of active video games on health outcomes among children and adolescents. *Obesity Reviews, 16*, 783–794. doi: 10.1111/obr.12287

Glegg, S.M.N., Holsti, L., Velikonja, D., Ansley, B., Brum, C., & Sartor, D. (2013). Factors influencing therapists' adopting of virtual reality for brain injury rehabilitation. *Cyberpsychology, Behaviour, and Social Networking, 16*, 385–401.

Griffiths, J. (2016). *How virtual reality is helping Team GB.* Retrieved from www.howit worksdaily.com/rio-2016-virtual-reality/

Hardy, L. (1990). A catastrophe model of anxiety and performance. In G. Jones & L. Hardy (Eds.), *Stress and performance in sport* (pp. 81–106). Chichester, West Sussex: Wiley.

Hardy, L. (1996). Testing the predictions of the cusp catastrophe model of anxiety and performance. *The Sport Psychologist, 10*, 140–156.

Hardy, L., Beeatie, S., & Woodman, T. (2007). Anxiety-induced performance catastrophes: Investigating effort required as an asymmetry factor. *British Journal of Psychology, 98*, 15–31.

Hoffman, H.J., Chambers, G.T., Meyer III, W.J., Arceneaux, L.L., Russell, W.J., Seibel, E.J., Richards, T.L., Sharar, S.R., & Patterson, D.R. (2011). Virtual reality as an adjunctive non-pharmacologic analgesic for acute burn pain during medical procedures. *Annals of Behavioural Medicine, 41*, 183–191.

HTC Corporation. (2016). *Vive.* Retrieved from www.htcvive.com/eu/

Hurley, O.A. (2003). *Psychological understanding of, and responses to, sporting injuries in elite athletes.* Unpublished PhD thesis, University College Dublin, Ireland.

Hurley, O.A. (2016a). Impact of player injuries, on the mental states, and subsequent team performances, at the Rugby World Cup 2015. *Frontiers in Psychology – Movement Science and Sport Psychology* [Opinion Article], 7(807). doi: 10.3389/fpsyg.2016.00807

Hurley, O.A. (2016b). Sport and health cyberpsychology. In I. Connolly, M. Palmer, H. Barton, & G. Kirwan (Eds.), *An introduction to cyberpsychology* (pp. 167–180). London: Routledge.

Hurley, O.A., Moran, A., & Guerin, S. (2007). Exploring athletes' experience of their injuries: A qualitative investigation. *Sport and Exercise Psychology Review, 3*(2), 14–22.

IJsselsteinijn, W.A., de Kort, Y.A.W., Westerink, J., de Jager, M., & Bonants, R. (2006). Virtual fitness: Stimulating exercise behaviour through media technology. *Presence, Teleoperators and Virtual Environments, 15*, 688–698.

Irish Examiner. (2008). *Nacewa plays through pain barrier.* Retrieved from www.irishexaminer.com/sport/rugby/nacewa-plays-through-pain-barrier-73060.html

Kirwan, G. (2016). Psychological applications of virtual reality. In I. Connolly, M. Palmer, H. Barton, & H. Kirwan (Eds.), *An introduction to cyberpsychology* (pp. 271–285). London: Routledge.

Kremer, J., & Moran, A. (2013). *Pure sport: Practical sport psychology.* London: Routledge.

Kyan, M., Sun, G., Li, H., Zhong, L., Muneesawang, P., Dong, N., Elder, B., & Guan, L. (2015). An approach to ballet dance training using MS Kinect and visualisation in a CAVE VR environment. *ACM Transactions ion Intelligent Systems and Technology, 6*, Article 2. Retrieved from http://dx.doi.org/10.1145/2735951

Lee, I.W., Kim, Y.N., & Lee, D.K. (2015a). Effect of a virtual reality exercise program accompanied by cognitive tasks on the balance and gait of stroke patients. *Journal of Physical Therapy Science, 27*(7), 2175–2177. doi: 10.1589/jpts.27.2175

Lee, N.Y., Lee, D.K., & Song, H.S. (2015b). Effect of virtual reality dance exercise on the balance, activities of daily living and depressive disorder status of Parkinson's disease patients. *Journal of Physical Therapy Science, 27*(1), 145–147. doi: 10.1589/jpts.27.145

Lewis, S. (2015). *The pain game: RWC's injury list.* Retrieved from www.irishexaminer.com/sport/rugby/the-pain-rwcs-list-356643.html

Lloréns, R., Noé, E., Colomer, C., & Alcañiz, M. (2014). Effectiveness, usability, and cost-benefit of a virtual reality-based telerehabilitation program for balance recovery after stroke: A randomized controlled trial. *Archives of Physical Medicine and Rehabilitation, 96*, 418–425. doi: 10.1016/j.apmr.2014.10.019

Masters, R.S.W. (1992). Knowledge, 'knerves' and know-how: The role of explicit versus implicit knowledge in the breakdown of a complex motor skills under pressure. *British Journal of Psychology, 83*, 343–358.

Masters, R.S.W., & Maxwell, J.P. (2008). Implicit motor learning, reinvestment and movement disruption: What you don't know won't hurt you. In A.M. Williams & N.J. Hodges (Eds.), *Skill acquisition in sport: Research, theory and practice* (pp. 207–228). London: Routledge.

McDermott, M. (2016). *Virtual reality app makes medical training available to all.* The Irish Times. Retrieved from www.irishtimes.com/news/science/virtual-reality-app-makes-medical-training-available-to-all-1.2728622

Meldzack, R., & Wall, P.D. (1967). Pain mechanisms: A new theory. *Survey of Anaesthesiology, 11*(2), 89–90.

Moran, A.P. (2012). *Sport and exercise psychology: A critical introduction.* London: Routledge.

Moran, A.P., & Toner, J. (2017). *A critical introduction to sport psychology.* London: Routledge.

Neil, R., Mellalieu, S., & Roberts, R. (2016). It's good to talk. *Sport & Exercise Psychology Review, 12*, 69–76.

Oculus. (2016). *RCSI medical training sim.* Retrieved from www.oculus.com/experiences/gear-vr/878262692296965/

Oculus VR. (2016). *Oculus Rift.* Retrieved from www.oculus.com/en-us/

Pasco, D., Roure, C., Kermarrec, G., Pope, Z., & Gao, Z. (2017). The effects if a bike active video game on players' physical activity and motivation. *Journal of Sport and Health Science, 6*, 25–32.

Pearson, L., & Jones, G. (1992). Emotional effects of sports injuries: Implications for physiotherapists. *Journal of Physiotherapy, 78*, 762–770.

Pessoa, T.M., Coutinho, D.S., Pereira, V.M., Pinho de Oliveira Ribeiro, N., Nardi, A.E., & Cardoso deOliveira e Silva, A. (2014). The Nintendo Wii as a tool for neurocognitive rehabilitation, training and health promotion. *Computers in Human Behaviour, 31*, 384–392.

Rizzo, A., Ford-Morie, J., Williams, J., Pair, J., & Galen-Buckwalter, J. (2005). *Human emotional state and its relevance for military VR training.* Proceedings of the 11th International Conference on Human Computer Interaction, Las Vegas, Nevada.

Royal College of Surgeons in Ireland (RCSI). (2016). *RCSI develops world's first virtual reality medical training simulator.* Retrieved from www.rcsi.ie/index.jsp?p=164&n=2553&a=7927

Sharp, L.A., Woodcock, C., Holland, M.J.G., Cummings, J., & Duda, J.L. (2013). A qualitative evaluation of the effectiveness of a mental skills training program for youth athletes. *The Sport Psychologist, 27*, 219–232.

Shim, J., & Carlton, L.G. (2006). Perception of kinematic characteristics of tennis strokes for anticipating stroke type and direction. *Research Quarterly for Exercise and Sport, 77*, 326–329.

Starrs, P., Chohan, A., Fewtrell, D., Richards, J., & Selfe, J. (2012). Biomechanical differences between experienced and inexperienced wheelchair users during sport. *Prosthetics and Orthotics International, 36*, 324–331.

Unimersiv. (2016). How the military is incorporating VR into troop training. *Virtual Reality.* Retrieved from https://unimersiv.com/military-incorporating-vr-troop-training/

Watson, G., Brault, S., Kulpa, R., Bideau, B., Butterfield, J., & Craig, C. (2011). Judging the 'passability' of dynamic gaps in a virtual rugby environment. *Human Movement Science, 30*, 942–956.

Wiederhold, B. (2016). Lessons learned as we begin the third decade of virtual reality. *Cyberpsychology, Behaviour and Social Networking, 19*(10), 577–578.

Wiederhold, B.K., & Wiederhold, M.D. (2014). How can virtual reality interventions help reduce prescription opioid drug misuse? *Cyberpsychology, Behaviour and Social Networking, 17,* 331–332.

Wilkinson, J. (2006). *My world.* London: Headline.

Yerkes, R.M., & Dodson, J.D. (1908). The relationship of strength of stimulus to rapidity of habit formation. *Journal of Comparative Neurology & Psychology, 18,* 459–482.

5

THE ROLE OF TECHNOLOGY IN ATHLETE–SPORT PSYCHOLOGY CONSULTING

CASE STUDY 5

Ian is a professional 23-year-old soccer player who is travelling away with his team to another country to play in a major soccer tournament. Ian is going to be away from his training base for six weeks for this tournament. He usually attends a weekly consultancy session with his sport psychologist, who is located at his home training base. Ian would like to remain in contact with his sport psychologist while he is away competing. He suggests that they communicate with each other using Skype and WhatsApp for the duration of the tournament. His sport psychologist agrees to this arrangement while Ian is away playing at the tournament.

(i)   Why could making such an arrangement with his sport psychologist be important for Ian?

(ii) What arrangements should his sport psychologist put in place to help ensure this consulting arrangement works well for both Ian and his sport psychologist?

(iii) How could this arrangement impact on Ian and his sport psychologist's relationship after the tournament has concluded?

5.1 Overview

This chapter is devoted to the athlete–sport psychology consultant relationship. It examines issues related to the use of new technologies in potentially enhancing the athlete–consultant working relationship. Within the demanding world of elite sport, increasingly busy time schedules and training/competition locations now often act as barriers to the traditional face-to-face meetings between athletes and their sport psychologists taking place. The technological advances of the modern digital era have provided solutions to overcome such space and time issues for these individuals. To date, however, little empirical research within the sport psychology literature has evaluated the strengths and potential risks for practitioners using such new technologies with their sport-based clients. Indeed, the ethical challenges that technological advances have posed for the consultation process, especially within professional sport settings, could be a timely research 'test case' study, in order to determine whether some sport psychologists are actually 'fit' to practice using such advances in technology. The term 'fit' to practice (Hays & Brown, 2004) is a well-suited term in such contexts too in sport psychology because a substantial amount of the applied work sport psychology consultants do is with individuals considered to be the 'gold standard' of physical fitness and, with the advice and help of sport psychologists, they can set high standards for their mental fitness as well.

While, as previously mentioned, a distinct lack of research findings exist to date examining the use of technology in sport psychology consulting, a small number of researchers, for example, Stewart Cotterill and Rebecca Symes (2014) have published some comprehensive discussion papers on this specific topic of technology use within the sport psychology consultant-athlete process. Cotterill and Symes (2014) remarked that new technologies, such as Skype and FaceTime, for example, are now popular tools used by many practitioners when working with their athletes, who may be in different locations to them. Athletes are often away on training camps without their sport psychologists for many reasons (such as due to cost issues or different commitments or schedules) and technological advances have helped to overcome the barriers for psychological service provisions in such incidences. However, the risks associated with the use of new technologies cannot be ignored (Cotterill & Symes, 2014). As such, professional practice considerations (e.g., ethical, boundary and security issues) for consultants of all kinds, not just sport psychologists, should be to the forefront of consultants' minds when using technology to deliver services to their clients. These risks are discussed in some detail in this chapter in the content of Section 5.5 more specifically. Potential future research directions for more exploration of this area (i.e., more detailed evaluations of traditional service delivery formats compared to the delivery of such services by sport psychologists in the digital age), are proposed in the final section of this chapter.

5.2 Learning objectives

1   To define some key terms relevant to the topic of sport cyberpsychology consulting practices
2   To introduce the reader to the most common pieces of technology used within sport settings to assist sport psychologists consulting with their athlete clients

(as well as with clients who are not athletes, for example, coaches, refereeing officials and medical professionals who work alongside the athletes within the sport arena)

3 To explain the strengths and limitations of technological devices used in the consulting process by some sport psychology consultants and their clients

4 To highlight possible exciting, future developments and research study suggestions in this area of technology-assisted sport psychology consultancy practices and service delivery

5.3 Definitions of relevant terms

Blogs (also known as weblogs)

These are written pieces on the Internet, usually opinion pieces, on topics of potential interest to readers, communicated to national and international audiences. They often allow for comments to be written in response to the pieces beneath them so that the entire piece becomes a form of interconnected text between the writer and responders.

Emoji (sometimes referred to as a smiley face)

This is a small digital facial expression, or symbol, used to convey an emotion or idea to another person within a digital conversation (i.e., within a text, a Facebook or Twitter message or a WhatsApp message).

Facebook

This is a social networking website that any individual or organisation can join for free. On one's Facebook page, an individual can post photos, share information and link to other information posted by their friends (i.e., other Facebook members they have accepted friend requests from, for example).

FaceTime

Technology which allows video calling to take place via the Internet, with or without a visual image of those communicating with one another being present.

LinkedIn

This is a professional networking site often used by individuals as a type of professional online curriculum vitae (CV). Employers and employees can use LinkedIn to view each others' activities and interests online. It is sometimes considered the professional version of Facebook, with individuals sending others they are interested in connecting with, for professional purposes mainly, requests to be accepted into their LinkedIn network. Once two individuals or organisations are linked, they can also send each other private messages via the LinkedIn network.

Podcast

A podcast is typically a series of audio and/or video pieces recorded for free, or for a subscription, that can be downloaded to various devices from the Internet.

Skype

This is software and an online application that allows individuals to communicate with each other, in a similar way to a telephone call, but with visual images also available of the individuals as part of the communication process.

Text (SMS)

This is typically a facility used mainly by individuals on their mobile phone devices to send short written messages to one another.

Webinar

This term refers to a seminar that is conducted using the Internet. It allows individuals not physically present at the seminar to 'tune in', to see and hear the seminar content using their digital devices (i.e., their smartphones, laptops or tablets) once they have an Internet connection.

WhatsApp

This is an instant messaging service downloadable on all smartphone devices. It requires an Internet connection to be open and available in order for messages, photos and other information to be shared between smartphone-connected individuals. WhatsApp groups are now common. These are collections of individuals who communicate with each other at the same time, in a type of group conversation.

WiFi

This term refers to a wireless Internet facility which allows computers, smartphones and other devices such as tablets to connect to the Internet, wire free, from particular areas with such WiFi coverage. Many public places and hotels, for example, offer this facility for free to individuals located therein, hence the term 'free WiFi'. While such access is free, it often requires a password from the venue personnel in order to gain access to the Internet for communication purposes on those premises.

5.4 Introduction

"I'll skype you", "I'll text you", "I'll Facebook you", I'll tweet you" and "I'll WhatsApp you" have become popular phrases, used in abundance in modern-day communications. They are all forms of digital communication used by millions of people every day in the same way the phrase, "I'll call you", would have been used perhaps 20 years ago. In fact, they have, in many cases, become the preferred modes of communication between individuals who are not in face-to-face proximity at any point in time. On many mobile communication devices today, the 'call' function is actually one of the least-selected options used for communicating (OFCOM, 2012; Papp, 2014). Why might this be the case? One reason proposed is the cost associated with making a call compared to free communication options offered by, for example, WhatsApp messaging services, once free WiFi access is available too. Internet access is available without WiFi on many mobile devices with built-in 3G, 4G, and 5G software (the G stands for Generation and refers to generations of wireless technologies, with each higher number considered to represent faster, more secure and more reliable software). The typically lower costs associated with text messaging have also made it a more attractive communication option over making a call, which can be expensive, depending on the contracts individuals have with their mobile phone and Internet providers. Across Europe now, the charges applied by many mobile Internet service providers, to enable their customers to access the Internet, make calls and send texts using their 3G, 4G and 5G facilities (known as roaming charges) outside of their home country have been removed, leading to free roaming services being widely available to most individuals (European Council, 2017).

As cited earlier, most mobile devices with Internet access software built into them, such as smartphones or tablet computers (tablets) have the capability for Internet-based messaging, including video messaging, on them and many people have a preference for using them. Athletes are no different in their use of these popular forms of communication. Cotterill and Symes (2014) noted,

> The use of social media in society has increased significantly in recent years and as a result is something that sport psychology consultants need to be aware of even if they choose not to embrace its use. The number of users of these forms of communication and technology are increasing across all age groups and in particular in the younger demographic groups, who in turn will provide the athletes of the future.
>
> *(p. 62)*

Athletes use these Internet-based communication forms regularly in the same way that members of the general population do. Therefore, a number of questions should be asked, such as: (i) what impact do such devices and communication options have on the interactions between athletes and their sport psychology consultants; (ii) what benefits and risks for the consulting process do all of these methods of communication pose; (iii) why should all practicing sport psychologists be aware of these methods and options for communicating with their clients, even if they do not personally embrace their use themselves with their athletes within their consultancy practices; (iv) is it a good thing that consultants are available to their clients on a constant basis, using texting and Skype or FaceTime; (v) should consultants and athletes follow each other on Twitter or be friends on Facebook; and (vi) are there times when consultants should text their clients, but, equally, are there times when such texting behaviour could be inappropriate? These are all important questions for practicing sport psychologists to consider, yet many of these questions do not have easy or simple answers (Cotterill, 2014).

This chapter aims to attempt to answer some of these important questions. Explanations of the different modes of digital communication often used are presented. However, first, some consideration is given to the point raised in the overview of this chapter, that of the ethical practices involved in sport psychology consultation settings and what professional standards are expected for a consultant to be considered fit to practice, regardless of the devices they use to engage in this consulting process with their clients (Hays & Brown, 2004).

5.5 Professional and ethical considerations within sport psychology

The importance of establishing guidelines for good professional practices, regardless of the consultancy format used, should be a very real and important consideration for consultants and their professional representative bodies, who help to train and accredit such individuals. The British Psychological Society's (2009) Code of Ethics and Conduct for Psychologists is one such document where issues such as respect, responsibility, competence and integrity are outlined. Important ethical issues such as confidentiality and establishing professional boundaries, for example, also remain core considerations for well-trained, professional sport psychologists, regardless of their methods of communication with their clients.

In their 2014 article, Cotterill and Symes highlighted the importance of considering such professional issues when using Internet-based facilities for consultation purposes. This has become a real and important focus for many sport organisations, including those who represent sport psychologists in a professional capacity. For example, the British Psychological Society (BPS) ran a masterclass workshop by three experienced practitioners in the summer of 2016 to assist and advise their members in how to use telephone and Skype methods within their service delivery with their athletes. This workshop was seen as an exercise in the continued professional development of their members within the BPS (2016).

Ethical principles and standards are often regarded as the directives that professional organisations, such as the BPS (2009) and the APA (2003), issue with regard to how their members should behave when working in a professional capacity with their clients. For sport psychologists, such clients, as previously cited, typically include athletes, but also can include coaches and other individuals associated with the sport environment, such as match officials and medical personnel (including physiotherapists and doctors, for example). Etzel and Watson (2017) listed what they considered to be the most important ethical issues for consideration when consulting in such sport settings as: *professional values, confidentiality, competence* and *multiple role relationships*. These issues are considered in more detail in the paragraphs that follow. The impact of technological advances, as an additional consideration today for practitioners and their professional bodies, is discussed in the content of these issues.

Professional values in sport psychology consulting practices, as outlined by the American Psychological Association (APA), the International Society for Sport Psychology (ISSP) and the British Psychological Society (BPS), for example, are similar to those in place in other helping professions (e.g., medicine, nursing and social care). Six general professional values are frequently cited for these professions, namely: (i) doing good for others (beneficence), (ii) doing no harm (non-maleficence), (iii) respecting the autonomy and independence of clients, (iv) being fair and objective, (v) being caring and compassionate and (vi) being responsible and accountable (see Etzel & Watson, 2017, and Koocher & Keith-Spiegal, 2009, for a more detailed review of these issues). Sometimes these values and principles come into conflict with those of professional sport organisations who may employ a sport psychology consultant to work with their teams and athletes, usually with the ultimate goal of performance enhancement. Such performance enhancement focused work may help to ensure the sport success of the organisation and, through that, increase its revenue or profits. Sport psychology consultants working in such environments, especially within an elite professional sport, should have a clear and confident capacity to manage the situations they find themselves in, while meeting the preceding six principles of their profession, perhaps most especially, the principle of protecting the *confidentiality* of the information imparted to them by their athlete clients. This principle often forms the cornerstone of the trusting relationship clients should have with their consultants (Cotterill, 2014). Such trust is also based on consultants displaying integrity in their roles as consultants with their clients.

While one would hope the welfare of the athlete is the most important consideration for both the consultant and the sport organisation the athlete is affiliated with, this may not always be evident from the behaviours of some sport organisations. For example, playing players who are suspected of being injured or concussed can happen in some sports (Etzel & Watson, 2017). Sometimes this is due to the athletes themselves under-reporting their symptoms, perhaps because they think the condition is not serious enough or that they may be viewed differently within their team or organisation if they admit to their condition (Delaney, Lamfookon, Bloom, Al-Kashmiri, & Correa, 2015). Sport psychology consultants should to be mindful of these issues that can arise within some sport organisations and be clear on the stance they take in relation to such situations (i.e., that of always putting the welfare of their athlete clients above all other performance and organisational considerations).

It is sometimes difficult for sport psychologists, especially those who are in training or have just finished the most basic level of training required to commence working in a consultant capacity, to determine if they are indeed ready to work, *competently*, as sport psychologists in certain high-pressure, elite sport settings where conflicts may arise, such as those highlighted earlier as 'hot' topics (i.e., with regard to injury, and concussion specifically, for example). This is why supervision by a more experienced practitioner is often required for a number of years as a necessary criterion before being formally accredited as a sport psychologist by various professional sport psychology bodies (Cotterill, 2012; Psychological Society of Ireland, 2017).

Many established practitioners and their governing organisations, such as the APA, BPS, IISP and the British Association of Sport and Exercise Sciences (BASES) agree that sport psychology consultants working with athletes should be required to undergo professional training, to a Master's standard of study at least, for example, in order to work with athletes and elite sport personnel. Some studies examining the preferred qualifications of individuals working as sport psychology consultants highlighted that degree holding psychologists often co-exist with other individuals who have 'mental skills training' and with those who have no speciality training in the area of sport psychology at all (Sanchez, Godin, & DeZanet, 2005; Wylleman, Harwood, Elbe, Reints, & de Caluwe, 2009). While this trend still exists today, it is encouraging to see that Lubker et al. (2012) noted that those employing the services of sport psychology consultants seem to now be indicating a preference for practitioners who have advanced degree qualifications and are certified by an accrediting body. However, the issue of titles and certification regarding who should, and should not, be permitted to work with elite athletes remains one in need of reform according to many working, governing and advising individuals who are considering, or have entered into, the profession of applied sport psychology (Oliver, 2010; Stapleton, Hankes, Hays, & Parham, 2010; Woolway & Harwood, 2017). Perhaps some guidelines regarding the use of digital devices within the consulting process could also be included in such reform processes?

Part of the requirements for professional programmes of postgraduate training for sport psychologists, and indeed across all psychology training speciality programmes, should include considerable training in ethics, especially an understanding of what constitutes ethical behaviour when working with clients, and also good consulting skills in general. The APA (2003) published a *Sport Psychology Proficiency* guide which is useful in determining if an individual has the basic knowledge, skills and procedural understanding required to work in the often high-pressured, elite sport setting. However, this guide was published before the rapid advances in technology which is now an additional consideration within the consultancy settings of many practitioners and their athletes. Therefore, guides such as the *Sport Psychology Proficiency* guide are probably in need of updating, to include some of the suggestions of Cotterill and Symes (2014), for example.

But first, what constitutes good general consulting skills? *Good communication skills* in any consulting process cannot be overemphasised. Communication skills include, *good listening skills* and an *awareness of body language*. These skills are emphasised to sport psychology consultants working with athletes and sport personnel. Face-to-face communications are considered to have advantages over all other kinds of communication explored in more depth later in this chapter because such communications provide the greatest opportunities for 'cues' to be available regarding the exchange between the individuals. For example, pauses in conversations or periods of silence are often reported to be 'less awkward' when individuals are engaged in face-to-face conversations than when they are on a tele- or Internet based-form of communication (such as a voice on a voice-only Skype communication or on a telephone; Hawker, 2012). The issue of background noise and telephone line or online Internet interferences, which may make the words spoken by either party difficult to hear and/or see, is also a concern in such interactions. In face-to-face communications, the brain acts as a filter to block out these frequent disruptions, often resulting in more of the communication being heard or understood. There is a greater probability of the real meaning in such communications being more accurately conveyed as a result of this filter process (Hawker, 2012). Cotterill (2014) remarked that anything other than a face-to-face conversation should be considered a compromise when referring to the athlete–sport psychology consultancy process. Although this statement may be true, there are a number of advantages offered by remote forms of communication involving the use, and sometimes necessity, of technological devices (Hawker, 2012). These advantages are outlined next.

The advantages of remote forms of communication, using advanced digital technology, are that: (i) they are less costly and (ii) they offer time efficiencies for both parties (Heaney, 2013). Travel expenses are typically not a consideration in such situations, unless one or both parties have to travel to access a viable Internet connection for such communications to take place. However, in order to use these new digital forms of communication, both individuals must first be sufficiently skilled in how to operate them (Hawker, 2012). This may be difficult for either party, but more especially for those from older generations of athletes or consultants who were not born into the modern digital age.

As mentioned earlier, establishing professional boundaries also remains a core issue for well-trained, professional sport psychologists. Such boundary considerations with regard to the use of technology within the consulting process is also important and is now considered.

5.5.1 Boundary considerations

How to cope with the sometimes difficult issue of boundary considerations between clients and their consultants working in sport arenas is important for a number of reasons, especially when technology is an added ingredient in the process. The implications and complexities of social media use (Facebook and Twitter, for example) is one reason (Cotterill & Symes, 2014). Other professions, such as medicine and social work, have published various policy documents advising their professional members on 'good practice' when using social media (Cheston, Flickinger, & Chisolm, 2013; Kimball & Kim, 2013). Within psychology, the BPS clinical branch of the discipline has provided a document titled *e-Professionalism: Guidance on the Use of Social Media by Clinical Psychologists* for their professional members (BPS, 2009). In this guide, they highlight some of the concerns posed within the questions in the introduction section of this chapter, specifically those related to boundary concerns (such as when individuals join each others' social networks). Some sports organisations have also advised their athletes on best practices and rules for using social media, and technology in general, within their sport, with a number of them even taking steps such as fining their athletes for infringing their social media use rules (Gardiner, 2015).

However, while some organisations, such as the International Society of Sport Psychology (ISSP; Watson, Tenenbaum, Lidor, & Alfermann, n.d.) and the Association for Applied Sport Psychology (AASP, 2011) have published some advice for sport psychologists using the Internet as part of their sport psychology consulting practices, many sport psychology bodies have yet to follow their clinical colleagues in developing their own specific set of e-professional guidelines for their members working with athletes (Cotterill, 2014). So the question of what such guidelines should contain specifically for sport psychologists consulting with athletes remains.

One boundary issue in the athlete–consultant process that should be considered in such guidelines is an examination of the specific risks for sport psychology consultants' mental health and well-being, since the added pressure of being potentially available to their clients on a constant basis via technology and social media tools has arisen. This constant access can place a strain on practitioners' work–life balance, which many practitioners struggled to maintain even before technological advances and social media entered the process (McCormack, MacIntyre, O'Shea, Campbell, & Igou, 2015). This issue of work–life balance for sport psychology consultants is explored in more detail at the end of this chapter. But for now, apart from boundary issues, other important ethical considerations when using technology include security and privacy issues within the consulting process. These are considered next.

5.5.2 Security and privacy issues

The ISSP, as mentioned earlier, recently published a position paper on the use of the Internet in sport psychology. In this paper, Watson et al. (n.d.) commented on the dangers associated with Internet misuse by individuals working within the profession of sport psychology. They outlined some professional, ethical practices that sport psychology consultants should employ when using the Internet as a resource. For example, they stressed that great care should be taken to inform clients of the limitations of technology, especially in relation to ensuring complete confidentiality when using any electronic form of communication. As such, where possible, Watson et al. advised that, for example, only secure sites should be used for private email communications with clients, with appropriate firewalls and anti-virus software maintained, to help prevent breaches in security and to minimise the risk of clients' personal records being hacked.

In their codes of conduct, the AASP (2011) outlined the best practices for sport psychology consultants integrating new technologies into their professional consulting and scientific work within the domains of sport, exercise and performance psychology. They highlighted the importance of consultants only using the technologies they are specifically comfortable with and have the correct training in using. They also advised consultants on their responsibilities for communicating the limitations of using telecommunications to their clients, in advance of consulting with their clients using these methods, especially with regard to the privacy issues and ethical practices as outlined earlier by Watson et al. (n.d.).

However, despite the boundary, security and privacy concerns outlined previously, one cannot ignore the position of technology within today's sport environment, and as Wiederhold (cited in Connolly, Palmer, Barton, & Kirwan, 2016, p. xix) was quoted at the beginning of this text, "Technology, as opined by Carl Jung, is neutral. It is how we use that technology that determines whether it will be positive or negative". With this statement in mind, some of the popular forms of digital communication that may be used within consultancy practices are presented, along with a discussion of their specific benefits and risks.

5.6 Most popular forms of communication used in consultancy practices

5.6.1 Skype and FaceTime

Defined at the start of this chapter, Skype and FaceTime are currently two of the most popular video messaging options used by many individuals to communicate. Such communications are employed when individuals are not within the same physical location and, thus, prevent them from having a face-to-face conversation. Skype offers athletes and their consultants with one way to overcome such constraints of location and time, by enabling them to speak with each other, while also seeing each other on a digital screen, if they wish to do so. This means the consulting services provided by their sport psychologists remain available to athletes even when they are away on training camps or at foreign-based competitions. Indeed, "knowing their sport science support team personnel, including their sport psychologists, as well as their families and their friends, are accessible via their mobile devices can act as a great source of comfort for many athletes" (Hurley, 2016, p. 170).

However, Skyping, like many forms of telecommunication, requires an Internet connection to be in place in order for the communication to occur. On many occasions, that connection may be unreliable. It may be disrupted during the interaction, resulting in disjointed conversations, with words said sometimes being missed or the images on the screens breaking down. The danger of information being misinterpreted as a result of such interruptions in the Internet signal is real, as are the frustrations that could result for the individuals trying to communicate using this type of technology (Hawker, 2012).

Skype communications (or FaceTime) do allow for voice and body movements to be conveyed on the computer or mobile device screen, and could, perhaps, be considered the nearest form of communication to the face-to-face traditional consulting sessions which have dominated such consulting practices in the past. Therefore, they may be the most effective ways to maintain the highest degree of communication in the consulting process, because of the availability of language and body cues – highlighted as important in the consulting process in the early part of this chapter).

One of the most important things to occur between sport psychologists and their client athletes, as well as clear, understood, communication as emphasised earlier, is the establishment of a rapport, a sense of trust, between the athlete and the practitioner (Cotterill, 2014). Often this is best facilitated using face-to-face meetings, at least in the early stages, when this relationship is being established. After rapport and trust have been established between the two parties, perhaps then communications via Skype and FaceTime can occur, if both parties express a wish to use them to communicate. However, it is important to be aware that some practitioners have reported their communications between themselves and their clients have suffered when they moved to these video-based communications, away from the more traditional face-to-face meetings. This is unsurprising to some degree given Cotterill's (2014) comment that anything other than a face-to-face conversation is a compromise. This view was contradicted, however, by Heaney (2013) who, having used a solely remote method of consulting, concluded that Skype consulting was a viable and equally effective method of delivering sport psychology services when compared to the traditional face-to-face method for such service provision. But what if such video-based communication is not available for use by the practitioner and the athlete? Other methods such as texting and emailing are alternative technology-assisted options for use within the consultancy process. These are explored next as viable options instead of the video-based communications of Skype and FaceTime.

5.6.2 Text

Texting provides users with the facility to send typically short instant messages and has, in some cases, overtaken phone calls as a popular mode of communication, especially among young people (Lenhart, Ling, Campbell, & Purcell, 2010). For sport psychology consultants, texting can provide a quick and easy way to 'check-in' with an athlete to see how a training session went, for example, after a consultancy session may have taken place already (where a particular issue an athlete may have been having in training, for example, was discussed). Texting also offers a quick way to gather feedback on how an athlete may be feeling, as many individuals are well versed in the use of the emoji facility on their mobile devices. This facility, defined at the start of this chapter, is often used in short text messages to express emotions, and in the case of athletes, can be used to convey feelings about a particular situation they have experienced in their sport setting. Of course, such emoji use is open to misinterpretation, therefore, the meaning behind each emoji is something the athlete and the practitioner need to be well trained in, if the facility is to be used effectively as part of the athlete–consultant process.

Social networking facilities, such as LinkedIn, Twitter and Facebook, for example, also have private text-like messaging options as part of their communication facility. This enables their users to send brief text-like messages to each other too. Such messages remain invisible to other members of those particular social networks. Consultants can, therefore, use such messaging facilities in these networks in the same way they use mobile phone text messaging. But, again, the necessary Internet connection must be available in order to send such web-based short messages.

The transfer of emotions through tone of voice is typically missing from communications that occur via text messaging, email and Skype or FaceTime communications. When the telephone is the chosen mode of communication, voice tone is an added element in the communication process. However, body language is omitted then too. Skype and FaceTime communications allow for voice and body movements to be conveyed on the computer or mobile device screen, and can, perhaps, be considered the nearest form of communication to the face-to-face traditional consulting practice format which dominated consulting practices in the past, as was highlighted earlier in this chapter. However, the Internet connection must be present or such options for communicating with athlete clients not in the same physical location as their consultants is not viable.

If sport psychology consultants wish to convey lengthier pieces of information to their clients, or indeed to a wider global audience, ways of doing this could include writing emails and blogs or recording podcasts and webinars on topics of interest to their clients, their students – if working in academic settings – and to the wider sport community also. Email, as a method of communication, one would assume is well understood by most audiences at this point in time, and its strengths and limitations have been well documented (see Derkes & Bakker, 2010, for a review of such email communications). However, these other methods of communication (e.g., blogs, podcasts and webinars) are now considered as communication options by sport psychologists within their practice settings.

5.6.3 Blogs

Blogs (or more formally known as weblogs), compared to emails, are a more recent communication development. Blog 'articles' are typically placed on a hosted website (such as Wordpress or Wired, for example) and resemble, in their structure, a newspaper piece often seen in the opinion section of such publications. Blogs offer practitioners a way to communicate their opinions and ideas while also being effective marketing tools for a consultant's professional services (Cotterill & Symes, 2014). Blogs should be interesting and should generate some discussion regarding the topic being presented. Some notes of caution when writing blogs include making sure to proofread such pieces and to consider how the content could be viewed by the audience reading it, as once the blog is posted online it is available for all individuals with Internet access to read, form an opinion on and comment on.

5.6.4 Podcasts

Podcasts, as defined at the outset of this chapter, are also useful ways for individuals to educate interested parties about topics related to their professions. Podcasting has become popular among sport psychologists for this reason but also because, like blogging, it can be a beneficial way to attract potential future clients, who, upon hearing a podcast, may seek out the sport psychologist's services. A podcast has advantages over blogging because it allows the audience to listen and/or watch the individual hosting the podcast. The communication is not just words written on a page for individuals to read.

Podcasting in educational settings has also become a popular way to facilitate distance-learning (or e-learning), with lecturers recording their classes so that individuals who cannot physically attend those classes may do so remotely, via the Internet. This could be especially beneficial for student athletes who, for example, may be away training and competing during the academic year (see Chapter 6 for a more lengthy discussion regarding this use of the Internet for educational purposes).

5.6.5 Webinars

For consultants, the age of technology has also led to the use of webinars as a way to continue their professional development. As defined at the start of this chapter, webinars are seminars carried out over/or using the Internet. Individuals who wish to 'attend' such webinars typically register to obtain a method to login online in order to take part or view the session live, or as an alternative, to access a playback facility, which may be available free of charge, or by paying a fee. Registered attendees of webinars are able to hear and often see the session being presented by the host individual(s). Registered attendees are also typically able to engage with the presenter(s) of the webinar as it is occurring live, by sending in questions and/or comments throughout the webinar session, which the presenter(s) of the webinar may answer if there is time during or at the end of the session. Such remote opportunities for learning and upskilling by practitioners, and their clients alike, are now used in a variety of educational settings (Jozwiak, 2017).

But with all of this focus on providing the best and most varied options, using lots of technologies, for consulting services for athlete clients, maintaining a work–life balance as a sport psychologist can be a real challenge for many practitioners (McCormack et al., 2015). This important issue is now discussed.

5.7 Work–life balance considerations for sport psychologists using technology when consulting

One of the greatest difficulties for many practicing sport psychologists working with athletes is maintaining an appropriate work–life balance (McCormack et al., 2015). Many sport psychology consultants are passionate about their careers and the work they carry out with their clients (Sebbens, Hassmen, Crisp, & Wensley, 2016; Sharp, Hodge, & Danish, 2015). However, such passion and commitment, while commendable, has resulted in many consultants being on duty 24/7. Advances in technology have allowed for consultants to be in constant contact with their clients. In some ways, it has also probably helped to facilitate cases of psychological over-attachment and over-contact between clients and their consultants. It could be leading to a lack of real psychological detachment for consultants from their work-related activities. It may even be placing such individuals at risk of psychological distress and burnout (similar to the burnout their athletes may experience if they are overtrain in their sport).

In 2015, McCormack et al. spoke of the importance of sport psychology consultants looking after their own mental health and well-being in order to be in the best state to help their athlete clients. Social support from peers, family members and friends has long been advocated as a 'stress buffer' for athletes (DeFreese & Smith, 2014). The same could, and perhaps should, be said for sport psychology consultants working with their athlete clients. McCormack et al. commented that their online survey and interview data revealed cases of consultants living up to the label suggested by Schein (as cited in Aoyagi & Portenga, 2010, p. 256) that "a consultant is always consulting". Burnout and a lack of detachment from work-related issues did appear to be a problem for some of the participants in their study, especially those involved in travelling with teams to training camps, where access to all individuals on a 24/7 basis was facilitated by the very nature of the environment.

Perhaps an over-concern by sport psychologists to provide constant support to their clients, to have a non-stop duty of care towards them, has steamed from the new focus for consultants as mentioned in Chapter 1, that of the mental health and well-being of their athlete clients. It is, and should be one of, if not the, most important ethical consideration for consultants. However, it is a departure from the more dominant focus for consultants in the past, of performance enhancement (Andersen & Speed, 2010).

However, consultants should realise that tired or burnt-out consultants are of little or no benefit to their clients, in a similar way that overworked employees of any kind are not able to perform to the best of their ability for their employers (Schaufeli, Taris, & Rhenen, 2008). Sport psychology consultants need to be aware of the importance of maintaining a degree of separation between their work and personal lives. If that means having a self-enforced rule of not using or checking work-related devices, such as smartphones where text messages, WhatsApp messages and email appear, for the night-time hours or between specific set times that their clients are also aware of, then so be it. Once the consultant has been clear about his/her degree of availability to a client and the expectations of the client are also understood, the relationship should not suffer when the consultant is not 'at work'. In such situations, the health of both the athlete and the consultant could then be prioritised, protected and regarded as equal.

There may of course also be pressure, real or imaginary, exerted on practitioners from external forces, such as by their sport setting employers. If not consulting in a private capacity, being seen to be accessible at practically all times to the athletes in their care may become an issue for practitioners who perhaps fear being viewed as uncaring or not providing 'value for money' if they are not providing such extensive access to their services. McDugall, Nesti, and Richardson (2015) illustrated, in their qualitative study with six experienced sport psychology consultants, that such individuals can experience feelings of 'immense pressure', along with 'working long hours'. One individual stated that working at major sport competitions felt like being "under siege" and "through a warzone" (p. 271). These potential experiences of consultants should be made known to sport organisations who hire such individuals, so that clear consulting expectations and boundaries, to protect not only the athletes but also the consultant, can be established from the outset of the relationship between the consultant and the employing organisation.

5.8 Conclusion and suggestions for future research

As highlighted earlier, Cotterill and Symes (2014) were among the first sport psychology practitioners to comprehensively write about the benefits and dangers of using a range of technological offerings when consulting with athletes. What is apparent is that specific difficulties may arise when new technologies enter the consulting relationships. Specific risk factors associated with remote consultations may include the blurring of boundaries in the consultant–client relationship, as well as security and privacy issues (Cotterill, 2012, 2014; Cotterill & Symes, 2014). For sport psychologists, an added pressure of being potentially available to clients on a constant basis can place a strain on their work–life balance, which many consultants have struggled to maintain, even before technology entered the process (McCormack et al., 2015).

In relation to these issues, all of the important questions for practicing sport psychologists to consider, posed at the start of this chapter, remain because as was stated, they do not have easy or simple answers despite this chapter aiming to address answers to some of them (Cotterill, 2014). However, such questions could form the basis for new exciting sport cyberpsychology research studies in the future. Empirical explorations of such important topics for consultants and their clients alike, would be a welcome addition to the sport cyberpsychology literature.

5.9 Open-ended discussion questions

1   What role can new communication technologies play in helping sport psychology consultants support their clients within the elite world of sport?
2   Discuss the advantages and disadvantages of current communication devices for helping consultants support their clients.
3   What advice could be given to sport psychology consultants to help them maintain a healthy work–life balance when consulting with their clients?

5.10 Practical exercise

Complete a role-playing paired exercise where one individual acts as the client and the other person acts as the consultant. Use the conversation to establish boundaries and discuss ethical issues relevant to both the client and the consultant in the use of technology within their consulting relationship. What difficulties arose during the conversation regarding both individuals' expectations? How might such difficulties be overcome, especially with regard to the use of technology as a method of communication between them?

References

American Psychological Association. (2003, 2010). *APA sport psychology proficiency*. Retrieved from www.apadivisions.org/dividion_47/about/sport-psychology/index.aspx

Andersen, M.B., & Speed, H.D. (2010). Therapeutic relationships in applied sport psychology. In M.B. Andersen & S. Hanarahan (Eds.), *Routledge handbook of applied sport psychology* (pp. 3–11). New York: Routledge.

Aoyagi, M.W., & Portenga, S.T. (2010). The role of positive ethics and virtues in the content of sport and performance psychology service delivery. *Professional Psychology: Research & Practice, 41*, 253–259. doi: 10.1037/a0019483

Association for the Applied Sport Psychology (AASP). (2011). *Ethics code: AASP ethical principles and standards*. Retrieved from www.appliedsportpsych.org/about/ethics/ethics-code/

British Psychological Society (BPS). (2009). *E-Professionalism: Guidance on the use of socialmedia by clinical psychologists*. Leicester: British Psychological Society.

British Psychological Society (BPS). (2016). *A masterclass workshop in applied sport psychology – 'Conducting telephone & Skype consultancy with athletes'*. Retrieved from http://www.golfmind.co.uk/wp-content/uploads/2016/02/1-Day-Masterclass_-Conducting-Telephone-Skype-Consultancy.pdf

Cheston, C.C., Flickinger, T.E., & Chisolm, M.S. (2013). Social media in use in medical education: A systematic review. *Academic Medicine: Journal of Association of American Medical Colleges, 88*, 893–901.

Connolly, I., Palmer, M., Barton, H., & Kirwan, G. (Eds.). (2016). *An introduction to cyberpsychology*. London, UK: Routledge-Taylor and Francis Group.

Cotterill, S. (2012). Routes to practising as a sport and exercise psychologist. *The Sport & Exercise Scientist, 29*, 18–19.

Cotterill, S. (2014). *Applied sport psychology and social media*. Retrieved from https://stewartcotterill.co.uk/2014/08/15/applied-sport-psychology-and-social-media/

Cotterill, S.T., & Symes, R. (2014). Integrating social media and new technologies into your practice as a sport psychology consultant. *Sport & Exercise Psychology Review, 10*, 55–64.

DeFreese, J., & Smith, A.L. (2014). Athlete social support, negative social interactions, and psychological health across a competitive sport season. *Journal of Sport and Exercise Psychology, 36*, 619–630.

Delaney, J.S., Lamfookon, C., Bloom, G.A., Al-Kashmiri, A., & Correa, J.A. (2015). Why university athletes choose not to reveal their concussion symptoms during a practice or game. *Clinical Journal of Sports Medicine, 25*, 113–125.

Derkes, D., & Bakker, A. (2010). The impact of E-mail communication on organisational life. *Cyberpsychology: Journal of Psychosocial Research on Cyberspace, 4*(1), Article 4. Retrieved from https://cyberpsychology.eu/article/view/4233/3277

Etzel, E.F., & Watson, J.C. (2017). Ethical practice challenges of consultation in professional sport. In R.J. Schinke & D. Hackfort (Eds.), *Psychology in professional sports and the performing arts* (pp. 63–73). London: Routledge.

European Council. (2017). *EU all set for free roaming from June*. Retrieved from www.consilium.europa.eu/en/press/press-releases/2017/04/25-free-roaming-from-june/

Gardiner, C. (2015). *Social media in sport*. Retrieved from http://believeperform.com/wellbeing/social-media-in-sport/

Hawker, D. (2012). *Support by phone or Internet: Good practice*. Retrieved from www.global-connections.org.uk/sites/newgc.localhost/files/papers/Remote%20Member%20Care%20Good%20Practice%20-%20Debbie%20Hawker%20-%20June%202012%20(pdf).pdf

Hays, K., & Brown, C. (2004). *You're on! Consulting for peak performance*. Washington, DC: American Psychological Association.

Heaney, C. (2013). Keeping sport and exercise scientists 'appy' – online and mobile technologies in sport and exercise science. *The Sport & Exercise Scientist, 37*, 14–15.

Hurley, O. (2016). Sport and health cyberpsychology. In I. Connolly, M. Palmer, H. Barton, & G. Kirwan (Eds.), *An introduction to cyberpsychology* (pp. 167–180). London: Routledge.

Jozwiak, A. (2017). *How to overcome barriers in education with webinars*. Retrieved from https://blog.clickmeeting.com/use-webinars-education

Kimball, E., & Kim, J. (2013). Virtual boundaries: Ethical considerations for the use of social media in social work. *Social Work, 58*, 185–188.

Koocher, G., & Keith-Spiegal, P. (2009). *Ethics in psychology and the mental health professions: Standards and cases* (3rd ed.). New York: Oxford University Press.

Lenhart, A., Ling, R., Campbell, S., & Purcell, K. (2010). *Teens and mobile phones*. Retrieved from http://www.pewinternet.org/2010/04/20/teens-and-mobile-phones/

Lubker, J.R., Visek, A.J., Watson, J.C., & Singpurwalla, D. (2012). Athletes' preferred characteristics and qualifications of sport psychology practitioners: a consumer market analysis. *Journal of Applied Sport Psychology, 24*, 465–480.

McCormack, H.M., MacIntyre, T.E., O'Shea, D., Campbell, M.J., & Igou, E.R. (2015). Practicing what we preach: Investigating the role of social support in sport psychologists' well-being. *Frontiers in Psychology, 6*, 1854. doi: 10.3389/fpsyg.2015.01854

McDugall, M., Nesti, M., & Richardson, D. (2015). The challenges of sport psychology delivery in elite and professional sport: Reflections from experienced sport psychologists. *The Sport Psychologist, 29*, 265–277.

OFCOM. (2012). *Communications market report*. Retrieved from www.ofcom.org.uk/__data/assets/pdf_file/0013/20218/cmr_uk_2012.pdf

Oliver, J. (2010). Ethical practice in sport psychology: Challenges in the real world. In S.J. Hanarahan & M.B. Andersen (Eds.), *Routledge handbook of applied sport psychology* (pp. 60–68). Abingdon, Oxfordshire: Routledge.

Papp, D. (2014). *We no longer use the phones in our smartphones*. Retrieved from https://davidpapp.com/2014/10/21/we-no-longer-use-the-phone-in-our-smartphones/

Psychological Society of Ireland. (2017). *Guidelines for the accreditation of postgraduate academic courses*. Retrieved from www.psihq.ie/page/file_dwn/11/psi-accreditation-process-doc%20updated%202017.pdf

Sanchez, X., Godin, P., & DeZanet, F. (2005). Who delivers sport psychology services? Examining the field reality in Europe. *The Sport Psychologist, 19*, 81–92.

Schaufeli, W.B., Taris, T.W., & van Rhenen, W. (2008). Workaholism, burnout, and work engagement: Three of a kind or three different kinds of employee well-being? *Applied Psychology: An International Review, 57*, 173–203.

Sebbens, J., Hassmen, P., Crisp, D., & Wensley, K. (2016). Mental health in sport (MHS): Improving the early intervention, knowledge and confidence of elite sport staff. *Frontiers in Psychology, 7*, 911. doi: 10.3389/fpsyg.2016.00911

Sharp, L.-A., Hodge, K., & Danish, S. (2015). Ultimately it comes down to the relationship: Experienced consultants' views of effective sport psychology consulting. *The Sport Psychologist, 29*, 358–370.

Stapleton, A.B., Hankes, D.M., Hays, K.F., & Parham, W.D. (2010). Ethical dilemmas in sport psychology: A dialogue on the unique aspects impacting practice. *Professional Psychology: Research and Practice, 41*, 143–152.

Watson, J.C., Tenenbaum, G., Lidor, R., & Alfermann, D. (n.d.). *ISSP position stand on the use of the Internet in sport psychology.* Retrieved from www.issponline.org/documents/internet-position.pdf

Woolway, T., & Harwood, C. (2017). Do titles matter in sport psychology? Performer attitudes toward professional titles and the effect of a brief intervention. *The Sport Psychologist, 29*, 171–182.

Wylleman, P., Harwood, C.G., Elbe, A.M., Reints, A., & de Caluwe, D. (2009). A perspective on education and professional development in applied sport psychology. *Psychology of Sport & Exercise, 10*, 435–446.

PART III

Sport personnel in the online world

6

ATHLETES AND THE INTERNET

CASE STUDY 6

Paula is an elite, 24-year-old field hockey player. She competes both for a professional club team in Europe and for her national team. Paula has enrolled on a part-time sport psychology programme to further her studies while also playing her sport on a full-time basis. Such study is encouraged by Paula's national hockey players' union, in order to help prepare her for life after professional sport. Paula is required to attend one class each week for 20 weeks in her home town where the educational institute offering this programme is based in order to complete this Level 8 Certificate in Sport Psychology programme, Paula also has access to all of the class notes, readings and extra resources, such as video clips and weblinks, using an online virtual learning environment that the academic institute running this educational programme provides for all of the students enrolled in its courses of study.

(i) Describe how the Internet has enabled Paula to study on and complete such an academic programme, while also performing as a professional field hockey player?

(ii) Detail the benefits and limitations of this type of part-time study offered as an educational programme for athletes like Paula.

(iii) What future developments in technology-based learning could enhance the experiences of students, similar to Paula, who opt to study on such educational programmes?

6.1 Overview

This chapter discusses how and why athletes use the Internet as a resource (e.g., for interacting and communicating online, for information gathering, and for educational and training purposes). It outlines some of the benefits, as well as the negative consequences, of such Internet use by athletes. For example, as the quote on page 109 from Michael Joyner (cited in Loria, 2016) displays, the Internet has enabled athletes (and spectators too) from all over the world to see what other athletes are achieving and to raise their own standards in order to match and perhaps supersede such accomplishments. Many athletes may also choose to 'surf the web' for entertainment purposes during their rest times when they are not training or competing. Such behaviour may alleviate the boredom of their downtime, as reported by some athletes. This use of the Internet as a form of distraction and entertainment, and where the experience of time passing may be somewhat distorted, is a familiar concept to many psychology researchers too. It is a concept associated with the research findings of Csikszentmihalyi (1990) regarding 'flow' states, for example. However, while such Internet activities may be entertaining and informative for athletes, they may also lead to problematic uses of the Internet by athletes, such as excessive online gambling and inappropriate information searching (e.g., to access illegal substances). These specific problematic behaviours are discussed in Chapter 10, which focuses on the problematic behaviours sometimes observed in athletes' online use.

6.2 Learning objectives

1 To introduce the reader to some common reasons why athletes use the Internet
2 To explain the strengths and limitations of such Internet use for athletes
3 To highlight some future developments for the ways athletes may use the Internet for information sharing, communicating and training benefits, both from sport and educational perspectives

6.3 Definitions of relevant terms

Attention

This term relates to the activity of directing the mind to complete a specific task or to focus the mind on a particular thought or emotion.

Fanship

This term refers to the sense of connection that often exist between fans of a sport and the sport itself and/or its associated athletes.

Internet self-efficacy

This is the belief an individual has in his/her own ability to complete actions, using the Internet, in order to fulfil specific goals (Eastin & LaRose, 2000).

Meditation

This is a process of spending time in quiet thought or reflection.

Mindfulness

This popular term refers to the action of concentrating one's thoughts on a present moment, in a purposeful, non-judgemental way.

Virtual Learning Environment (VLE)

VLEs (also referred to as Learning Management Systems (LMSs) or Course Management Systems (CMSs); see Moore, Dickson-Deane, & Galyen, 2011) refer to online environments that typically contain lecture notes, reading materials, weblinks and video clips, for example, to support more formal, physical-presence-based traditional student learning environments provided in many academic institutions, such as schools and colleges or universities. VLEs often have facilities to enable: (i) online discussions between students and their instructors, as well as having (ii) direct emailing facilities, (iii) assessment submission uploading options (with plagiarism detection software included) and (iv) student assessment feedback functions. VLEs may be used to deliver exclusive online-based virtual education programmes.

6.4 Introduction

America Online (AOL) carried out a study of Internet use by 55,000 consumers and identified eight key reasons why individuals stated they engaged with Internet content (see Shanmugham, 2016). AOL referred to these eight reasons for seeking out content using the Internet as *content moments*. The eight content moments they identified were: (i) *to be inspired*, (ii) to be *in-the-know* (for example, to stay up-to-date on news and the most recent ideas), (iii) *to find information* (i.e., to seek out advice about issues of interest), (iv) *to be comforted* (i.e., to seek out social support from others), (v) *to connect with others* (i.e., to be, and feel, part of a wider community), (vi) *to feel good* (i.e., to improve mood and to help relax), (vii) *for entertainment purposes* and finally (viii) *to stay in touch* (i.e., to remain connected with family and friends). It appears logical that these eight reasons for using the Internet could also apply to athletes. However, an interesting question could also be: Do athletes' specific uses of the Internet differ in ways from those of non-athlete populations? Some research evidence will be presented in this chapter to determine if this is indeed the case. However, for now, let us begin by asking how and why athletes appear to be using the Internet.

6.5 How and why are athletes using the Internet?

Early Internet use research suggested that different age groups used the Internet as a resource in different ways (Kiel, 2005). Soon the global population will be one where every generation has grown up in the 'age of the Internet' (given that the Internet came into existence in 1977; Attrill, 2015). Studies that have shown

Internet use declines as people age (Kaare, Brandtzaeg, Endestad, & Heim, 2007; Weiser, 2000) may soon be overtaken by as many studies showing Internet use rising among older, perhaps more house-bound and less mobile, generations of adults too. The advances in the ease with which the Internet can now be used has helped to move its use in this direction perhaps. Indeed, the view that the Internet is only a playground for young people, sometimes referred to as the Net Generation (Net-Gen or N-Gen), is already being challenged, with individuals as old as 102 years of age being shown to be users of the Internet (Attrill, 2015). Some researchers have referred to Internet use as goal-related or goal-directed behaviour, across different ages and employment status groups (Akman & Mishra, 2010). Given that large numbers of elite athletes may comprise of a younger age demographic, their Internet use could be compared to those of the N-Gen. However, empirical research making such comparisons does not appear to be evident to date. Indeed, research on the different uses of the Internet today among older and younger generations is also still catching up with the advances in the Internet and has led to perhaps more similar, less distinctive, generation gaps being apparent with regard to Internet use across older and younger populations in today's society.

The Internet has also made it possible for today's academic institutions to offer their educational and training programmes in an online format so that students, including professional athletes, can enrol on and successfully complete courses using virtual learning environments (VLEs). Other individuals are also attracted to such programme offerings, including other elite performers such as professional dancers, musicians or indeed personnel in the defence forces, who, like their athlete colleagues, are also required to travel abroad frequently, thus preventing them from enrolling on traditional academic programmes that require their physical presence in a classroom setting for some continuous time period each year. These virtual learning environments allow student athletes and the previously mentioned performers to study at their own pace and in their own time. Some programmes (such as that outlined in the case study of Paula at the start of this chapter) have course offerings that also combine both the online and offline worlds for their programme delivery. Other programmes are offered using solely the VLE model of online delivery, where students are not required to attend classes physically. Instead, they interact online with their course lecturers and fellow students using the VLE.

It is probably no surprise, however, to discover that despite issues such as age and academic developments regarding the uses of the Internet being relevant as examples, there remains a lack of empirical research documenting the specific uses of the Internet by athletes. Given this position, this chapter considers the models and perspectives proposed to explain differences in Internet use between older and younger generations in general, as well as the perhaps differing needs and goals of athletes.

6.5.1 Meeting needs and goals

The *uses and gratification (U&G) theory* proposed by Blumler and Katz (1974) is often cited within cyberpsychology research to help explain the reasons why individuals use the Internet. This theory explains how Internet use has a purpose and that such purpose leads to a form of gratification for individuals when they engage in the practice of using the Internet. The goal, or purpose, of Internet use may not always originate from a motivation within an individual to want to discover information about a specific topic for its own sake, however (regarded as a type of internal motivation), without a specific external reward being available. Rather, the motivation for using the Internet by many individuals may originate from specific external motivations, such as a requirement to read a research article because it is required reading for a college course (e.g., in the case of Paula, presented at the start of this chapter).

How athletes specifically use the Internet, like any other group of individuals, is determined by their specific, individual needs and personal goals. This is considered the case for other individuals who engage with the Internet also (Spears, Postmes, Lea, & Wolbert, 2002). Athletes may, for example, use online resources (such as YouTube video clips and blogs) to *learn new skills* or to refine the techniques of their already accomplished skills in their sport (Guerin-Eagleman, 2015). The Internet, in such cases, offers athletes a vast array of media options through which they may view such sport content (e.g., videos, images, texts and audio resources), and as Dr Michael Joyner, physician and researcher in human performance and exercise physiology stated,

> You don't push the limits of human performance without being aware of what those supposed limits are, and the Internet has made us more aware than ever of any seemingly insane accomplishment out there. . . . Now it's possible for people all over the world to connect via the Internet, and people are getting into some very interesting things.
>
> *(cited in Loria, 2016)*

Athletes, like their non-athlete peers, may also use the Internet *to communicate* with others. This is typically achieved using their social media networks of Facebook, Twitter, Instagram and LinkedIn, for example. (Athletes' specific use of social media is discussed at length in the next chapter of this text). In brief, however, in relation to such online social media use, Gangadharbatla (2008) provided an overview of four main factors thought to influence many individuals' social networking behaviour. The four factors Gangadharbatla (2008) discussed are: (i) a need for belonging, (ii) a need for cognition, (iii) Internet self-efficacy and (iv) collective self-esteem. These factors are discussed here, prior to Chapter 7, however, because they could also be logically applied to athletes' general Internet uses.

Maslow (1943, 1968) discussed the *need for belonging* in his Hierarchy of Needs model of motivation. Maslow positioned this need to belong in his Hierarchy of Needs model after the more basic physiological human needs (such as eating and drinking for survival) had been met, as well as safety needs (i.e., having a secure, safe place in which to live – for example, a home). The need to belong, Maslow (1943, 1968) claimed, came after these two more 'urgent' needs had been met. Maslow paired the need to belong with the need to love and be loved. Maslow claimed these love and belonging needs centred round the human need to feel cared for, and to feel part of and accepted by a larger social network, that is, that of a family, a peer group, a community and a society at large (Baumeister & Leary, 1995). This need to feel a sense of belonging to such groups is considered a strong motivator for many human behaviours and may explain why individuals join groups, including online groups, for example (Chiu, Cheung, & Lee, 2008; Hurley, 2016). However, recent examinations of Maslow's model in relation to social media use, for example, has led to debates surrounding its application in explaining why individuals are motivated to join online groups (Asher, 2014; Chan, 2016; Cherry, 2015). Recognising that there may be valid arguments for how Maslow's (1943) hierarchy model may not satisfactory explain motivations for seeking out social interactions online, an important term to consider when examining such motivations for joining groups of any kind is *collective self-esteem*. This term refers to a person's self-identity being linked to the sense of belonging he or she feels as a result of being part of certain groups, both online and/or offline (see Flood et al., 2015, and Hurley, 2016, for more in-depth reviews of online groups).

A small number of researchers in recent years, employing this *U&G theory*, have examined these online communities and their specific uses (as cited previously; Blumler & Katz, 1974; Katz, Blumler, & Gurevitch, 1974). For example, in a study of masters' gymnasts, Guerin-Eagleman (2015) employed a mixed-methods approach to obtain both quantitative and qualitative data from 164 participants, from 17 countries, regarding their use of online groups. Masters' athletes typically range from 30 to 90 years of age (Weir, Baker, & Horton, 2010), although in her study, having consulted the competition policies of many countries for Master's level gymnastics, Geurin-Engleman allowed athletes from 20 years upwards to take part in her study, which actually comprised the largest age group – 67.5% of the sample were between 20 and 29 years of age. These Master's level athletes claimed to use online communities mainly to gain information and technical knowledge for their sport, as well as for fanship. Guerin-Eagleman reported that these athlete-specific online communities typically represented an extension of the athletes' in-person training groups and communities (i.e., they knew and interacted with their online group members in their offline worlds too). Guerin-Eagleman's (2015) study helped to address a gap in the sport literature by exploring some athletes' specific uses of the Internet, in this case to facilitate their generation of online communities, rather than focusing on the athletes' audiences or supporters' use of such online communities. Studies of these 'supporting individuals' had dominated the literature and research in the area up to that point (see Cheever, 2009; Clavio & Kian, 2010; Gantz & Wenner, 1995; Kim & Ross, 2006).

This research study by Guerin-Eagleman's (2015) of athletes' uses of online communities helps not only our understanding of the interactivities of athletes in such forums, but also could help sport clubs, as well as national and international sport governing bodies, determine how best to use the Internet in order to meet the needs of their athletes. On a related point, Hurley (2012) completed an online survey examining the tweet content preferences of followers of sport psychologists on Twitter. These followers were mainly athletes, coaches and academics.

The results of Hurley's study revealed that the followers of sport psychologists on Twitter wished to see these psychologists tweet research findings regarding psychological principles they applied in real life contexts with their athletes, as well as practical tips on how to apply the various psychological techniques they advocated with their athletes in order to enhance their sport performances. Such topics and issues regarding social media use by various individuals in sport environments is addressed in more depth in Chapters 7 and 8 of this text. However, as well as using the Internet for social, online group networking as well as for information seeking and sharing reasons via social media, athletes may also use the Internet for cognitive-based reasons. This reason for their Internet use is explored next.

Cognitive-based motivations and needs have been identified for Internet use and activities across many populations. One cited need is the *need for cognition*. This need for cognition refers to a person's need to apply cognitive effort to a task and to experience a reward for such mental effort. This cognition-based need could influence how a person (in this case an athlete) may use the Internet (Attrill, 2015). However, knowing *how* to use the Internet is an important factor in determining if the Internet is used by an individual and is referred to as Internet self-efficacy.

Internet self-efficacy describes the belief individuals may have regarding their ability to complete actions using the Internet in order to fulfil specific goals (Eastin & LaRose, 2000). If an individual lacks such belief, he or she is unlikely to use the Internet. Schofield-Clarke (2009) referred to a technological comfort zone. A lack of this comfort zone could result in the individual not interacting with the Internet at all. In today's society a large percentage of the global population do use some form of Internet engagement. However, there is still a small percentage of individuals (one in ten in the United Kingdom, for example, according to their National Statistics Office) who have not, to date, used the Internet (Dilworth, 2017). Age-related reasons for more or less Internet use, as mentioned at the outset of this chapter, have been proposed across a number of research studies, although these findings have been questioned, as was also mentioned earlier (see Attrill, 2015).

Considering the needs and goals of athletes, their uses of the Internet could be listed for the following reasons: (i) *for information sharing and communicating* (i.e., using social media to interact with fans, *promoting their own 'brand'* and their personal business offerings – see Chapter 7), (ii) *for educational purposes* (such as for online, distance learning), (iii) *for information seeking* (i.e., for training and medical information; for post-sport career support networking and/or information) as well as (iv) *for non-sport specific reasons* (i.e., for entertainment purposes). To return to the question posed earlier in this chapter then: Do such proposed reasons for athletes' specific Internet use differ substantially from those of non-athlete populations? Some evidence would suggest not, especially if one considers the findings of Shanmugham (2016) presented in the introduction section to this chapter. Therefore, some of these proposed main reasons for athletes' Internet use are explored later in more detail (Note: Athletes' *communication reasons* for their Internet use will be covered in depth in Chapter 7, which specifically examines athletes' social media use as a main form of their online communications).

6.5.2 Information sharing and communicating

What information athletes choose to share with others online can have a significant impact on their careers and lives in general. Different platforms online typically lead to individuals modifying their online information-sharing behaviour depending on who their audience is for those platforms. For example, some athletes may limit their Twitter information sharing to sport-related topics such as their team activities, team promotional or individual appearance events and training events, although some studies show this not to be the case. Some athletes actually appear to like to share non-sport related content online in many cases (Hambrick, Simmons, Greenhalgh, & Greenwell, 2010). Athletes' Twitter accounts often have thousands of followers (Social Bakers, 2017), and as such, athletes may tailor their online information sharing to match that specific platform as they are using it. One specific use athletes appear to have for the Internet, however, is for their own promotion and 'brand' exposure. This use is outlined in the next section.

6.5.3 Promotion options and athletes' brand exposure

The trend of celebrity athletes impacting significantly the ticket sales and products of teams is not a new phenomenon. In 1997, Hausman and Leonard examined the impact of professional athletes on such revenue and estimated that, for example, USA National Basketball Association (NBA) star, Michael Jordon, alone increased the revenue for his team, and that of the national basketball team of the USA, by 50 million dollars. In 2008, Lawson, Sheehan and Stephenson completed a similar study focusing on David Beckham's move to play soccer in USA major league soccer and similarly reported his contribution to the multi-million dollar increased revenue for his team (LA Galaxy) upon his arrival into that sport environment.

Given such opportunities, many athletes use the Internet now to promote products for their sponsors and corporate clients, while also using it as a way to self-promote their own athletic brand. Often athletes or their representatives (i.e., agents/agencies) establish websites detailing athletes' activities and offerings in order to attract potential sponsors. Some athletes may employ public relations (PR) agencies to run these websites. However, the athletes often have a direct input regarding what is displayed on their websites too.

The growth in Internet use in recent years has greatly increased the potential for sponsorship opportunities for athletes, enabling them to secure attractive endorsement contracts. Such opportunities have had varying degrees of success for both the athletes and their employing sponsors. For example, in 2011, Hambrick and Mahoney examined the Twitter accounts of Lance Armstrong and Serena Williams to examine their use of this online platform to promote various products, as well as advertising their own sport activities and charitable work. Of the 7,202 tweets Hambrick and Mahoney (2011) analysed that were posted by these two athletes, 12% of them were promotional tweets that included references to some of their sponsors. Interestingly, within these tweets the two athletes failed to mention six of their sponsors. If such companies are paying the athletes to promote them, this may not be a good return on their investment.

E-vending has also become an increasingly popular way to sell products to the public. However, the decision to purchase a product is often influenced by a number of important factors, such as the reliability of the product to do what it reports to do. Well-known athletes are some of the most used individuals for such purposes. They are hired by companies to share their assumed knowledge and expertise of their sport in order to influence the public in purchasing the product associated with their sport that they themselves report using. This phenomenon is known as electronic word of mouth or eWOM (Do-Hyung, Jumin, & Ingoo, 2007; Hajli, 2016). The use of social media platforms to communicate such product 'reviews' by well-known sport athletes has increased the use of the term social word of mouth (or sWOM for short; Hajli, Lin, Featherman, & Wang, 2014). Of interest here, is that this phenomenon of product endorsement online by athletes and its potential impact on the athletes' mental well-being or indeed its impact on their sport performances does not appear to have been the subject of empirical study by psychology researchers to date. The potential of this research avenue is returned to in the conclusion of this chapter. However, athletes may also use the Internet to enhance their later, non-sport, careers in other ways, such as for educational purposes. This reason for their Internet use is explored next.

6.5.4 Educational opportunities

Athletes, as a group, are a somewhat unique collection of individuals whose lifestyles may challenge the traditional delivery of education that requires students to be available on a full-time basis to physically attend lectures, coursework sessions, meetings and other institutional events. Athletes often cannot fulfil such academic commitments due to their training and competition schedules. They are sometimes required to be away from their 'base' for lengthy periods of time, at training camps abroad and at competitions held in venues around the world. Such events also may take place during the academic year. As a result, student athletes may become disheartened and disengaged with their studies because of their lack of availability to meet the course requirements and many may withdraw from their courses of study as a result (Kreb & Lockee, 2009). This is not an ideal situation as such actions may negatively impact upon the athletes' career options later in life when they formally retire from professional sport participation, for example. One of the most obvious uses of the Internet by such student athletes then is for online study. Online educational options provide athletes with opportunities to pursue their sport goals while also achieving their academic aspirations. Such options are something many sport organisations and support groups are encouraging athletes to pursue, given the uncertain nature of a sport career, which can end suddenly due to a serious injury, for example (Reiner, 2017; Simonson, Smaldino, Albiright, & Zvacek, 2006).

Kreb and Lockee (2009) examined the perceptions of student athletes regarding these online educational options. They specifically examined the benefits and barriers experienced using such online learning options. Kreb and Lockee (2009) hoped their study would help educators to determine the best way to cater for this specific group of individuals so that the education they receive in the future is a positive one and of the best possible quality. Using a mixed research methodology involving individual and group interviews, as well as a survey design, Kreb and Lockee (2009) reported that the majority of the athletes who participated in their study unsurprisingly reported that, due to significant time constraints, online learning options provided them with a way to manage their time so that they could fit in their training and competitions, as well as their educational commitments. As mentioned earlier, athletes often have irregular schedules and different rest times compared to other students – such as during long travel journeys on trains, buses and airplanes to and from training camps or competitions, for example. Online learning afforded these athletes the opportunity to pass this travel time in a productive way, by allowing them to catch-up on course work and complete assignments, while also helping to alleviate the anxiety sometimes caused in the past by worrying about missed classes and not being able to catch-up on their educational course work at busy sport performance times. The anonymity online learning can provide was also mentioned as an advantage by the participants in Kreb and Lockee's (2009) study. To elaborate, some of their athlete participants remarked that online learning options helped them to avoid being labelled as less capable or being given special treatment due to their athletic status, when compared to their non-athlete peers.

Of course, as with all forms of programme delivery, online programmes have barriers and limitations too. The athletes in Kreb and Lockee's (2009) study reported the lack of: (i) structure, (ii) access to academic staff (lecturers/professors/tutors) in a face-to-face environment and (iii) some freedom from accountability, as potential barriers to them successfully completing their academic courses of study, as well as their sometimes lower regard for the online learning option when they compared it to more traditional, physically-attended, offline academic options. But despite these recognised limitations of online study, athletes are encouraged to invest in their education using such online options, while competing at a high level in their sport. It is an important activity for them to engage in, in order to prepare them for life after sport, especially professional sport, where their source of income comes directly from taking part in their sport.

This transition from professional athlete to a second career as a non-athlete has been documented as, potentially, one of the most demanding phases in an athlete's life. Many athletes have described this time as one of grieving, for the loss of their athletic careers, and also one of uncertainty, for what the future may hold for them as they move onto another career (Gillick, 2017). Athletes who have not prepared well for the inevitable end of their full-time sport careers have been at the centre of some recently reported tragic stories in the media (Williams, 2017). Some athletes have taken their own lives when they failed to find ways to cope with the transition from their professional athletic career to a second career. One recent high profile tragic case of this was that of Australian rugby player, Dan Vickerman, who died in February 2017, through suicide. This former professional rugby player had given a number of talks prior to his death to current players about the difficulties in transitioning from life as an elite player to life after a professional sport career. However, the culture within some traditionally male-dominated sports still have some work to do before such cases are reduced (Williams, 2017; see Section 6.5.6 on athletes' Internet use for retirement information and support networks for more information related to this important topic).

In summary then, why are athletes choosing 'virtual schools' for their educational opportunities? Some of the reasons cited previously were outlined also by Reiner (2017; see Box 6.1 and Box 6.2 for summaries of the strengths and limitations of distance/virtual learning for athletes).

BOX 6.1 A SUMMARY OF THE STRENGTHS OF DISTANCE/VIRTUAL LEARNING FOR ATHLETES

1   They facilitate athletes' busy training schedules and their need to rest at times that are typically different to non-athlete students.
2   They enable athletes to pursue their sport goals and their academic goals at the same time.
3   They accommodate learning from any location, once the location has Internet-facilitated access.
4   They are often cost-effective for student athletes, and also for the academic institutions offering these online programme options for athletes, as they typically have less overhead costs associated with them.

BOX 6.2 A SUMMARY OF THE LIMITATIONS OF DISTANCE/VIRTUAL LEARNING FOR ATHLETES

1   They prevent athletes from interacting in a physical way with their student peers (despite allowing them to interact remotely/virtually via discussion boards, etc.).
2   They may prevent young athletes from developing their social skills to the same level as their non-virtually schooled peers.
3   They sometimes require expensive technologies and equipment to be purchased to enable such learning options to take place (e.g., laptop computers, high-speed Internet access, etc.).

6.5.5 Information seeking (anti-doping information)

The Internet can also be a valuable source of information for athletes regarding injury and anti-doping information, two topics closely associated with elite sport performances. However, similar to any kind of Google search for such information, they carry a note of caution for athletes, that is, to only access reliable sources for such health and performance-related information. It can be difficult for athletes to know what information is reliable on the Internet. It is, therefore, the responsibility of their support organisations and rule enforcers to also inform athletes of where to locate such information on the Internet. However, even with such advice available to athletes from such bodies, for example, on the website of the World Anti-Doping Agency (WADA), numerous high profile cases of athletes testing positive for banned substances have occurred in recent times. In some cases, the athletes have claimed they did not consult the most up-to-date information online on such sites for the correct information, for various reasons.

The recent case of female Russian tennis player, Maria Sharapova, is perhaps one of the most high-profile of such cases in the past few years. Sharapova tested positive for the banned substance meldonium (also called mildronate). This substance is prohibited for use by athletes because of its ability to increase the exercise capacity of the user (by increasing blood flow to the muscles, thus allowing for increased oxygen levels to reach the muscles and enabling the athletes to train at higher volumes than fellow competitors not taking the drug; The Guardian, 2016). Sharapova claimed she had been taking the drug for medical reasons (for a magnesium deficiency and the risk of diabetes, due to a genetic predisposition) for ten years – since 2006. Sharapova stated in a press conference when her positive test was reported to the media in June 2016 that she had not educated herself on the recently added substances to WADA's list of banned substances, which now includes meldonium. Sharapova received a two-year ban from tennis which was subsequently reduced to 15 months.

Such incidences of athletes failing to access the required information online regarding important matters related to their sport performances, focuses a spotlight on the use of the Internet to convey such information to athletes in a prompt, immediate way, but then relying on these individuals to access the information and educate themselves on this most up-to-date online information (as Sharapova claimed not to have done). The way in which important information is communicated online may not always be user friendly. Therefore, some athletes could argue that they could not find the relevant information in the online source. With recent cyberattacks being reported (Ingle, 2016), what safeguards are in place to stop hackers from accessing the information of such important sport performance consulted websites such as WADA and making changes to the information online that athletes then consult? How often is such information checked by the personnel in such organisations to make sure that it is accurate and correct? These are important questions in need of some consideration by sport organisations as the digital age advances, and as more information is placed online (replacing traditional published copies of such documents).

6.5.6 *Retirement information and support networks*

As previously mentioned, many sport bodies – professional, semi-professional and amateur in status – have established athlete support organisations for their members. Such organisations are important sources of support for athletes during their sport careers and, perhaps even more so, post retirement from their sport (for the tragic reasons cited earlier). Many of these organisations, such as Rugby Players Ireland (formally known as the Irish Rugby Union Players Association), the Gaelic Players Association (GPA) and the Jockeys Education and Training Scheme (JETS) offer very useful online information and network options for their athletes to search through in order to locate suitable training and educational opportunities, both during their sport careers and post retirement. Some businesses may also partner with such organisations to provide athletes with apprenticeship opportunities to work in their companies while they are still competing as athletes. These support organisations typically offer both online and offline supports for athletes, the aim being to prevent the athletes falling victim to the mental health, physical health, and sometimes financial difficulties some of their previous members have suffered. For examples of such support organisations, see Table 6.1.

TABLE 6.1 Athlete support organisations for various sports from around the world

Organisation	Country and Sport	Website
Association of Tennis Professionals (ATP) World Tour	Men's Tennis; International	www.atpworldtour.com/
Women's Tennis Association (WTA)	Women's Tennis; International	www.wtatennis.com/
FIFIPro World Players Union	Soccer; International	www.fifpro.org/en/
Gaelic Players Association (GPA)	Ireland; Gaelic Games – Football, Hurling and Camogie	www.gaelicplayers.com/
Irish Jockey' Trust (IJT) Jockeys Work Education and Training Scheme (JWETS)	Ireland; Horse Racing	http://ijt.ie/ http://ijt.ie/jwets/
Jockeys Education and Training Scheme (JETS; UK)	United Kingdom; Horse Racing	www.jets-uk.org/
National Basketball Players Association (NBPA)	USA; Professional Basketball	https://nbpa.com/
National Football League Players Association (NFLPA)	USA; National Football League (American Football)	www.nflpa.com/
National Hockey League Players' Association (NHLPA)	USA & Canada; Ice Hockey	www.nhlpa.com/
Major League Baseball Players Association (MLBPA)	USA; Baseball	www.mlbpa.org/

(Continued)

TABLE 6.1 (Continued)

Organisation	Country and Sport	Website
Professional Cricketers' Association (PCA)	United Kingdom; Cricket	www.thepca.co.uk/
Professional Footballers' Association of Ireland (PFAI)	Ireland; Soccer	www.pfai.ie/
Professional Footballers' Association (PFA) (Established in 1907, the PFA is the world's oldest professional sportsperson's union)	United Kingdom; Soccer	www.thepfa.com/
Rugby Players Ireland	Ireland; rugby union	www.rugbyplayersireland.ie/
The Rugby Players' Association	United Kingdom; rugby union	https://therpa.co.uk/
Track and Field Athletics Association (TFAA)	Athletics; International	www.trackfieldaa.com/

As highlighted in the content of this chapter, athletes can use the Internet in many positive ways. While the Internet could now even be considered a vital resource for such elite athletes for their sport preparations (in facilitating their information seeking, information sharing and communicating, as well as for educational purposes), its uses by athletes in a negative context cannot be overlooked. Though it would be wrong to vilify the Internet, its disadvantages and limitations should also be acknowledged in the case of athletes' uses of it as a resource. Such negative Internet uses, not exclusive to athletes it should be noted, include using it: (i) *as a source of negative distraction, taking them away from their training, competition and education* (i.e., it can facilitate procrastination), (ii) *as a source of misinformation*, (iii) for *information overload* and (iv) for *Internet misuse and abuse* (discussed in greater depth in Chapters 9 and 10). The first three negative aspects of Internet use cited here will be presented next in the context of athletes.

6.6 Athletes' negative Internet use

For athletes, the ability to concentrate on the tasks they are engaging in while performing in their sport is considered a key mental skill for them to be able to develop and control (Durand-Busch, Salmela, & Green-Demers, 2001; Northcroft, 2009), especially during training and competition, as described in Chapters 1 and 3. However, like all human brains, athletes' brains are not designed to remain focused on any one task all of the time. Therefore, taking mental breaks should also feature as part of an athlete's training and competition schedule. For many athletes, the Internet can be a positive source of entertainment and information during such mental downtime (e.g., to facilitate educational opportunities). It can also act as a source of entertainment and a way to pass time in order to alleviate general boredom. However, do Internet activities distract athletes from performing at their best?

Stone (2009) refers to the term continuous partial attention (CPA) to describe where individuals engage in a number of activities at one time without fully devoting all of their available attentional resources to any one of the tasks being carried out. The term is referred to in cognitive science as 'complex multi-tasking'. Stone (2009) stated, CPA relates to the notion that many individuals 'want it all and want it now' when they engage in the online world, where there is a need to be connected, through the various forms of connecting platforms available, such as email, WhatsApp messaging and social media. However, such needs come at a cognitive cost, one of these being that of distraction, potentially resulting in such individuals being in a stressed state, on high alert all the time, similar to the 'always on' mentality (Kirwan, 2015). One of the key mental skills for athletes to master within their sport environments is being able to monitor when they need to be 'on' and when they can afford to 'switch off' (Moran & Toner, 2017). Most successful athletes have discovered strategies to enable them to achieve this important 'switch-on/switch-off' mental state – strategies such as the use of task-focused goal setting through the application of the SMART goal principle, for example (Bull, Albinson, & Shambrook, 1996; explained in Chapter 1). Such strategies enable athletes to focus on specific motor skills being attempted, rather than allowing their thoughts to drift onto tasks to be completed in the future or tasks that have already been completed in the past, perhaps not successfully so. In the case of their Internet use, perhaps athletes need to also be reminded to apply these similar goal-setting strategies when online, in order to avoid becoming distracted by the many attractions the online world offers.

6.6.1 Attention and distraction

Other strategies athletes may use to help them avoid distractions, including digital or technology based ones, are self-talk strategies (Kremer & Moran, 2013) and mental imagery strategies (MacIntyre et al., 2013). Pre-performance routines, incorporating a number of these techniques, are also applied by many athletes in an attempt to maintain their attention on what is important at that point in time in training or in competition, for example, rather than allowing themselves to be distracted by irrelevant stimuli (Gilleece, 1996). So, athletes are actually in a good position when it comes to digital, Internet-based distractors, as they may apply the same strategies they use to facilitate their sport performances in order to manage and overcome their Internet-based distractions that they may also be exposed to on a regular basis. How might athletes train their brains even better to exert more attention on such tasks than they currently do? Greaney (2016) suggested individuals can *train their attention* using mindfulness meditation. Mindfulness is a popular area of research and application today within psychology. It has been shown to enhance attention in undergraduate students (Tang et al., 2007) as well as having cognitive and behavioural benefits (greater self-control and planning) for children (Posner, Rothbart, & Tang, 2013). Young athletes could also be encouraged to use such mindfulness techniques to enable them to exert self-control and delayed gratification with regard to their technology use, thus perhaps preventing them from developing into more digitally distracted elite professional athletes.

6.6.2 Misinformation

One of the greatest limitations of the Internet, as mentioned previously in relation to doping offences, is the lack of a watch-dog presence to prevent inaccurate or misleading information from being posted on the Internet without it being verified as correct information. For athletes, sourcing misinformation can be very damaging, especially information that is health and training related. Athletes may uncover incorrect information on injuries and illnesses, supplements and diet, training methods and recovery strategies. Such information could result in athletes placing their bodies in harmful positions, under negative training loads, or at risk of competition or participation bans from their sport due to positive drug tests as a result of contaminated products ingested, either on purpose or without their knowledge. Perhaps one reason athletes fall victim to misinformation online is because there is such a vast amount of information available to them on the Internet. As a consequence of this, information overload is a real danger for any person engaging with the online world, and will be considered in the next section.

6.6.3 Information overload

As mentioned previously, there is such a vast amount of information available in the online world, it is possible for individuals to experience stress about what information they should attend to and what information they should filter out. For many, Google is the first port of call when wishing to find out information on practically anything in today's world, but how much of what 'Google knows' is actually true (Hadlington, 2015)? Athletes are constantly in search of those fine margins that could result in very successful performance outcomes, and one extra stressor for many of them is the potential for Internet searches to result in information overload. A Google search for any number of types of sport-related information, technology based or otherwise, can result in hundreds, if not thousands, of search results, making it difficult for athletes to determine what is and what is not credible information. Those who support such athletes should encourage them to seek out advice on what information they deem credible and what information should be filtered out. An interesting research study could involve exploring how much credibility 'expert' athletes place on information related to their sport that comes via online searches.

6.7 Conclusion, including future directions for research

The goal of this chapter was to explore athletes' uses of the Internet, and as is evident from the material presented, athletes derive many advantages from their online interactions that have become part of their daily lives as elite professionals.

This chapter identified some of the main reasons athletes, like many other individuals, use the Internet, such as: (i) for interacting and communicating online, (ii) for information gathering and (iii) for educational and training purposes. Although it could be said that in today's society it is impossible for athletes to train and compete in the way that they do without access to the Internet, the dangers or risks associated with Internet use specifically for athletes should also be highlighted. It can be a source of: (i) negative distraction from their training, competition and education (i.e., facilitating procrastination); (ii) misinformation; (iii) information overload and increased stress associated with this, and also (iv) opportunities for athletes to engage in Internet misuse and abuse (discussed in detail in Chapters 9 and 10).

Future research in this area could include more in-depth investigations of athletes' specific uses of the Internet compared to their non-athlete peers, in order to determine if there are any substantial differences in the ways athletes of differing levels of expertise engage with the Internet. Studies examining how much credibility 'expert' athletes place on information related to their sport that comes via online searches could also be interesting. Finally, the potential of the Internet to facilitate athletes' education and career opportunities shows how the online world can facilitate their lives after sport. This avenue should be extended to ensure the term 'student athlete' becomes more widespread as a description of *all* professional athletes, so that they can be properly prepared for life after sport also.

6.8 Open-ended discussion questions

1   What role has the Internet played in transforming the lives of athletes?
2   Discuss the advantages and risks of information seeking by athletes using the Internet.
3   What advice should be given to athletes who are considering studying online?

6.9 Practical exercise

Carry out a debate on the following motion with your class of students, with half of the group arguing in favour of the motion and the other half of the group arguing against the motion;

The motion: Internet use for information seeking should be supported and promoted among athletes.

References

Akman, I., & Mishra, A. (2010). Gender, age and income differences in internet usage among employees in organisations. *Computers in Human Behaviour, 26,* 482–490.

Asher, N. (2014). *Maslow's hierarchy of needs in social media.* Retrieved January 29, 2016 from http://roarlocal.com/maslows-hierarchy-social-media/

Attrill, A. (2015). Introduction. In A. Attrill (Ed.), *Cyberpsychology* (pp. 1–6). Oxford, UK: Oxford University Press.

Baumeister, R.F., & Leary, M.R. (1995). The need to belong: Desire for interpersonal attachments as a fundamental human motivation. *Psychological Bulletin, 117,* 497–529.

Blumler, J.G., & Katz, E. (1974). *The uses of mass communication.* Thousand Oaks, CA: Sage Publications.

Bull, S.J., Albinson, J.G., & Shambrook, C.J. (1996). *The mental game plan.* Eastbourne, East Sussex: Sports Dynamics.

Chan, M. (2016). *Maslow's model as applied to social media (or how Maslow got it wrong).* Retrieved from https://medium.com/@MarshaChan/applying-some-psychology-to-social-media-9deb505f678

Cheever, N. (2009). The uses and gratification of viewing mixed martial arts. *Journal of Sports Media, 4,* 235–253.

Cherry, K. (2015). *Updating Maslow's hierarchy of needs.* Retrieved January 29, 2016 from http://psychology.about.com/od/humanist-personality/fl/Updating-Maslowrsquos-Hierarchy-of-Needs.htm

Chiu, P.Y., Cheung, C.M.K., & Lee, M.K.O. (2008). Online social networking: Why do 'we' use Facebook? *Communications in Computer and Information Science, 19,* 67–74.

Clavio, G.E., & Kian, T.M. (2010). Uses and gratification of a retired female athlete's Twitter followers. *International Journal of Sport Communication, 3,* 485–500.

Csikszentmihalyi, M. (1990). *Flow: The psychology of optimal experience.* New York: Cambridge University Press.

Dilworth, M. (2017). *1 in 10 has never used the Internet.* Retrieved from www.independent.co.uk/news/business/news/adults-never-use-internet-one-in-ten-office-national-statistics-ons-a7744636.html

Do-Hyung, P., Jumin, L., & Ingoo, H. (2007). The effect of on-line consumer reviews on consumer purchasing intention: The moderating role of involvement. *International Journal of Electronic Commerce, 11,* 125–148. doi: 10.2753/jec1086–4415110405

Durand-Busch, N., Salmela, J., & Green-Demers, I. (2001). The Ottewa Mental Skills Assessment Tool (OMSAT-3). *The Sport Psychologist, 15,* 1–9.

Eastin, M.S., & LaRose, R. (2000). Internet self-efficacy and the psychology of the digital divide. *Journal of Computer Mediated Communication, 61.* Retrieved from http://onlinelibrary.wiley.com/doi/10.1111/j.1083-6101.2000.tb00110.x/full

Flood, C., Rooney, B., & Barton, H. (2015). Online groups. In A. Attrill. (Ed.) *Cyberpsychology* (pp. 72–87). Oxford, UK: Oxford University Press.

Gangadharbatla, H. (2008). Facebook Me: Collective self-esteem, need to belong, and Internet self-efficacy as predictors of the iGeneration's attitudes towards social networking sites. *Journal of Interactive Advertising, 8,* 5–15.

Gantz, W., & Wenner, L.A. (1995). Fanship and the television sport viewing experience. *Sociology of Sport Journal, 12,* 56–74.

Gilleece, D. (1996). *Breathe deeply and be happy with second.* The Irish Times, 27 September. Retrieved from www.irishtimes.com/sport/breathe-deep-and-be-happy-with-second-1.71529

Gillick, D. (2017). *When people said I should go talk to someone, I told them to shut up. I thought I was right, but I was weak and lost.* Retrieved from www.the42.ie/david-gillick-mental-health-interview-3350266-Apr2017/

Greaney, J. (2016). Attention and distraction online. In I. Connolly, M. Palmer, H. Barton, & G. Kirwan (Eds.), *An introduction to cyberpsychology* (pp. 86–97). London, UK: Routledge-Taylor and Francis Group.

The Guardian. (2016). *What is meldonium and why did Maria Sharpapova take it?* Retrieved from www.theguardian.com/sport/2016/mar/08/meldonium-maria-sharapova-failed-drugs-test

Guerin-Eagleman, A. (2015). Online communities among international Masters gymnastics participants: A uses and gratifications analysis. *International Journal of Sport Communication, 8,* 313–329.

Hadlington, L. (2015). Cognitive factors in online behaviours. In A. Attrill (Ed.), *Cyberpsychology* (pp. 249–267). Oxford, UK: Oxford University Press.

Hajli, N. (2016). Ethical environment in the online communities by information credibility: A social media perspective. *Journal of Business Ethics,* 1–12. doi: 10.1007/s10551-016-3036-7

Hajli, N., Lin, X., Featherman, M., & Wang, Y. (2014). Social word of mouth: How trust develops in the market. *International Journal of Market Research, 56,* 673–678.

Hambrick, M.E., & Mahoney, T.Q. (2011). It's incredible – trust me': Exploring the role of celebrity athletes as marketers in online social networks. *International Journal of Sport Management and Marketing, 10,* 161–179.

Hambrick, M.E., Simmons, J.M., Greenhalgh, G.P., & Greenwell, C.T. (2010). Understanding professional athletes' use of Twitter: A content analysis of athlete tweets. *International Journal of Sport Communication, 3,* 454–471.

Hausman, J.A., & Leonard, G.K. (1997). Superstars in the National Basketball Association: Economic value and policy. *Journal of Labour Economics, 15,* 586–624.

Hurley, O. (2012). The sport psychologist tweeter: What information do followers want? *Perspectives II, 46*–55. Retrieved from https://issuu.com/myiadt/docs/iadt_perspectives_ii_-_an_anthology

Hurley, O. (2016). Sport and health cyberpsychology. In I. Connolly, M. Palmer, H. Barton, & G. Kirwan (Eds.), *An introduction to cyberpsychology* (pp. 167–180). London: Routledge.

Ingle, S. (2016). *Fancy Bears hack again with attack on senior anti-doping officials.* Retrieved from www.theguardian.com/sport/2016/nov/25/fancy-bears-hack-again-with-attack-on-senior-anti-doping-officials

Kaare, B.H., Brandtzaeg, B., Endestad, T., & Heim, J. (2007). In the borderland between family orientation and peer-culture: The use of communication technologies among Norwegian tweens. *New Media & Society, 9,* 603–624.

Katz, E., Blumler, J.G., & Gurevitch, M. (1974). Uses and gratifications research. *Public Opinion Quarterly, 37,* 509–523.

Kiel, J.M. (2005). The digital divide: Internet and e-mail use by the elderly. *Medical Informatics and the Internet in Medicine, 30,* 19–23.

Kim, Y., & Ross, S. (2006). An exploration of motives in sport video gaming. *International Journal of Sports Marketing & Sponsorship, 8,* 34–46.

Kirwan, G. (2015). Health psychology online. In A. Attrill (Ed.), *Cyberpsychology* (pp. 164–182). Oxford, UK: Oxford University Press.

Kreb, S.G., & Lockee, B.B. (2009). *Supporting student-athletes through distance learning: A game plan for success.* Paper presented at the 25th Annual Conference on Distance Teaching and Learning, Madison, WI.

Kremer, J., & Moran, A. (2013). *Pure sport: Practical sport psychology.* London, UK: Routledge-Taylor and Francis Group.

Lawson, R.A., Sheehan, K., & Stephenson, E.F. (2008). Vend it like Beckham: David Beckham's effect on MLS ticket sales. *International Journal of Sport Finance, 3,* 189–195.

Loria, K. (2016). *The Internet is driving athletes to do crazy things no one knew were possible.* Retrieved from http://nordic.businessinsider.com/ultramarathon-freediving-extreme-sports-2016-8

MacIntyre, T., Moran, A., Collet, C., Guillot, A., Campbell, M., Matthews, J., Mahoney, C., & Lowther, J. (2013). *The BASES expert statement on the use of mental imagery in sport, exercise and rehabilitation contexts.* The Sport Scientist, 38. Retrieved from www.bases.org.uk/ Use-of-Mental-Imagery-in-Sport-Exercise-and-Rehabilitation-Contexts

Maslow, A.H. (1943). A theory of motivation. *Psychological Review, 50,* 370–396.

Maslow, A.H. (1968). *Towards a psychology of being.* New York: Von Nostrand.

Moore, J.L., Dickson-Deane, C., & Galyen, K. (2011). E-learning, online learning and distance learning environments: Are they the same? *Internet and Higher Education, 14,* 129–135.

Moran, A., & Toner, J. (2017). *A critical introduction to sport psychology.* London: Routledge.

Northcroft, J. (2009). They shall not pass. *The Sunday Times* (Sport), 8 February, pp. 12–13.

Posner, M.I., Rothbart, M.K., & Tang, Y. (2013). Developing self-regulation in early childhood. *Trends in Neuroscience and Education, 2,* 107–110.

Reiner, D. (2017). *Why student athletes choose the virtual school advantage.* Retrieved from http:// blog.connectionsacademy.com/why-student-athletes-choose-the-virtual-school-advantage/

Schofield-Clarke, L. (2009). Digital media and the generation gap. *Information, Communication & Society, 12,* 388–407.

Shanmugham, S. (2016). *Why do you use the Internet?* Retrieved from www.weforum.org/ agenda/2016/10/why-do-you-use-the-internet

Simonson, M., Smaldino, S., Albiright, M., & Zvacek, S. (2006). *Teaching and learning at a distance.* Upper Saddle River, NJ: Pearson Education.

Social Bakers. (2017). *Twitter statistics directory.* Retrieved from www.socialbakers.com/ statistics/twitter/

Spears, R., Postmes, T., Lea, M., & Wolbert, A. (2002). When are net effects gross products? The power of influence and the influence of power in computer-mediated communications. *Journal of Social Issues, 58,* 91–107.

Stone, L. (2009). *Beyond simple multitasking: Continuous partial attention.* Retrieved from https:// lindastone.net/2009/11/30/beyond-simple-multi-tasking-continuous-partial-attention/

Tang, Y., Ma, Y., Wang, J., Fan, Y., Feng, S., Lu, Q., Yu, Q., Sui, D., Rothbart, M.K., Fan, M., & Posner, M.I. (2007). Short-term meditation training improves attention and self-regulation. *Proceedings of the National Academy of Science, 104,* 17152–17156.

Weir, P., Baker, J., & Horton, S. (2010). The emergence of masters sport: participatory trends and historical developments. In J. Baker, S. Horton, & P. Weir. (Eds.), *The Masters athlete: Understanding the role of sport and exercise in optimizing aging* (pp. 7–14). London, UK: Routledge.

Weiser, E. (2000). Gender differences in Internet use patterns and Internet application preferences: A two sample comparison. *Cyberpsychology & Behaviour, 4,* 167–178.

Williams, M. (2017). *Dan Vickerman's death highlights the dangers of silence.* Retrieved from www.irishtimes.com/sport/rugby/international/matt-williams-dan-vickerman-s-death-highlights-dangers-of-silence-1.2987793

7

ATHLETES AND SOCIAL MEDIA

CASE STUDY 7

Sean is an elite, 27-year-old male rugby player on a well-known rugby team. He is also an active user of the social media networks Twitter and Facebook. Late one evening during pre-season training, Sean tweets a personal view about a sensitive political and societal issue that has been the focus of discussion within the wider media at that time. The following day, Sean wakes to find a large number of individuals who follow him on Twitter have responded negatively to his tweet, with many of these individuals stating they were 'hurt' by Sean's comment on Twitter. Sean responds to this situation by deleting his original tweet. He also tweets a public apology to those who reported they were offended by his remarks.

(i) How might such an incident impact on Sean's physical and psychological well-being, and on his sport performances?

(ii) How might such an incident impact on Sean's value as a brand within his sport (i.e., sponsorship deals, endorsements, future business partnerships, etc.)?

(iii) How should Sean's sport organisation respond to this incident? (Should Sean be fined or reprimanded in any way for his actions?)

(iv) What general lessons can be learned from this scenario? (What advice should be given to young athletes wishing to use social media platforms for social, entertainment and business purposes?)

7.1 Overview

Many sport psychology texts devote some of their content to discussions regarding the social psychology of sport. This chapter also focuses on some social psychology concepts, but from a sport cyberpsychology perspective. Specifically, the use of social media by athletes to communicate with one another and with their wider support networks, as well as the general public, are examined. Advantages of using online social media platforms such as Twitter, Facebook, LinkedIn, Instagram and YouTube are mainly highlighted. How athletes present themselves on such platforms and what information they decide to share with the public is discussed. Research from the cognitive psychology literature regarding the decision-making process involved in taking such communication options is also presented in order to attempt to explain athletes,' and their supporters', online social networking behaviour. Some of the risks associated with these online interactions are also mentioned. They are expanded upon in Chapters 9 and 10, in the final, fourth section of this text. This fourth section examines some specific problematic issues that may arise for athletes who use the Internet and social media (such as cyberbullying and online gambling).

7.2 Learning objectives

1   To introduce some of the common terms related to social media use by athletes to communicate with their peers and the public at large
2   To highlight the advantages and disadvantages of athletes' presence and interactions on social media
3   To explain the concept of self-presentation online and to consider the self-presentation of athletes specifically online
4   To highlight some of the cognitive processes that may influence athletes' decisions regarding what information they share on their social media platforms

7.3 Definitions of relevant terms

Facebook

This is a social networking online platform that allows 'friends' to follow each other on online in order to see their friends' online posts and to respond to them using a series of options. Initially, the only available responses were to 'like' or 'dislike' a post. However, Facebook changed these options in recent years, removing the 'dislike' option and instead included responses to friends' posts as: 'like', 'love', 'wow', 'sad' or 'anger'.

Instagram

This is an online platform that allows users to share photographs with friends and the public that appear on that specific platform. The content can also be linked to their other social media platforms such as Facebook and Twitter. Less popular platforms for sharing images include Tumblr and Flickr.

LinkedIn

This is a social networking application that allows individuals to communicate online with others in a way similar to the social network, Facebook. LinkedIn, however, is regarded as a more professional social network. Users must accept requests from other users to link up with them, similar to the way individuals using Facebook must accept the friend requests' of others wishing to 'friend' them online in order for the individuals to have access to the online posts they place on their Facebook pages.

Snapchat

This is a mobile messaging application that allows users to take photos and then send them to other users. The user can also insert text onto the image to be sent. The receiver of an image on Snapchat can take a screenshot of the image. Snapchat differs from other mobile applications because the images taken and sent out on the Internet using this social media communication device disappear after 10 seconds from the platform.

Twitter

This is a social media platform that allows users to send short, initially 140-character tweets, but as of November 2017, changed to 280-character tweets, or comments, out to their followers. It is a form of microblogging (blogging is explained in Chapter 5 as part of the athlete–consultant process). Users of Twitter can tweet, retweet (i.e., share public tweets) and favour/'love' tweets they see posted on their Twitter feed. They may also directly, and privately, message individuals they follow on Twitter who also follow them back (using a facility referred to as direct messaging, or DM. These DMs are not limited to the 280-character restriction that applies to public feed tweets). Other options on Twitter allow individuals to 'block' and 'mute' individuals who follow them or who they follow on Twitter.

7.4 Introduction

As Boehmer and Lacy (2014) stated, "The impact of social media on the current media landscape is undeniable" (p. 1). Social media has become one of, if not the, most popular 'go-to' sources for breaking news in today's society. This trend has transferred across to the sport setting also, with many fans now appearing to go to social media sites to obtain the most current news on the teams, athletes and sport events they support or have an interest in (Whiteside, Yu, & Hardin, 2012).

'Following' athletes on social media platforms such as Twitter, Snapchat and Instagram has also become very popular. In June of 2017, Social Bakers announced figures for the most followed Twitter accounts across many countries. Ireland's figures, for example, showed that of the top four most followed accounts, three of them, located in positions 2 to 4 of the most followed accounts, were the Twitter accounts of Irish athletes, namely, Conor McGregor (Ultimate Fighting Championship, UFC, at number 2), Sheamus O'Shaunessy (World Wrestling Entertainment, WWE, at number 3) and Rory McIlroy (golf) at number 4. Interestingly, in the number 1 position in Ireland for Twitter, with the most followers, was the account of the former boy band One Direction singer, Niall Horan. By comparison, in the USA, three of the top four followed Twitter accounts at that same time were also musicians, namely, Katy Perry (at number 1), Justin Bieber (at number 2) and Taylor Swift (at number 4). Former USA President, Barack Obama, held the third position at that time. In the United Kingdom too in 2017, three of the top four followed Twitter account positions were held by musical acts, namely, by another of the singers from the former boy band, One Direction – Harry Styles (at number 2). At number 3, Niall Horan of the same boy band (and at positon 1 in Ireland), while the female singer Adele was at number 4. Interestingly, in the UK, the most followed account on Twitter in 2017 was the 'Breaking News' account of the British Broadcasting Channel (known as the BBC; Social Bakers, 2017). It would appear, therefore, that individuals from the sport and entertainment industries attract some of the most social media followers worldwide, according to the Twitter social media platform statistics anyway.

According to Samford University Sports Business Report (The Business Side of Sports, 2016), social media also appears to have changed the face of sport. Most people today recognise and acknowledge the impact of social and digital media on the sport landscape. Many individuals, including athletes, coaches, fans and sponsors, for example, now obtain much of their information from such social media platforms (Whiteside et al., 2012). Indeed, the statistic cited above referring to the UK's most followed Twitter account being the BBC's 'Breaking News' supports this point. Another point that reinforces this trend in recent times comes from the way in which some sport events in recent years have been referred to, according to their social media traffic generation. For example, the London 2012 Summer Olympic Games were commonly referred to as the Twitterlympics (Adebayo, 2013) or the 'Social Media' Olympics (Androich, 2012). Indeed, the 2012 Summer London Olympic Games were perhaps the first global sport event to really embrace the social media age.

In light of these new developments regarding the way people communicate and interact with each other using these social networks, questions of interest to sport psychologists and cyberpsychologists in this regard have arisen; they include: (i) what are athletes using social media for, (ii) what impact can this social media use have on these athletes' sport preparations and performances, (iii) what impact can social media have on athletes' public personas, (iv) what role does social media play in athletes' abilities to attract sponsors and (v) why do so many individuals follow athletes, especially in the case of Ireland, for example, on various social media platforms? These issues are explored in sections of this chapter on athletes' social media use.

7.5 Uses of social media by athletes

Before exploring possible answers to questions like why so many people follow athletes on social media today, let us first consider some of the *reasons why* athletes claim to use social media. The personal, social networking behaviours of athletes are examined next under the following sub-headings: (i) personal social networking, (ii) professional networking, (iii) brand management and (iv) fan communication. Issues such as self-presentation by athletes, privacy and trust issues, as well as athletes' decision-making processes regarding what information they elect to share online will be included in these discussions.

7.5.1 Personal social networking

Many current athletes, retired athletes and other 'elite performers' have a social networking presence today (Narcum, Havard, & Mason, 2016; see Fieldhouse Media's 2016 survey of social media use by student athletes also for some figures on this trend). The attractions such media use holds for the athletes who use them are, in some ways, no different to their attractiveness for other social media members from non-sport backgrounds who also use them. For example, they can use them to seek out information, to share information, to communicate with others and also for entertainment purposes (reasons highlighted for general Internet use too in Chapter 6).

Social media platforms specifically allow athletes to communicate with each other and share their life experiences, while also giving their fans and supporters an insight into their lives, which, for athletes, can be from the perspective of within and/or outside of their sport/performance arenas (Narcum et al., 2016). Of course, not all athletes have a social media presence. However, such a presence is perhaps considered desirable if these individuals hope to secure additional earnings from sponsorship and endorsement deals, rather than just from their sport performances (Pegoraro & Jinnah, 2012). While such reasons for having a social media presence are likely to influence some athletes' decisions to join certain social media networks, other important influences on their decision-making process to use such media may also exist. For example, whether or not they decide to join their peers in using such social media may come from their decisions to conform to their peers' behaviour.

It is commonly accepted that in the teenage years especially, the most influential individuals in teenagers' lives are often not their parents or siblings, but rather their friends and peers. These peers seem to be some of the greatest influencers in young peoples' lives around this time in their social, cognitive and emotional development (Steinberg, 2012). Young individuals, including young athletes, do appear to really care about what their peers think and say about them around this time. Therefore, they often conform and participate in the same kinds of activities as these peers, such as having a presence, and interacting, on social media. This conformity behaviour, also known as 'majority influence', is a powerful motivator for many individuals in determining how they behave, both on and offline (Asch, 1951; Barton, 2016). However, similar to many human behaviours, such influences are not the only motivators or reasons for athletes' decisions to join online social networks. Instead, such behaviours can be determined by multiple motives, both internal and external to the individual (Moran & Toner, 2017). For example, athletes may often be motivated to pursue professional sport careers for internal reasons, such as experiencing great enjoyment from participating in their sport activities. However, athletes often state the high-earning potentials sport careers may also offer, as well as the social status they provide if athletes become highly accomplished within their sport, as other, externally driven, motivations for pursuing a professional sport career. Therefore, in such circumstances, another advantage of having a social media presence for an athlete can be its ability to showcase their sport accomplishments, as identified by Hambrick, Simmons, Greenhalgh, and Greenwell (2010) and Pegoraro (2010) in their studies of athletes' social media posts, as reasons why athletes use social media, specifically the platform, Twitter. How athletes' sport organisations view their uses of such social media varies. A somewhat neutral view, perhaps, was stated by Russell Stopford, Head of Digital at Manchester City FC in 2012 and now Digital Director of FC Barcelona, who was quoted as saying,

> Manchester City is now a digital-first brand. . . . Social media fits with the brand values of the club: transparency and giving the fans something unique. . . . We don't actively encourage players to be on Twitter – it is up to them. But, if they want to be on social, we support them with best practice.
> *(cited in Reynolds, 2012)*

Other coaches' and managers' comments regarding social media use by athletes and within sport environments are explored more in Chapter 8, where sport organisations' specific uses of social media are discussed, as well as in Chapter 9, where the cyberbullying and harassment of athletes is discussed.

Hambrick et al. (2010) and Pegoraro (2010) both identified six categories of tweets that describe athletes' typical uses of Twitter. These categories included tweets related to: (i) their personal lives, (ii) their business lives, (iii) their sport lives, (iv) their fans, (v) other athletes and (vi) for "pop culture or landmark references" (Pegoraro, 2010, p. 507). With regard to their business lives, such uses of social media for professional networking has become popular among athletes, especially in relation to their brand management and the ways they interact with others on such media. These reasons for athletes using social media are presented next.

7.5.2 Professional networking

The decision to create a social media presence may indeed come from athletes' awareness of the potential, professional impact such a media presence could have on their personal brand as athletes (Narcum et al., 2016). A social media presence can help athletes to, as was mentioned earlier, attract business and sponsorship interest from companies who often like to be aligned, and associated, with the sport role model persona and general attractiveness of an athlete's status (Narcum et al., 2016; Figure 7.1).

FIGURE 7.1 Mike Ross, brand ambassador for Subaru

Source: Courtesy of Inpho Photography, with thanks to retired Irish rugby player, Mike Ross, and Subaru.

Therefore, many athletes use social media platforms for this 'business' brand purpose. The main business or corporate-focused social media network currently available is LinkedIn. It is often described as the Facebook social media equivalent for business or professional communities. It typically contains posts from members that relate to their professional practices. The platform itself encourages its users to develop a form of abbreviated curriculum vitae (CV) on the site and to establish connections with other linked professionals working in related areas (Skeels & Grudin, 2009). LinkedIn describes itself as a network for professionals. Individuals connect and communicate on LinkedIn, typically, in a more formal and career-oriented way than they perhaps would do on other social networks such as Facebook, Instagram or Snapchat. Athletes, similarly, can use LinkedIn in this way, to develop connections, communicate and share information about their professional, career-oriented activities with other interested parties. This may be especially useful to them when they decide to retire as athletes. The connections they make on LinkedIn can help them to establish their new professional second careers after their sport careers have concluded.

A social media presence may also be an effective way to sell brands and services. Publically known athletes can be used to communicate with their global audiences regarding a range of products. Many companies pay athletes to send out promotional tweets advocating their products (Narcum et al., 2016). Athletes can use social media in this way to 'sell' their own brands too (Arai, Ko, & Kaplanidou, 2013).

7.5.3 Brand management

As previously mentioned, many athletes now see the benefits of having an online presence to attract sponsors and to secure endorsement deals (Narcum et al., 2016). Such income has the power to significantly add to athletes' 'on-field/in-sport' contract earnings obtained through their main jobs of performing within their sport arena. Many athletes have dedicated websites where interested parties can go to research more about them as athletes and to determine if an athlete is a good fit for their brand, for example (Narcum et al., 2016). It may be somewhat surprising to hear it is not always the most successful athletes that secure the most lucrative endorsement deals. Many investors consider an athlete's personality and public attractiveness and/or popularity when deciding if they wish to hire that individual to promote their products. One such athlete who secured many endorsement deals without being especially successful within her chosen sport was female professional tennis player, Anna Kournicova, who famously never won an individual Grand Slam tennis event during her tennis career, yet continues to receive lucrative endorsement contracts, based on her attractiveness as a former female athlete (Manish, 2015).

However, as previously mentioned, sponsors of athletes are not only attracted to such athletes in a business sense because of their public attractiveness or likability. Some companies opt to hire athletes to endorse their products because of these athletes' ability to generate controversy. One such athlete is, perhaps, the notorious Conor McGregor in MMA. McGregor is known for being a controversial individual who divides public opinion regarding his likeability. Other examples exist, such as in the English Premiership Football League. A number of this league's soccer players from high-profile teams have used social media platforms to communicate with their public in often bizarre and unconventional ways. For example, Joey Barton (who currently plays for Burnley Football Club, but who has played for Manchester City FC and Newcastle United FC), MUFC retired player, Rio Ferdinand, and Wayne Rooney (currently a player at Everton Football Club, but who spent 13 seasons at Manchester United) have all been the subject of Twitter controversies (Morrissey, 2014; MailOnline, 2011). However, such athletes' styles of communication on their social media platforms do not appear to have prevented them from securing valuable endorsement contracts from successful sport brands (Wayne Rooney, for example, has a football boot sponsorship deal with the sportswear brand Nike, reported to be worth in the region of 1 million pounds per year; Davis, 2015; Figure 7.2).

Athletes, of course, as mentioned earlier, also may have other motives for creating an online social media presence, such as for communicating with their fans, as was reported by Hambrick et al. (2010) and Pegoraro (2010). This specific reason for why athletes use social media will now be explored.

7.5.4 Fan communication

Many athletes use the social media platforms of Facebook, Twitter and Instagram to communicate with their supporters. These social media platforms have

FIGURE 7.2 Wayne Rooney, wearing Nike boots

Source: Courtesy of Pexels.

far-reaching effects, according to the Global WebIndex (2013). It reported that over 1.15 billion individuals are Facebook users, while Twitter estimates it has over 328 million active monthly users (Fortune, 2017), with 1.5 billion registered users, up from 500 million in 2013. According to Sanderson and Kissing (2011), Twitter appeared to be the most popular social media platform used by athletes then, perhaps because it provides users with immediate and direct ways to connect, and communicate, with their other individuals.

In 2016, according to Hookit, Portuguese soccer star Cristiano Ronaldo became the first athlete to amass over 200 million followers across his social media platforms (Twitter, Facebook and Instagram). Hookit, a database that tracks, measures and values the social and digital media used within sport environments

(Hookit, 2016) stated that, by amassing over 200 million followers across his social media channels, this placed Ronaldo, in 2016, in the same league as the globally popular music stars Justin Bieber and Taylor Swift (two of the most followed individuals in the world across their social media platforms). Thus, the potential impact, and reach, of social media for athletes is undeniable.

Athletes and elite performers rarely need to be reminded of the importance of their supporters in helping them to achieve their brand and earning potential (as previously discussed). So, what kinds of communications with fans do athletes typically engage in? It is important to remember that athletes' self-disclosures online via their social media platforms can impact the perceptions of their supporters, as well as their sponsors. Kim and Song (2016) examined this issue by studying the para-social relationship between celebrities, including athletes, and their supporters. Kim and Song (2016, p. 573) referred to a 'celebrity' in their study as a person who received popular fame and public attention, including actors, actresses, singers, comedians, models and athletes. Five hundred seventy-two undergraduate students from a public university in the United States took part in their study. Kim and Song reported that celebrities' self-disclosures about their lives on Twitter increased their followers' feelings of those celebrities being a part of their own social lives too. This phenomenon is known as social presence.

Social presence is a term that generally refers to a feeling individuals have of being somewhat psychologically connected with another individual in a mediated environment (Biocca, Harms, & Burgoon, 2003). Social media facilitates this psychological feeling sport fans often report (that is, feeling directly connected with, and having a sense of togetherness with, the celebrity idols, including athletes, that they follow on social media platforms such as Twitter and Instagram). So, one reason fans are drawn to follow sport stars online, similar to their reason for following celebrities in other areas, such as in the music industry, include this perception of them having a relationship with those 'desirable' individuals. Many athletes do interact directly with their supporters online via their social media too, rather than employing a member of a marketing firm to do so for them, for example. According to Pegoraro (2010), athletes said they interact with their supporters in this direct way in order to share aspects of their daily lives with them and to answer their supporters' questions. The athletes recruited for Pegoraro's study reported that they considered social media to be a good way to interact in such ways with their supporters, removing the need for a 'middle person' to be in place (such as an interviewer, who typically in the past may have posed questions to the athlete, that supporters may have been interested in, in face-to-face interviews that then appeared in newspapers, on radio and on television). Now, in this digital age, fans can ask questions of their athlete idols using Twitter, Instagram and Facebook, in the hope that such athletes will respond to their questions directly. Such direct interactions between athletes and their supporters may also increase their fans' status among their own peer groups, who may be 'impressed' by their friends' interactions with such athletes on social media.

But, having discussed some of the reasons why athletes often use social media, namely, for communication and professional purposes, how they present themselves online, using such media interactions, can be very interesting and is discussed in more depth in the following section.

7.6 Self-presentation by athletes using social media

One should remember that how individuals present themselves online can be very different from the way they appear in person. Many theories of self-presentation online have been proposed within the cyberpsychology literature to explain these discrepancies (Ellison, Heino, & Gibbs, 2006; Higgins, 1987; Markus & Nurius, 1986). Topics such as identity, impression formation and impression management have been explored within this context. But how do these issues relate to athletes online?

Identity often refers to an individual's views and feelings about him or herself. 'The self' is a complex concept as it is possible for an individual to possess a number of versions of the self. As a result of this view, terms such as the 'actual self', the 'ideal self' and the 'ought self' have been proposed, and studied, within social psychology and social cyberpsychology. Indeed, the online versions of all these possible versions of the self have been the focus of much cyberpsychology research in recent years (see Connolly, 2016, and Fullwood, 2015, for reviews on this topic). The ways in which different representations of the self may be portrayed and manipulated in some very controlled ways by individuals in the online world means individuals, including athletes, can regulate what others view of their lives. Most individuals wish to portray only the best versions of themselves in their online contexts and activities, such as in images of themselves, and in their posts regarding their achievements (Fullwood, 2015). Anything less than such positive portrayals could be perceived by individuals as potentially damaging for the way others form impressions of them, known as *impression formation.* This is distinct from *impression management* (which is described as how individuals attempt to control the impressions others have formed of them, as opposed to how such impressions were initially generated; Fullwood, 2015). Some athletes, and indeed their sport organisations, may view any kind of social media transgression as potentially damaging to their marketability and to the brand from which they generate a substantial amount of their earnings (see case study 7 at the beginning of this chapter as an example of such a social media transgression that could be committed by an athlete).

In spite of this, surprisingly, athletes may often need to be reminded that when interacting with the public using their social media, they are representing themselves and others, in many cases, such as their teammates, their coaches, managers, parents, extended family and possibly friends, not to mention their province or country perhaps. Social media transgressions by athletes can, therefore, have farreaching effects beyond those of the athlete, and as such, training in the proper and most beneficial uses of this media is now advised (Hambrick et al., 2010; Narcum et al., 2016). Such social media training is now carried out by many teams and sport organisations (see Stopford's quote, cited in Reynolds, 2012, at the beginning of this chapter as an example of this position by sport clubs today). Indeed, one of the complaints many coaches and managers have about athletes using social media is that they do not, in some cases, use it in an appropriate or well-considered way. They also claim athletes spend too much time on such social media, in their opinion (Narcum et al., 2016). This raises the issue of social media being potentially a source of negative distraction for athletes (as mentioned in Chapter 6) and is perhaps one reason why many clubs and teams now have in place social media 'blackouts' for their athletes around and during sport events.

In a further development with regard to such athletes' social media use, many professional athletes' behaviours on their social media accounts are now bound by clauses in their contracts. These clauses prohibit such athletes from posting negative comments online about issues related to their teams and their sport in general, for example. Once case where an athlete breached this rule, with costly consequences for himself both financial and for his reputation, was soccer player, Ashley Cole. Cole was fined 90,000 pounds for referring to the Football Association (FA) as a 'bunch of twats' on his Twitter account in 2012 (The Telegraph, 2012). In fact, between 2011 and 2014 alone, the FA in England collected social media Twitter-related player fines of over 350,000 pounds (Hytner, 2014). Such social media transgressions by athletes have prompted some coaches to implore their athletes to keep their communications 'clean' and refrain from posting content that they would 'not wish their grandmothers' to see (Sara Federico, Weber State University golf coach, cited in Denby, 2017). Considering these transgressions, are there aspects of athletes' lives they are not willing to share or discuss on their social media platforms? These issues related to privacy are outlined next.

7.7 Privacy-related issues for athletes' social media use

Many athletes, while willing to share a portion of their lives with their public and supporters, also go to some lengths to maintain a degree of privacy within their personal and family lives. However, in some cases they still appear to lack understanding of what information remains private, and what does not, in online settings. Many sport organisations recognise this too and go to some lengths to educate their athletes about the risks and dangers of sharing information online. Such education is warranted, as research in the area of cyberpsychology has shown there is often a *knowing-doing gap* (this term refers to a disproportionate assessment of risk by an individual regarding the likelihood of an event occurring as a result of a behaviour – for example, the likelihood of an athlete's privacy and security being placed in jeopardy as a result of posting a comment on a social media platform such as Facebook, Instagram or Twitter). Athletes' awareness and estimations of the impact and reach of their online posts, like many other social media users, may be flawed (Cox, 2012; Kirwan, 2016). While athletes and performers may appear to value their privacy, as is often evident in their comments to the media, such as refusing to speak about their personal lives and relationships, they then often fail in their actions to safeguard these important personal relationships in the online world. In an age where every behaviour may be recorded on a smartphone and shared with a global audience, why might athletes fail in their thinking in this regard, when it is something that appears to be important to them? This question could form the basis of an interesting research project in the future perhaps. One theory used to explain the behaviour of sharing information online is referred to as the communication privacy management theory (Petronio, 2002, 2013; Petronio & Durham, 2015). This theory outlines how many individuals believe they have the right to determine and control how their private information is shared online. However, in most cases, one should assume that any information placed online, in social media settings especially, does not remain private 'among friends and family only', for example. Once a person is 'friended' on Facebook, for example, that person's images and posts may be copied, pasted and saved by other 'friends' and then redistributed, even without the knowledge or consent of the person who initially shared the content. Some software on mobile devices is capable of sourcing the locations of individuals at a certain points in time when they are using their mobile digital devices too. Therefore, posting information regarding holiday locations in real-time can be costly, as some athletes (and other celebrity individuals) have discovered recently. For example, opportunistic criminals may gain access to athletes' properties when they know, as a result of their social media postings, that they are away on holiday; Sabur, 2017).

When athletes are the victims of such crimes, they may then become hyper-vigilant regarding their online presence. Tversky and Kahneman (1973) described this phenomenon, when such (in this case, negative) experiences are readily available to a person's conscious thinking as 'availability heuristics'. If an individual does not experience such negative events and then does not have its implications to bring to mind, the person is more likely to consider the event, or crime in this case, as less likely to happen to him/her and may engage in risky behaviour, such as posting his/her location on online social media platforms for anyone to see. Of course, cybercrime also makes the risk of personal information being 'hacked' or accessed via the online world a real threat today too (as was seen in the case of the hacking by 'Fancy Bears'; Ingle, 2016; referred to in Chapter 2 also). The take-home message is: athletes need to remain vigilant and aware of who has access to their information, once they share it on their social media online, for their own safety, and for the security of the important individuals in their lives also.

If athletes are aware of the potential dangers and risks to their personal lives and their own reputations by having a social media presence, then another question that could follows is, why do, and should, such athletes continue to share personal information online in their social media posts? Empirical research that addresses such connected topics and provides definitive answers to such questions is, to date, lacking within the sport cyberpsychology related literature. A number of potential answers to these questions could be posed, however, and they are presented next, based on the limited currently available literature.

Hurley (2016), having reviewed some of this research within the cyberpsychology field related to online groups specifically, discussed a number of reasons why individuals interact with others online, and specifically why they join online groups quite readily, despite some of the risks mentioned above. The reasons commonly cited by such online group members included: (i) the desire to present a particular version of the self to the wider public (as alluded to in Chapter 6) and also (ii) to alleviate loneliness and boredom.

Being lonely and/or bored can be a real problem for athletes, and it is often during such times that they are most likely to entertain themselves using technology-based devices, such as smartphones and tablets. Many athletes have a lot of their time scheduled for them by their coaches, physiotherapists and managers as part of their training/work timetable. Such schedules often include their eating and rest times. It is a potential problem then for these individuals, whose lives are often dominated by such strict routines of training, refuelling (a term commonly used to refer to eating for sport performances) and rest, to perhaps manage their own time effectively. In the small amount of remaining time they have to decide upon their own social activities or interactions, athletes may not make the best or most well-thought out decisions (as some of their previously cited social media transgressions indicate), perhaps because they are not used to having to do so (i.e., they are out of practice at having to make such decisions for themselves and then 'lose' the ability to think clearly when they do have such opportunities). This is not an ideal situation for athletes especially (not to be skilled at thinking for themselves within their competitive and training environments), yet they may not be provided with sufficient opportunities to practice such individual thinking and decision making, by their coaches and management personnel. An important skill for athletes to master is the ability to cope with the sport environment and to be adaptable (see Chapter 1 regarding mental skills and mental fitness). They may often need to apply a different competition or game plan – a strategy sometimes necessary during many sport events when an initial game plan may not be having the desired impact within the event. Such practice of their own decision making for their sport performances could be included in their social media training. Presenting athletes with 'what if' social media–related scenarios and having them discuss and devise ways to manage or cope with social media transgressions, like Sean's, as presented at the start of this chapter, could be valuable for them.

But even understanding the distractions and risks associated with social media use and agreeing to social media bans or 'blackouts' does not mean athletes will adhere to them. The desire to hear and read what others are saying about them on social media could be too strong a desire for some athletes to resist, especially during important sport events. Could athletes be susceptible to the phenomenon described in cyber language as the 'fear of missing out' (or FOMO; Vanden Abeele & van Rooij, 2016)? Perhaps this could provide an interesting avenue for future research on athletes' social media behaviour and motivations?

7.8 The decision-making process for sharing information on social media

Given the risks to security and privacy, as well as the distractibility of social media use, what then influences the decisions of athletes to share information online, for the reasons outlined earlier, such as for personal and professional networking, for brand management and for communicating with fans, for example. Assuming they are aware of the potential dangers posed by their many social media online interactions, what cognitive processes take place that could explain some of their decisions and behaviours? Psychologists have examined the cognitive decision-making process involved in online information-sharing behaviours. Daniel Kahneman (2011) has, for example, described two 'systems' he considered to be involved in this decision-making process. Kahneman (2011) referred to the process as involving a System 1 and a System 2. System 1 Kahneman considered to be the 'fast' system, referred to as such because it is the system thought to be activated when a person responds quickly to posts or messages online, without giving too much thought to the consequences of the content or interactions that follow from it. System 2 is referred to as the 'slow' system because it is typified by a longer, more well-considered process of thinking by the individual about the interaction before responding to it. When engaging in *System 2 thinking*, an individual will typically consider the consequences of the interaction before responding. It is clear that in some cases where athletes posted content online they may have used their System 1 thought process when, in fact, their System 2 would have been the better system to employ for that interaction. If System 2 is used, an ill-advised post on Twitter or Facebook may be less likely to reach the online world (as the case study example at the outset of this chapter described in relation to the rugby player, Sean) because the individual may have considered the potential impact of the tweet's content on himself, and also on the lives of others in his social network (e.g., teammates) and in the wider public also before posting his opinions on the topic in question. When athletes do make ill-advised online comments on their social media, can it really be 'deleted' and how does the response to their comments socially and emotionally impact on them?

7.9 Athletes removing online profiles

This question of how athletes respond to negative social media comments is an interesting one for psychologists to consider. As the case study of Sean at the start of this chapter illustrates, athletes do, and have, posted ill-considered comments online on media such as Twitter and Facebook which have then evoked negative responses from the public. As Kahneman (2011) explained, this could be when the fast System 1 is used in error when, in fact, the slower System 2 was required. Such incidences may prompt athletes to remove their online profiles completely, by closing down their Facebook, Twitter and Instagram accounts, for example. This phenomenon is known as virtual identity suicide (Steiger, Burger, Bohn, & Voracek, 2013). Recent high-profile, although not athlete, cases of this have included popular musician, Ed Sheeran, who closed down his social media Twitter and Instagram accounts following online criticism of his acting performance in the popular *Game of Thrones* television series (O'Connor, 2017). It would be a shame if many athletes, who have an online presence for all of the reasons previously cited made the decision to do the same. However, this is unlikely given the statement of Samford University Sports Business Report cited at the outset of this chapter (The Business Side of Sports, 2016), that social media also 'changed the face of sport'. Sport is 'Big Business' and athletes are aware of this, so their social media presence, once it continues to help their 'business', is unlikely to disappear completely.

7.10 Conclusion, including future research suggestions

This chapter attempted to outline some of the reasons athletes use social media (for networking, communicating and attracting sponsors, for example). Their decisions to use such platforms, while known to be 'risky' at times for their sport lives (e.g., distraction issues) and their personal lives (e.g., security and privacy issues), were also discussed.

Based on these topics, a key area for research could be to conduct in-depth qualitative studies with athletes, examining their specific decisions to use, and interact on, social media. Specifically, different athletes' uses of such media (i.e., cultural differences; male versus female athletes' uses of social media and team versus individual athletes' uses) in relation to their different sports could be an interesting focus for some empirical studies. Attempts to explain cases of athletes sometimes making poor decisions when considering what they do and do not post on their social media platforms is also an area where future investigations would be welcomed, especially if effective evidence-based and research-focused training in social media use is to be provided to such athletes in the future.

7.11 Open-ended discussion questions

1   Discuss the advantages and disadvantages of social media use for athletes, specifically in relation to their sport performances.
2   What advice could be given to athletes to help them present the 'best' version of themselves on their social media platforms?
3   What role may social media play in helping athletes market themselves to potential sponsors in the future?

7.12 Practical exercise

In groups of three, complete a case study task, where the student groups select one male and one female performer from the world of sport and examine these individuals' online presences, specifically outlining the potential reasons for the individual's online presence. Discuss the possible impressions (using their online post as evidence) that the public may form of such individuals, based on their communications on their social media platforms.

References

Adebayo, D. (2013). Eye on the stars: Twitter and the sporting hero. *Index on Censorship, 42*(1), 62–65.

Androich, A. (2012). Demanding their share. *Marketing Magazine, 117*(12), 8–10.

Arai, A., Ko, Y.J., & Kaplanidou, K. (2013). Athlete brand image: Scale development and model test. *European Sport Management Quarterly, 13*, 383–403.

Asch, S.E. (1951). Effects of group pressure upon the modification and distortion of judgements. In H. Guetzkow (Ed.), *Groups, leadership and men: Research in human relations* (pp. 177–190). Oxford: Carnegie Press.

Barton, H. (2016). Persuasion and influence in cyberspace. In I. Connolly, M. Palmer, H. Barton, & G. Kirwan (Eds.), *An introduction to cyberpsychology* (pp. 111–123). London, UK: Routledge-Taylor and Francis Group.

Biocca, F., Harms, C., & Burgoon, J.K. (2003). Towards a more robust theory and measure of social presence: Review and suggested criteria. *Presence: Tele-Operators and Virtual Environments, 12*, 456–480.

Boehmer, J., & Lacy, S. (2014). Sports news on Facebook: The relationship between interactivity and readers' browsing behaviour. *International Journal of Sport Communication, 7*, 1–15.

The Business Side of Sports. (2016). *Samford University Sports Business report: Social media has changed the sport's world.* Retrieved from https://businesssideofsports.com/2016/03/10/social-media-has-changed-the-sports-world/

Connolly, I. (2016). Young people and the Internet. In I. Connolly, M. Palmer, H. Barton, & G. Kirwan (Eds.), *An introduction to cyberpsychology* (pp. 224–238). London, UK: Routledge-Taylor and Francis Group.

Cox, J. (2012). Information system user security: A structured model of the knowing-doing gap. *Computers in Human Behaviour, 28*, 1849–1858.

Davis, C. (2015). *Wayne Rooney could make multi-million pound move from Nike to Adidas.* Retrieved from www.telegraph.co.uk/sport/football/players/wayne-rooney/11968793/Wayne-Rooney-could-make-multi-million-pound-move-from-Nike-to-Adidas.html

Denby, D. (2017). *Social media can be a double-edged sword.* Retrieved from http://signpost.mywebermedia.com/2017/02/15/social-media-can-be-a-double-edged-sword-for-athletes/

Ellison, N., Heino, R., & Gibbs, J. (2006). Managing impression online: Self-presentation processes in the online dating environment. *Journal of Computer Mediated Communication, 11*, Article 2. Retrieved from http://jcmc.indiana.edu/vol11/issue2/ellison.hyml

Fieldhouse Media. (2016). *Social media use of student athletes: 2016 survey results.* Retrieved from www.fieldhousemedia.net/social-media-use-of-student-athletes-2016-survey-results/

Fortune. (2017). *Twitter gains more followers.* Retrieved from www.emarketer.com/Article/Twitter-Gains-More-Followers/1015764

Fullwood, C. (2015). The role of personality in online self-presentation. In A. Attrill (Ed.), *Cyberpsychology* (pp. 9–28). Oxford, UK: Oxford University Press.

Global WebIndex. (2013). *Global WebIndex Stram Social report-Q2.* Retrieved from www.globalwebindex.net/product/stream-social-global-report-q2-2013-withembedded-data/

Hambrick, M.E., Simmons, J.M., Greenhalgh, G.P., & Greenwell, C.T. (2010). Understanding professional athletes' use of Twitter: A content analysis of athlete tweets. *International Journal of Sports Communication, 3*, 454–471.

Higgins, E.T. (1987). Self-discrepancy: A theory of relating self and affect. *Psychological Review, 94*, 319–340.

Hookit. (2016). *Cristiano Ronaldo: The most influential figure in sports.* Retrieved from www. hookit.com/brands/hookit/news/cristiano-ronaldo-first-athlete-with-200-million-followers/

Hurley, O. (2016). Sport and health cyberpsychology. In I. Connolly, M. Palmer, H. Barton, & G. Kirwan (Eds.), *An introduction to cyberpsychology* (pp. 167–180). London: Routledge.

Hytner, D. (2014). *Think before you tweet: FA has made £350,000 in Twitter fines since 2011.* The Guardian. Retrieved from www.theguardian.com/football/2014/oct/30/fa-fines-rio-ferdinand-twitter

Ingle, S. (2016). *Fancy Bears hack again with attack on senior anti-doping officials.* Retrieved from www.theguardian.com/sport/2016/nov/25/fancy-bears-hack-again-with-attack-on-senior-anti-doping-officials

Kahneman, D. (2011). *Thinking fast and slow.* London: Penguin.

Kim, J., & Song, H. (2016). Celebrity's self-disclosure on Twitter and parasocial relationships: A mediating role of social presence. *Computers in Human Behaviour, 62*, 570–577.

Kirwan, G. (2016). Privacy and trust online. In I. Connolly, M. Palmer, H. Barton, & G. Kirwan (Eds.), *An introduction to cyberpsychology* (pp. 124–136). London, UK: Routledge-Taylor and Francis Group.

MailOnline. (2011). *Rooney at centre of Twitter row after offering to fight 'fan'.* Retrieved from www.dailymail.co.uk/news/article-1388602/Wayne-Rooney-centre-Twitter-row-offering-fight-fan.html

Manish. (2015). *Anna Kournikova: The most famous tennis player never to have won a singles title.* Sportskeeda. Retrieved from www.sportskeeda.com/tennis/anna-kournikova-most-famous-tennis-player-never-won-singles-title

Markus, H., & Nurius, P. (1986). Possible selves. *American Psychologist, 41*, 954–969.

Moran, A.P., & Toner, J. (2017). *A critical introduction to sport psychology.* East Sussex: Routledge.

Morrissey, P. (2014). *Joey Barton slams FA for Rio's £25k per tweet fine & ban, Ferdinand joins in, says 'sket' was meant to be a joke [Tweets].* Retrieved from www.101greatgoals.com/blog/joey-barton-slams-fa-for-rios-25k-per-tweet-fine-ban-ferdinand-joins-in-says-sket-was-meant-as-a-joke-tweets/

Narcum, J.A., Havard, C.T., & Mason, K.H. (2016). The impacts of Twitter transgressions on an athlete's brand. *Journal of Business Administration,* (Fall 2016), 1–8.

O'Connor, R. (2017). *Ed Sheeran deletes Twitter account after Game of Thrones backlash.* Retrieved from www.independent.co.uk/arts-entertainment/music/news/ed-sheeran-twitter-delete-account-game-thrones-cameo-backlash-loop-glastonbury-arya-stark-a7846421.html

Pegoraro, A. (2010). Look who's talking: Athletes on Twitter: A case study. *International Journal of Sport Communication, 3*, 501–514.

Pegoraro, A., & Jinnah, N. (2012). Tweet'em and reap'em: The impact of professional athletes' use of Twitter on current and potential sponsorship opportunities. *Journal of Brand Strategy, 1*, 85–97.

Petronio, S. (2002). *Boundaries of privacy: Dialectics of disclosure.* Albany, NY: SUNY Press.

Petronio, S. (2013). Brief status of report on communication privacy management theory. *Journal of Family Communications, 13*, 6–14.

Petronio, S., & Durham, W.T. (2015). Communication privacy management theory: Significance for interpersonal communication. In D.O. Braithwaite & P. Schrodt (Eds.), *Engaging theories in interpersonal communications: Multiple perspectives* (2nd ed., pp. 335–347). Thousand Oaks, CA: Sage Publications.

Reynolds, J. (2012). *Manchester City's Russell Stopford on how the club achieves digital dominance.* Campaign. Retrieved from www.campaignlive.co.uk/article/manchester-citys-russell-stopford-club-achieved-digital-dominance/1145120

Sabur, R. (2017). *John Terry's mansion burgled while footballer posted holiday pictures on social media.* Retrieved from www.telegraph.co.uk/news/2017/03/04/john-terrys-mansion-burgled-footballer-posted-holiday-pictures/

Sanderson, J., & Kissing, J.W. (2011). Tweets and blogs: Transformative, adversarial, and integrative developments in sports media. In A.C. Billings (Ed.), *Sports media: Transformation, integration, consumption* (pp. 114–127). New York: Routledge.

Skeels, M.M., & Grudin, J. (2009). When social networks cross boundaries: A case study of workplace use of Facebook and LinkedIn. *Group '09*, May 10–13, Sanibel Island, Florida, USA.

Social Bakers. (2017). *Twitter statistics directory.* Retrieved from www.socialbakers.com/statistics/twitter/

Steiger, S., Burger, C., Bohn, M., & Voracek, M. (2013). Who commits virtual identity suicide? Differences in privacy concerns, internet addiction and personality between Facebook users and quitters. *Cyberpsychology, Behaviour and Social Networking, 16*, 629–634.

Steinberg, L. (2012). *A social neuroscience perspective on adolescent risk taking.* Retrieved from www.youtube.com/watch?v=LrVPKYsRxMw

The Telegraph. (2012). *Ashley Cole fined £90,000 by FA . . . and Chelsea discipline Terry.* Retrieved from www.theguardian.com/football/2012/oct/18/ashley-cole-fined-chelsea-terry

Tversky, A., & Kahneman, D. (1973). Availability: A heuristic for judging frequency and probability. *Cognitive Psychology, 5*(1), 207–232.

Vanden Abeele, M., & van Rooij, T. (2016). *Fear of missing out (FOMO) as a predictor of problematic social media use among teenagers.* International Conference on Behavioural Addictions, Geneva.

Whiteside, E., Yu, N., & Hardin, M. (2012). The new 'toy department'? A case on differences in sports coverage between traditional and new media. *Journal of Sports Media, 7*, 23–38.

8

USE OF THE ONLINE WORLD BY TEAMS, COACHES AND ORGANISATIONS

CASE STUDY 8

Katherine is the Public Relations Officer (PRO) for a high-profile team sport organisation. Her job involves publicising all of the organisation's events, both on and off the field of play, that the teams within the organisation participate in. Katherine is also involved in designing the media training for the players, coaches and support staff employed by her organisation.

  (i) What specific online media could Katherine use to help her in her job as the PRO for her sport organisation; how could such media be best used by Katherine's organisation to the greatest advantage?

 (ii) What risks are associated with the use of online media by sport organisations such as Katherine's?

(iii) What material could Katherine cover with the athletes, coaches and support staff of her organisation to help them use the online world to their best advantage, while avoiding the potential dangers such online engagement may pose for some individuals?

(iv) How might Katherine advise others within her organisation to use the online world for their continued professional development (CPD) both for themselves and for other staff members (i.e., for the upskilling of the coaches working within the organisation)?

8.1 Overview

Many successful sport teams and organisations are now using the online world in a very direct and beneficial way to expand their fan base. This chapter addresses issues related to the use of the online world by such sport organisations, their teams, their support staff and their supporters to communicate with one another. The advantages of using online platforms such as Twitter, Facebook, Instagram and YouTube by these groups are highlighted. Potential uses include: (i) showcasing athletes, (ii) recruiting athletes, (iii) sharing news about athletic teams, (iv) establishing partnerships with charity organisations and (v) providing support networks for retired athletes (i.e., through organisations such as Rugby Players Ireland, the Gaelic Players Association (GPA) and the Jockeys Education and Training Scheme (JETS), for example; see Table 6.1 for some more examples of support organisations for athletes across many sports around the world). Topics such as how teams and sport bodies present themselves online and what information they share with the public online are discussed. Research findings from the cognitive and social psychology literature, as well as the sport marketing literature, regarding the benefits and risks associated with such presentations of information online are discussed. The decision-making process involved in determining what and why such sport groups behave in particular ways online is also considered, having introduced similar topics in Chapter 6 in relation to athletes' online interactions. In the latter parts of the chapter, the discussion moves to topics such as how coaches, managers, support staff and large sport organisations use the online world for social support, mentoring and continuing professional development (CPD).

8.2 Learning objectives

1   To introduce the reader to the most common uses of the online world by sport organisations, their associated teams and their staff
2   To explain some of the advantages and disadvantages of various online platforms used by such groups
3   To outline some best practices employed by sport teams and organisations who have made use of the online world to successfully expand their sport brand
4   To make some suggestions for future research in this area and how the online world may be further utilised to bridge the gap between the public and the sport teams they support

8.3 Definitions of relevant terms

Motivational climate

This term refers to the perceived structure of the sport environment in this case, generally established by the attitudes and behaviours of the coach. Two types of motivational climate are generally referred to in the context of sport – mastery climate and ego-oriented climate (see Ames, 1992, and Moran, 2012).

Relationship marketing

This refers to the enduring relationship between the consumer and the individual or organisation engaged in marketing a product or brand.

Social capital

This term refers to the network of relationships between individuals within a society that enables that society to function in an efficient and effective way, with resources and benefits provided by others (Attrill, 2015).

Sport Twitter consumption

The use of Twitter to obtain information related to a sport environment of interest – for example: (i) information regarding individual athletes who compete in a sport, (ii) information about sport events or (iii) information about sport organisations.

8.4 Introduction

The Internet has provided a level playing field for all sports, teams and their associated organisations to market themselves to their public. Practically every sport team and association has a website or online presence in today's society on free platforms such as Facebook, Twitter, Instagram, Snapchat and YouTube. These groups use these platforms to market themselves, their sport, their teams and their athletes. Technology tools such as WordPress have enabled websites to be generated relatively easily by such sport organisations, with technical designers typically assisting them with such tasks. Indeed, their website is often the first place sport organisations direct their supporters to go to for information related to their teams and athletes. For example, Leinster Rugby stated in 2015 to their supporters, "Did you know that the first place to see your Leinster team news will always be leinsterrugby.ie?" (cited in The Irish Independent, 2015).

Given the high usage of social media tools, already explained extensively in Chapter 7 with regard to athletes' uses of them (i.e., Twitter, Facebook and Instagram or Snapchat), their advantageous use by teams and those associated with them is also worthy of recognition. Academics working and researching in the worlds of sport psychology and cyberpsychology have also become interested in studying the impact of teams' uses of the online world. In this chapter, the uses and impacts of the online world by teams, organisations and their associated personnel, such as their coaching staff, are presented.

8.5 Use of social media by sport organisations and teams – the best and the how

According to Deloitte's Money League in 2017, Manchester United Football Club (MUFC; Figure 8.1) was the biggest sport team in the world, based on its revenue generation of $774 million (more than $74 million over its closest rival, the Dallas Cowboys NFL team; Ozanian, 2017). Such revenue has been generated with the help of MUFC's use of various online social media platforms, as is demonstrated from the figures for its social media platforms in 2017, recorded as: Twitter (10 million followers), Facebook (72.9 million friends) and Instagram (16.8 million followers; Sokkaa, 2017). Interestingly, these figures only placed MUFC third

FIGURE 8.1 Old Trafford, the home of Manchester United Football Club

Source: Courtesy of Pexels.

in terms of their actual social media following, behind Real Madrid (at number 2) and the FC Barcelona (positioned at number 1), who in 2017 had 20 million Twitter followers, 97 million Facebook friends and 47 million Instagram followers (Mackenzie, 2017). What these figures illustrate is the extent of the social media following these sport organisations have amassed in a relatively short period of time since the emergence of these online platforms. Many sport teams, coaches and organisations have in that time realised and harnessed the potential to expand their fan base, and revenue, by using such online platforms.

Some sport teams, such as the three just cited, seem to be more knowledgeable in how to use their online social media to their greatest advantage. They employ good psychological and marketing principles, and strategies, to obtain the greatest benefits from their online presence and interactions with the public. Interesting questions then arise, such as: (i) what makes such sport teams effective in their use of the online world? and (ii) can the activities of sport teams and organisations on various online and social media platforms be, in some cases, harmful to their teams' and their individual athletes' performances? These questions are considered and form the rationale for some of the subject matter presented in this chapter.

8.5.1 Why do sport organisations use online social media platforms?

One of the most obvious reasons for sport teams and organisations to use online social media is that it provides free and generally easy-to-use tools to extensively market their teams. Before the advent of social media, and indeed the Internet itself, direct interactions between sport organisations and their audiences were expensive (especially using television and print media advertising to achieve such interactions). The Internet and social media have changed that situation completely, making it much less costly for sport organisations to interact with their target audiences.

According to Witkemper, Hoon Lim, and Waldburger (2012), Twitter, Facebook and YouTube were the three most common types of social media linked to many official sport teams' websites. Based on the Irish Sport Social Media Report (Sport for Business, 2017b), Twitter now appears to be the most popular medium sport fans go to first for their sport-related content. However, this report also encouraged sport-related businesses and organisations to post more videos and images from their sports on their online media, as this content appeared to be the most sought after by supporter audiences across these social media platforms. YouTube, Instagram and Snapchat are typically the video- and image-based tools employed most for presenting such visual content by sport teams and organisations.

In accordance with these new forms of communication in sport settings, the skills of the sport communication professionals working for many sport organisations has also changed in recent years (see the case study example posed at the beginning of this chapter as an illustration of this). Expertise in the generation and use of social media content, as well as the monitoring of online communities' interactions is now a requirement for most, if not all, employees working in such public relations (PR) positions (Boehmer & Lacy, 2014).

A number of studies have attempted to examine the use of such social media by various companies and organisations in order to determine their actual impact on customers' behaviours. For example, in a café-based study, Dholakia and Durham (2010) reported a positive relationship between increased social media activity on their social media platforms and increased offline store visits. Boehmer and Lacy (2014) also studied the use of Facebook, as part of a specific interactive social-customer relationship-management (SCRM) strategy to determine, for example, what happened when an individual clicked on a sport news link in a social media platform (in this case, Facebook) which then directed the individual to the organisation's own website. Boehmer and Lacy (2014), however, reported no positive relationship between increased interactivity on the organisations' Facebook page as a result of individuals clinking on the sport news link (see Abeza, 2016, for a more in-depth review of social media's role in relationship marketing in a professional sport context).

Interestingly, while Facebook remains very popular as a social media platform, with over 2 billion monthly users and over 1 billion daily mobile users (Zephoria, 2017), Twitter appears to be gaining in popularity as the 'go to' media of preference for many sport fans. With this in mind, Box 8.1 presents some specific reasons for this particular growth in Sport Twitter Consumption by such audiences.

BOX 8.1 REASONS FOR THE SPECIFIC GROWTH IN SPORT TWITTER CONSUMPTION

According to Pedersen, Parks, Quarterman, and Thibault (2010), social media is being used more frequently by sport organisations and teams to communicate with their fans. The social media platform, Twitter, is still behind Facebook and Instagram in the number of overall followers on its platform (supported by the figures for the most-followed sport team, namely FC Barcelona; cited in Mackenzie, 2017). More recently, however, Twitter does appear to have 'gripped' the minds of sport team supporters, and is perhaps growing at a rate that will soon see it become the most popular form of social media used by sport team supporters (Sport for Business, 2017a). Many sport teams have begun to use Twitter because it provides them with a mechanism to communicate and interact directly with their fans in a very immediate way. According to Schäferhoff (2016), "no other industry has embraced the microblogging platform as readily as sports teams and their fans". Many reasons for this situation have been identified, but the most common appear to be that Twitter provides sport teams with an effective way to promote their teams, reach out to new supporters and achieve instant contact with such individuals.

So, for fans of sport teams and spectators of sport in general, the social media platform, Twitter, can potentially narrow the gap between them and their sport idols. It allows both groups to interact and converse with each other in a very direct way not possible in the pre-social media age. If this is the case, then: (i) what do such sport organisations/teams tweet about, (ii) what impact could such tweets have on an organisations' athletes and (iii) do different sport organisations differ in their tweet content?

Healy (2014) attempted to answer these questions by analysing the tweet content from the Twitter accounts of 17 Irish sport clubs and organisations (representing intermediate level Irish soccer, rugby, and GAA clubs) in order to determine their specific use of Twitter, as well as examining if such organisations' tweet content could possibly impact upon the motivational climate of the organisations' teams. Healy (2014) identified four themes from the 6,410 tweets analysed in his study, namely, 'news', 'match updates', 'public relations', and 'team interactions'. Tweets classified as news were considered factual tweets (i.e., they gave the team's followers updates on club events). While these types of tweets were relatively common (i.e., 1,704 out of 6,410 tweets analysed, corresponding to 26.5% of all tweets examined), they rarely mentioned a specific team from the organisation/club, or a specific player. Tweets categorised as 'match updates' were the most frequent types of tweets posted by the 17 sport teams (equating to 35% of the overall tweets examined). The 'match updates' tweets typically contained real-time information about 'live' matches (i.e., match score updates). According to Healy (2014), such tweets could have an effect on a team's motivational climate, because in some of these tweets, references were made to the performance of the club's specific teams, or individual athletes playing on those teams. If such tweets were read back after a match by the teams' athletes, they could impact upon their future motivational states. Therefore, individuals responsible for posting sport clubs' or organisations' tweets should be trained in what content they should include in their tweets and be made aware of the potential impact such posts could have on the clubs' or organisations' athletes who read them typically after their sport events.

Healy (2014) also sought to establish if clubs from different sports used Twitter in different ways. To achieve this, the tweeting habits of the clubs across the three sports were compared. For GAA clubs, the most common type of tweet was classified as a 'match update' (38%). The least common type of tweet posted was the 'team interactions' type (corresponding to 9% of the tweets analysed). Similar to GAA clubs, the most common theme to emerge from the tweets of rugby clubs was 'match updates' (38%). In contrast to GAA and rugby clubs, the most common Twitter theme for soccer clubs' tweets was 'public relations' based (accounting for 41% of all their tweets). 'Match updates' were also common Twitter content for such soccer teams (at 33%). 'News'-related tweets were less frequent for soccer organisations, but they were not considered disproportionally so (at 25%). Healy (2014) suggested that more extensive, qualitative and multicultural studies should be carried out, incorporating more sport types than the three Irish team sports included in his study, in order to give a clearer picture of sport clubs' and organisations' overall uses of Twitter to communicate with their target audiences.

Burst Media (cited in Polese, 2014) reported that 45% of 18- to 35-year-olds follow sport teams and athletes on various forms of social media in order to keep 'in the loop' regarding up-to-date news about their teams. Perhaps, given the results of Healy's (2014) study, some sport teams and organisations should consider increasing the news content on their social media platforms in order to increase their consumers' satisfaction levels with their brand's social media content. Polese (2014) reported that 35% of the same age range of social media users reported they used social media to tweet, retweet and share online links containing sport-related content. This information highlights the awareness needed by teams, organisations and indeed all of their employed personnel, their coaches and athletes included, regarding the potential impact their online posts can have, given the likelihood of them being extensively viewed and shared by their young fan base.

A number of sport teams have recognised the power of the impact of their online presence and especially that of the social media platforms they use. Some teams have embraced the growth of Twitter so much, for example, they have replaced the names of their players on the backs of their jerseys with their Twitter handles (Knapp, 2011). Many sport organisations also use hashtags to encourage and generate discussions around their sport events on their Twitter accounts. They can also use these hashtags as a tool to monitor the extent of the discussions generated about their event and their athletes online (referred to as 'trending on Twitter', for example). It is interesting to note that despite terms such as 'trending on

Twitter' now being part of everyday conversations, such phrases would probably not have been used or understood in conversations 10 to 12 years ago. This point alone also illustrates the impact of the digital world on the media landscape in recent years (Boehmer & Lacy, 2014).

At the other end of the relationship between sport organisations and their online content consumers, an important consideration for sport organisations centres around the reasons *why* their customers use the online world. Holmlund (1997) explained that the interactions between fans and sport organisations can develop into a substantial relationship by progressing through a series of stages. For example, invitations to interact with a sport organisation, using various social media, can lead to 'episodes' (one encounter) and then 'sequences' of interactions. Such sequences of interactions can then lead to the establishment of the desired 'strong' relationship between the fan and the sport organisation. Today, marketing professionals working for sport teams are aware that the social media they use, such as Twitter, Facebook, Snapchat or Instagram, can trigger this relationship-generating sequence of events. Therefore, sending out that initial invitation to an individual via social media, or other online methods such as email, to interact with the organisation is the first important step in initiating this possible chain of events to potentially establish a strong future relationship between the fan and the organisation.

One study by Witkemper et al. (2012) did examine the motives, and constraints, of sport Twitter consumers who engaged in sport Twitter consumption (STC). Specifically, Witkemper et al. (2012) studied the different motivations for why social media users used Twitter for sport-related reasons (i.e., to follow certain athletes on Twitter). They examined various use motivations, namely: (i) information motivation, (ii) pass-time motivation, (iii) fanship motivation and (iv) entertainment motivation. Witkemper et al. also appeared to be the first researchers to empirically examine user constraints when interacting with social media for such sport-related purposes. Their rational for choosing to study constraints too as a key issue in the STC process is understood by their statement that, "By identifying which specific constraints limit participation in following athletes' Twitter accounts, sport governing bodies, leagues, and individual teams' front offices may better decide how to change their social media marketing strategies", given that, "Twitter as a marketing strategy is a relatively new tactic, so information is needed on how best to utilize it" (p. 171). As two of the most sought after results of any sport marketing strategy are often: (i) to maintain consumers' awareness of a brand and (ii) to establish a strong connectivity between the consumer and the brand, this aspect of Witkemper et al.'s (2012) study, examining the constraints for why such brand awareness and connectivity does not happen, would be welcomed by many marketers working in this sport arena. As Witkemper et al. (2012) commented "There are many options for sport organisations to grow their relationships with fans, and Twitter represents a new avenue through which a relationship can be enhanced" (p. 180).

However, Witkemper et al. (2012) also cited some limitations of their study. Their use of a student population as their participants was one such limitation, because the findings may not generalise to other non-student populations. Witkemper et al. (2012) also saw their survey-based study as only a first, exploratory study in this area. As such, they encouraged other researchers to carry out more extensive studies in this area, including a detailed study of other types of social media, such as Facebook, Instagram and YouTube, in order to establish a greater understanding of social media's impact on sport consumers too. Of course, sport organisations can also use the online world for reasons other than expanding their fan base. They also can use it to help: (i) expand their athlete roster and (ii) for training purposes (of their coaches and officials). These uses are presented next.

8.6 Use of the online world for player recruitment

The Internet and online social media have created many opportunities for sport organisations to potentially recruit athletes for their teams (Rahmati, 2016). Within such settings, the benefits of their websites and social media platforms include: (i) generating awareness of their organisation or club's mission, culture and values, as well as, (ii) showcasing their training programmes and facilities. It also enables such sport organisations to screen athletes they may be interested in recruiting, by viewing the athlete's website and social media/online interactions. Such 'research' can enable them to determine if an athlete is a suitable candidate or employee for their club, team or organisation. This is, again, one of the reasons why athletes need to be mindful of their interactions online, as was explored in Chapter 7, especially with regard to student athletes' social media uses and behaviours. Sport organisations also need to be careful how they handle such recruitment strategies, by keeping within the rules of their sports' governing bodies, as the penalties for sport organisations using social media for recruitment purposes in incorrect ways can also be costly (Rahmati, 2016).

8.7 Coaches' use of online platforms

Of course, while the overall sport organisations' and teams' uses of social media and the online world are important to consider, so too are the ways such organisations can use the online world to benefit their own coaching and support staff. The interactions such personnel can experience and benefit from, using the online world, are vast. One area where the world of technology can and is being used effectively is in the area of e-learning in sport for coach development and training opportunities. The training of coaches using programmes delivered in a virtual learning environment in the main, with some face-to-face sessions then added to solidify the learning, as deemed necessary, is becoming popular in the same way that such uses of the online world for providing education and training opportunities are used by athletes (see Chapter 6). These coaches who train athletes on a day-to-day basis can also advance their education options by using virtual learning environments (VLEs), while meeting their training and coaching commitments (Leinster Rugby, 2017). Such uses of the online world for the delivery of coach-training programmes are beneficial for a number of reasons. One important reason is that they are cost-effective for sport organisations who are attempting to upskill and grow their coaching staff, especially when such personnel and finances too may be in short supply, and also when many of the 'target' coaches are not based within close proximity of the physical headquarters of the sport organisation itself, for example (as discussed in Chapter 6 also).

The online world specifically provides coaches with opportunities to: (i) communicate with each other, creating extensive and helpful support networks, (ii) share information and their coaching experiences, as well as (iii) providing formal continuing professional development (CPD) and training for individuals across a spectrum of coaching standards from professional down to novice coaching personnel.

8.8 Conclusion, including future directions for research

The aims of this chapter included outlining some of the advantages and disadvantages of various online platforms used by sport teams and organisations, some best practices employed by such groups who have made use of the online world to successfully expand their sport brand, as well as to make some suggestions for future research in this area for how the online world may be further utilised to bridge the gap between the public and the sport teams they support.

As can be seen from the content of this chapter, the opportunities for sport organisations, teams and their coaches to use the online world to their benefit are potentially vast. However, given this area of opportunity is somewhat new for many of these groups, more research is needed to specifically understand the impact of the digital world and social media on sport organisations and the individuals associated with them (such as their athletes, their supporters and their coaching staff).

Some limitations of the studies cited in this chapter have been identified, such as the use of only one type of social media and only three types of team sports by Healy (2014), and again only Twitter and students included for examination in Witkemper et al.'s (2012) study. These researchers, completing new, exploratory studies have cited the need for more empirical research in the areas of sport organisations' uses of the online world in order to fully understand the impacts and benefits it can truly have for their organisations and associated personnel (such as their athletes and coaching staff). It is true that the impact of sport organisations' uses of the online world on their supporters has been studied somewhat (e.g., Witkemper et al., 2012), however, the impact of this use on the athletes performing within or for such organisations', and their teams as a whole, for example, has not been the subject of detailed empirical exploration and is an avenue for potential future study in this area.

8.9 Open-ended discussion questions

1   What role may the online world play in the future in helping sport teams and organisations to market themselves to as wide an audience as possible?

2   Discuss the advantages and disadvantages of using the online world to train
and upskill coaches and managers of teams.

8.10 Practical exercise

In groups of two or three, ask students to devise a series of training sessions to
deliver to sport coaches on their uses of the online world to enhance their job performances. What benefits could interaction in the online world potentially offer
such individuals in order to advance their careers? What notes of caution should
be highlighted to individuals using such digital environments?

References

Abeza, G. (2016). *Social media in relationship marketing: The professional sport context.* Unpublished
PhD Thesis, Ottawa, Canada. Retrieved from https://ruor.uottawa.ca/bitstream/10393/
35373/1/Abeza_Gashaw_%202016_thesis.pdf

Ames, C. (1992). Achievement goals, motivational climate, and motivational processes. In
G. Roberst (ed.) *Motivation in sport and exercise* (pp. 161–176). Champaign, IL: Human
Kinetics.

Attrill, A. (Ed.). (2015). *Cyberpsychology.* Oxford, UK: Oxford University Press.

Boehmer, J., & Lacy, S. (2014). Sports news on Facebook: The relationship between interactivity and readers' browsing behaviour. *International Journal of Sport Communication*, 7,
1–15.

Dholakia, U.M., & Durham, E. (2010). One café chain's Facebook experiment. *Harvard Business Review*, *88*, 26–27.

Healy, P. (2014). *An investigation of motivation in co-dependent team sport.* Unpublished Masters
Thesis, Institute of Art, Design and Technology, Dun Laoghaire, Co. Dublin, Ireland.

*Holmlund, M. (1997). *Perceived quality in business relationships.* Publications of Swedish
School of Economics and Business Administration No 66, Helsinki.

The Irish Independent. (2015). *Stay connected with Leinster Rugby – and let us tell your story.*
Retrieved from www.independent.ie/sport/rugby/leinster-rugby/stay-connected-with-
leinster-rugby-online-and-let-us-tell-your-story-31536105.html

Knapp, A. (December 2011). *Pro lacrosse team replaces names with Twitter handles on jerseys.*
Retrieved from www.forbes.ie

Leinster Rugby. (2017). *Leinster Rugby continues collaboration with St. Mary's University, Twick-
enham.* Retrieved from www.leinsterrugby.ie/leinster-rugby-continues-collaboration-
with-st-marys-university-twickenham/

Mackenzie. (2017). *Ranking the world's top ten most supported soccer teams by fans.* Trendrr. Retrieved
from www.trendrr.net/6110/top-10-best-most-popular-soccer-teams-football-club-largest-
fans/

Moran, A. (2012). *Sport and exercise psychology: A critical introduction.* London: Routledge.

Ozanian, P. (2017). *Manchester United now biggest sports team in the world.* Forbes. Retrieved from
www.forbes.com/sites/mikeozanian/2017/01/19/manchester-united-now-biggest-
sports-team-in-the-world/#ea99bc823d41

Pedersen, P., Parks, J., Quarterman, J., & Thibault, L. (2010). *Contemporary sport management*
(4th ed.). Champaign, IL: Human Kinetics.

Polese, L. (2014). *How Twitter is changing the way we experience sports.* Audiense. Retrieved from
https://audiense.com/how-twitter-is-changing-the-way-we-experience-sports/

Rahmati, R. (2016). *How social media is changing college recruiting.* Spredfast. Retrieved from www.spredfast.com/social-marketing-blog/how-social-media-changing-college-recruiting

Schäferhoff, N. (2016). *How to use Twitter to market and promote your sports team.* Retrieved from www.themeboy.com/blog/twitter-sports-team-marketing-promotion/

Seo, W. J., & Green, C. (2008). Development of the motivation scale for sport online consumption. *Journal of Sport Management, 22,* 82–109.

Sokkaa. (2017). *Top 7 football clubs with the biggest fanbase worldwide today.* Retrieved from http://sokkaa.com/2017/03/27/top-7-football-clubs-with-biggest-fanbase-worldwide-today/

Sport for Business. (2017a). *Irish sport social media report – March 2017.* Retrieved from http://sportforbusiness.com/25667-2/

Sport for Business (2017b). *Irish sport social media report – July.* Retrieved from http://sportforbusiness.com/irish-sport-social-media-july-2017/

Witkemper, C., Hoon Lim, C., & Waldburger, A. (2012). Social media and sports marketing: Examining the motivations and constraints of twitter users. *Sport Marketing Quarterly, 21,* 170–183.

Zephoria. (2017). *The top 20 valuable Facebook statistics – updated November 2017.* Retrieved from https://zephoria.com/top-15-valuable-facebook-statistics/

PART IV

The dark side of sport cyberpsychology

9

CYBERBULLYING AND CYBER HARASSMENT IN SPORT ENVIRONMENTS

CASE STUDY 9

Lee is a 26-year-old elite male swimmer. He is also an active user of Twitter, Instagram and Facebook. As Lee competes in one of the most important international competitions of his career, he receives some negative and threatening messages on his social media platforms from some of his followers. The content of these negative messages mainly question Lee's commitment to his sport and his patriotism.

  (i) How might such an incident impact on Lee's psychological well-being, as well as on his sport performances?
 (ii) How should Lee and his sport organisation respond to this incident?
(iii) How could such an incident potentially impact upon the lives of the individuals engaged in this negative online behaviour targeting Lee?
(iv) What general lessons can be learned from this scenario (i.e., what advice should be given to young athletes using social media platforms for social, sport, entertainment and business purposes who are bullied and harassed in this way)?

9.1 Overview

Many of the positive uses of new technologies have been detailed in the earlier chapters of this text. In this chapter, some of the specific, darker sides of the cyber world for athletes will be described. Issues such as cyberbullying, cyber harassment, cyberstalking and trolling are explained. Some incidences that have occurred of such behaviours aimed at well-known athletes in their sport environments are also presented. Possible reasons why athletes are popular targets for such negative online behaviours are suggested, based upon some of the available research findings of cyber psychologists, who have largely examined these issues within other settings (such as educational and organisational settings). Issues such as online disinhibition and de-individualisation will be discussed in these contexts. Strategies currently applied by athletes and sport organisations to cope with these negative incidences occurring in online interactions are also highlighted. For example, some sport teams attempt to manage such incidences by agreeing to short-term social media 'blackouts' with their athletes during the times around important matches or competitions in the hope that such actions will prevent their athletes from becoming aware of, and distracted or upset by, the negative behaviours of others directed at them during their important preparation and performance times. The final section of this chapter includes some future research suggestions that could help to advance our understanding of, and ways to manage, such issues within sport environments.

9.2 Learning objectives

1   To introduce the reader to the issues of cyberbullying, cyber harassment, cyberstalking and trolling sometimes experienced by athletes, as well as those associated with them (e.g., their coaches, parents, siblings, support staff and match officials) within their sport environment
2   To outline some methods commonly used to cyberbully, harass, troll and stalk athletes
3   To present some reasons why athletes are often the targets of such negative online behaviours, including an explanation of related issues from the cyberpsychology literature, such as online disinhibition and de-individualisation
4   To highlight some current strategies employed by sport teams, sport organisations and lawmakers to counteract the negative online behaviours athletes now appear to be frequently subjected to within their sport environments
5   To suggest some new ways such issues could be dealt with in the future, based upon research findings from other settings where such behaviours are also problematic, such as in educational and business settings

9.3 Definitions of relevant terms

Bullying

Bullying, or victimisation, as experienced in school settings, has typically been defined using the criteria of Olweus (1993). It is referred to as negative actions the targeted individual is repeatedly exposed to, over time, from one or more other individuals. The negative actions or behaviours are typically harassing, embarrassing and intimidating in nature, with physical harm also caused to the victim in some cases.

Cyberbullying

This behaviour is defined as the wilful use of electronic devices (typically smartphones and the Internet), by an individual or group of individuals, to intimidate, harass or embarrass another person or persons.

De-individualisation

This term refers to the tendency for individuals to become influenced by the behaviours, opinions and attitudes of others to the extent that they lose their own sense of being individuals, with the power to think for themselves. In such cases, a type of 'groupthink', typically originating from some dominant individual(s) within the group, takes over as the dominant opinion of the group and dictates the way all of the individuals appear to then think, feel and behave when they are part of that group.

Harassment

This is defined as the pestering or unpleasant bothering of another individual.

Online disinhibition

This term, introduced by Suler (2004), describes the tendency for some individuals to lose their sense of social etiquette and good behaviour when interacting in an online environment.

Stalking

Stalking is considered behaviour that occurs over a prolonged period of time and typically includes watching, following and harassing behaviour that is considered unpleasant by the targeted individual who is being stalked.

Trolling

This involves the posting of unpleasant comments online about an individual or individuals with the wilful intent of causing distress, and potentially psychologically harming that individual. It is often carried out in order to elicit a generally negative reaction from the target individual or individuals.

SimiSimi

This is an automated chat bot which operates by allowing users to teach it to answer in a certain way when specific questions are asked of the app, or when certain words or phrases are typed into the app. When another individual then asks this app a question using the same key words, it replies using this programmed negative, and sometimes explicit, language. All of this can be achieved anonymously, therefore, there is no way to identify the individual(s) telling the auto bot what to say and about whom.

9.4 Introduction

Cyberbullying has become a real problem for many athletes in today's digital world. They are often the subjects of online bullying, harassing and threatening comments from others, mainly, but not always, regarding their performances within their sport. For example, the American gymnast, Gabby Douglas, an Olympic and World Gold medallist commented, "When they talk about my hair, or not putting my hand over my heart or being salty in the stands, really criticising me . . . it was really hurtful" (cited in ABC News, 2016). A number of research studies have been published on the prevalence rates for cyberbullying within various environments such as education settings (Mishna, Cook, Gadalla, Daciuk, & Solomon, 2010; Wolke, Lee, & Guy, 2017) and organisational settings (i.e., in the workplace; Baruch, 2005), although available research in this specific area is somewhat limited (Coyne et al., 2015). Research investigating the prevalence of cyberbullying within sport environments, similar to workplace settings, is also limited. One of the first discussions regarding the issue of online maltreatment of athletes was by Kavanagh and Jones (2014), who referred to 'virtual maltreatment' and defined this as: "Direct or non-direct online communication that is stated in an aggressive, exploitative, manipulative, threatening or lewd manner and is designed to elicit fear, emotional or psychological upset, distress, alarm or feelings of inferiority" (p. 37). Kavanagh and Jones proposed four types of virtual maltreatment that could occur, namely, physical, sexual, emotional and discriminatory (of which such discrimination could be based upon gender, race, sexual orientation, religion or disability).

While research studies specifically presenting data on the prevalence rates and experiences of cyberbullying by athletes are scarce, much available anecdotal evidence suggests that such virtual attacks on athletes are frequent, with cases such as that of gymnast, Gabby Douglas (ABC News, 2016), reported in the media on a frequent basis. For some athletes, such incidences of cyberbullying and cyber harassment could dissuade them from using the online world, especially social media, despite its many benefits for athletes, as highlighted by Hambrick, Simmons, Greenhalgh, and Greenwell (2010; also discussed at length in Chapter 6 of this text). This is an unfortunate situation and justifies the interest of researchers in carrying out more studies in this area in order to determine the prevalence and impact of such cyberbullying behaviour on its athlete victims.

Regardless of the reasons proposed for why athletes are the subject of cyberbullying and other negative online attacks (which will be discussed later in this chapter), the psychological responses these athlete victims have to such experiences appear to be similar, based on their anecdotal comments, to their non-athlete counterparts who have also been the target of such negative online behaviours. Victims of such cyberbullying can suffer numerous physical, social and psychological problems as a result of being bullied online (Corcoran, Connolly, & O'Moore, 2012), including difficulties such as increased substance use (Carbone-Lopez, Esbensen, & Brick, 2010), feelings of low self-esteem and depression (Juvonen & Gross, 2008; Katzer, Fetchenhauer, & Belschak, 2009) and emotional difficulties. Such emotionally impacted victims, for example, have reported feelings of anger, frustration and fear as a result of being bullied (Katzer & Fetchenhauer, 2007).

Cyberbullying has also been linked to declines in academic performance (Katzer et al., 2009; Rothon, Head, Klineberg, & Stansfield, 2011), with related issues such as difficultly concentrating (Yuvonen & Gross, 2008) and declines in academic attendance also reported (Ybarra, Diener-West, & Leaf, 2007). Numerous tragic cases of teenage deaths by suicide (sometimes referred to as cyberbullicide; Hinduja & Patchin, 2010) have also been linked to cyberbullying (Farberov, 2017; The Telegraph, 2015). In the case of athletes specifically, a response to cyberbullying for them could include an inability to perform well within their sport due to some of the physical, and psycho-social reasons already outlined for non-athlete victims, such as difficulty concentrating and lowered levels of self-esteem.

It may appear somewhat surprising that there remains such a lack of empirical research on the cyberbullying of athletes, given the high number of examples of cyberbullying and cyber harassment of well-known athletes online frequently reported in the general media, along with the potential damage to these athletes' mental states and sense of self that such attacks could cause. However, perhaps the fast pace of technological advances that enable these new forms of cyberbullying to take place has occurred quicker than sound empirical research, which can take some years to complete, can keep up with. The suggestion that this was a specific area of cyberbullying worthy of more study was noted two years ago by Rooney, Connolly, Hurley, Kirwan, and Power (2015) and remains a suggestion for researchers interested in this area of sport psychology in the digital age.

Traditional, offline bullying within sport has been the focus of some investigations. For example, Steinfeldt, Vaughan, LaFollette, and Steinfeldt (2011) studied bullying behaviour among adolescent football players. Steinfeldt et al. (2011) were interested in the role masculinity and moral atmosphere, two social norms, played in determining whether or not a player engaged in bullying behaviour in such a sport context. Steinfeldt et al. (2011) reported that the moral atmosphere within football (i.e., peer influence and influential male figure) and adherence to male role norms were predictors of whether or not bullying behaviour occurred in that setting, with the most significant predictor being whether or not the most influential male figure in the player's life approved of the bullying behaviour or not. It would be interesting to see if similar research findings were reported for online bullying behaviour within soccer and indeed within other sports also. The sports of rugby, soccer and tennis have all recently been the subject of scrutiny from individuals interested in examining the cultures within these sports to determine if they foster more or less tolerance for some types of bullying behaviour, for example bullying against individuals within their own sport from the lesbian, gay, bisexual and transgender (LGBT) communities (British Broadcasting Channel; BBC, 2011). Empirical research in this area is also seriously lacking, however. Given that much of the cyberbullying literature regarding athletes to date has been anecdotal in nature, some specific cases of athletes being bullied online as reported in the media, to support this call for more research in this area, are presented next.

9.5 Examples of cyberbullying of athletes

One known case of an athlete being bullied online involved the British diver, Tom Daley, who during the 2012 London Summer Olympic Games was the subject of harassment and negative comments by another young British male (BBC, 2012). The outcome of this behaviour for the then 17-year-old male bully was arrest and caution by the British police who were able to track the individual to his home address using computer detection software. Tom Daley also re-posted the remarks made by the young male on his own Twitter account. The comments included references to Daley's father who had passed away a short time prior to the 2012 Olympic Games in London.

A similar reference to the death of a family member was reported in the case, in 2017, involving the Bournemouth FC and Irish soccer player, Harry Arter. However, in this case the perpetrator of the online attack was a fellow soccer (non-league) Hitchin Town FC player, Alfie Barker (The Irish Independent, 2017). Barker sent negative tweets to Arter following Arter's team's loss during a game against Arsenal FC which Bournemouth were winning 3–0 at one point in the match. Arter had, in 2015, lost a child to a stillbirth. Barker referred to Arter's child's death in his series of tweets. His conduct resulted in Barker's contracts with his registered team and also with his on-loan team being terminated. In his public apology to Arter following the incident, Barker commented that his consumption of alcohol was one of the factors that perhaps contributed to what he, and his father, described as completely out of character behaviour for Barker.

These experiences for Daley and Arter, and also for Gabby Douglas, as referred to earlier in this chapter, are similar to many other athletes who have also suffered cyberbullying and cyber harassment online. These athletes appear to have experienced distress and upset as a result of these online attacks. However, the responses of their fellow athletes, as well as the general public at large, in their messages of support for these athlete-victims could also have helped the athlete-victims to cope with these negative situations. This illustrates one of the positive elements of the online community, that is, its capacity to be a source of positive social support too, with the potential to even increase the personal self-esteem of the recipients of such support (Ellison, Steinfield, & Lampe, 2007; Raacke & Bonds-Raacke, 2008).

In the case of the 17-year-old male who was found to have engaged in the negative online behaviour against Tom Daley, he too like Barker, issued an online apology after the incident. In this case, the then teenager stated that he was just disappointed with Tom, and his diving partner, Pete Waterfield's performance in the synchronised diving Olympic competition. The teen commented that he had been 'rooting for them'. The age of this individual, at the time of the incident, is perhaps noteworthy, as some research studies have shown that teenagers, given their age and lower level of cognitive maturity (Steinberg, 2012) may often engage in spontaneous, risky behaviour that could be a result of them using the System 1 proposed by Kahneman (2011; as described in Chapter 7), rather than employing perhaps the more appropriate System 2, where the consequences of their actions are considered for a longer period of time (such as before posting a comment online that may upset or harm another person, socially and/or emotionally, or indeed harm themselves through the repercussions of their actions – arrest and caution in this case).

Given the apparent prevalence with which these online attacks against athletes appear to occur, some have surmised that one plausible reason why such attacks happen may be because of other online-related behaviour, namely online gambling behaviour. Many individuals place bets on the performances of athletes and their associated teams, and these individuals may become angry when the athletes they bet on are not successful in their performances and result in these online gamblers losing large amounts of money. Thus, their anger at this situation may precipitate their online negative bullying or harassing behaviour against these athletes (Rossingh, 2017).

Before examining in greater detail this, and other reasons, why athletes may often be the targets for specific online attacks, as well as what strategies have been implemented to date to help combat these attacks on athletes, let us first consider the main methods used to initiate such negative behaviours of cyberbullying and cyber harassment against athletes.

9.6 Cyberbullying of athletes – methods used

As with cyberbullying that takes place within other populations, the cyberbullying of athletes and indeed others within their sport environments (i.e., their coaches and support personnel, as well as sport officials) can occur in various ways, using a number of formats. Typically cyberbullying is orchestrated using methods such as social media platforms (e.g., Twitter and Facebook), text messaging, email and digital images (such as those shared on Instagram and Snapchat). Any or all of these formats may be used if an individual, or group of individuals, has the use of a smartphone or a computer with an Internet connection. New applications (apps) have also been the subject of some recent news items as specific vehicles used for cyberbullying, namely SimiSimi (Higgins, 2017; see definition on p. 161). However, these apps appear to be used more prominently and problematically within education settings.

For athletes (and some sport officials, such as referees), the traditional forms of bullying, without the use of the online world, still occur within their sport arenas. This is perhaps not surprising as some of the bullying research involving young adult populations has indicated that bully victims are typically bullied using both online and offline methods – in essence that cyberbullying is just another type of traditional bullying – rather than a new kind of bullying that occurs in isolation to other forms of bullying (Cassidy, Faucher, & Jackson, 2013; O'Moore, 2012). Wolke et al. (2017) explored if this claim was indeed the case, that "cyberbullying creates very few new victims" (p. 899). Their UK-based study of 2,754 adolescents, between the ages of 11 and 16 years, did indeed support this assertion that 'pure' cyber victimisation is rare, with only 4% of their sample who reported to be victims of bullying citing cyberbullying as the sole type of bullying they were subjected to. But can the same be said in the case of athletes? Are athletes subjected to bullying on and offline? Or, are they an example of a unique group of victims who are subjected to cyberbullying alone? This is unlikely, as athletes are often subjected to verbal taunting (such as booing) and harassment by spectators, offline, at their sport events (Morse, 2016). This kind of behaviour may be witnessed at soccer games in the English Premiership, for example. Some former athletes have spoken about the negative impact such spectators' actions can have on players' mental health and well-being (Hattenstone, 2012). Athletes typically experience online forms of bullying and harassment via their social media platforms such as Twitter and Facebook, as well as their image-based media of Instagram and Snapchat. Perhaps in order to understand the potential differences in their bullying landscape, however, compared to their non-athlete counterparts, the reasons *why* athletes may be victims of online bullying, and other similar negative abusive behaviours, should be explained. This is the focus of the next section.

9.7 Why are athletes popular targets for online bullying and harassment?

One question psychologists have been interested in answering regarding online bullying of any individual, athlete or non-athlete, is what motivates a bully to engage in negative behaviour towards other individuals (in the cases of athletes, individuals they have often never even met; Hambrick et al., 2010).

Based on previous research findings of cyberbullying online from which to draw comparisons, and acknowledging that many of these studies have been conducted in non-athlete contexts, some reasons why athletes may also be popular targets for negative online attention from others could be explained as due to phenomena such as *moral disengagement, diffusion and displacement of responsibility* as well as *dehumanisation of the victim*. Other reasons for the cyberbullying behaviour of athletes could be linked to feelings of *envy*, the *athlete not being physically present* to defend him or herself, or to challenge the bully, the *behaviour being perceived as easy* and *not really harmful* to the athlete-victim, the *anonymity assurances* that the online world often provides the bully with (although not always the case, as the Tom Daley example, cited above, demonstrated) and *anger* because of other sport-related behaviour outcomes as referred to earlier (e.g., gambling losses). These reasons are all explored here.

Some of the psychological literature and research findings available on moral behaviour has, in ways, helped to provide an answer to the question of why online bullying occurs. Cyberbullying itself, as a term, did not exist in everyday vocabulary prior to the early 2000s and some of the recent research on cyberbullying and cyber aggression has been informed by the study of moral behaviour, or more specifically, moral disengagement. *Moral disengagement* refers to situations where individuals' tendencies to judge themselves as morally wrong for their actions, and where emotions such as guilt and shame are experienced, are effectively switched off. The switching off of these judgements and emotions is what is thought to enable such individuals to behave in ways they might consider immoral within other contexts (Runions & Bak, 2015). Research on traditional bullying, on aggressive behaviour and on cyberbullying have all shown that bullies, and those that facilitate their negative behaviours (referred to in the psychology literature as 'bystanders'), typically exhibit high levels of this moral disengagement during such events (Runions & Bak, 2015).

Some interesting debates among researchers of bullying behaviour specifically carried out in online settings have focused on the topic of whether moral disengagement may actually be as relevant in online contexts because of the ease with which a person can act anonymously online (Pornari & Wood, 2010). Some researchers have argued that the technological world, where many young people now socialise, does indeed facilitate moral disengagement (Bauman, 2010). However, as a result of the somewhat confusing research perspective of whether or not moral disengagement is an important feature of online bullying, Runions and Bak (2015) attempted to examine how the features of the online world may facilitate moral disengagement. They suggested that the ease of disseminating information in the online world, as well as the often diffusion or displacement of responsibility reasons given by online bullies to explain away their actions (see the examples given in the preceding cases of Tom Daley and Harry Arter), as well as the dehumanisation of the victim, are some examples of how the online world can assist in this moral disengagement of online bullies. Some moral disengagement scales have also been recently adapted in an attempt to measure this potential moral disengagement of individuals in specific environments such as the online world (see Boardley & Kavussanu, 2011).

Apart from moral disengagement, other psychological concepts to explain online cyberbullying, as referred to by Runions and Bak (2015), such as diffusion of responsibility, displacement of responsibility, as well as revenge motives have been considered. Some of these concepts have been indicated more commonly than moral disengagement when aggressive behaviours occur, along with behaviours such as victim blaming (White-Ajmani & Bursik, 2014). The increased distance between the online victim and bully, created by the logistics of the online world (i.e., the inability of the bully to physically see the victim), has also been considered as a reason why online bullies have later reported that they did not regard their online actions as having caused any real harm to their victims (Pornari & Wood, 2010).

Another feature of the online world in potentially facilitating online bullying behaviour is that it allows for a degree of acceptance to take place of certain kinds of other potentially negative online behaviours that, if carried out in-person, would be considered serious and disturbing. For example, stalking a person in the middle of the night would typically be seen as extreme and unacceptable behaviour. However, portable technologies such as smartphones and tablets have made it appear as nothing unusual for a person to be reading another individual's online posts on social media, for example, in the middle of the night and then replying to them in a negative way. Runions, Shapka, Dooley, and Modecki (2013) referred to this phenomenon as *the affordances* that technology and the online world provides so many of its users, including individuals who follow athletes on social media, for example.

Somewhat related to the online bullying of athletes is research on bullying behaviour using computer-mediated communication devices that has included the exploration of these negative online behaviours in settings such as team competition online games (Kwak, Blackburn, & Hun, 2015). In their study, Kwak et al. analysed numerous online reports of toxic behaviours players engaged in while playing one of the most popular online games, 'The League of Legends'. Kwak et al. (2015) reported significant differences in participants' opinions regarding what actually constituted toxic behaviour by players in such contexts. They uncovered cultural differences in these opinions also. Is it then possible that similar cultural differences and perceptions or understanding of what really constitutes toxic behaviour in sport contexts could also exist for individuals who engage in the bullying and harassment of athletes online? Perhaps this is also an area worth investigating in the future in order to increase our understanding of why cyberbullying of many successful athletes takes place?

The 'envy' reason proposed for why individuals may engage in online bullying behaviour toward athletes could stem from a belief that athletes represent individuals who are some of society's best examples of individuals possessing expertise, health, wellness and prosperity qualities. Indeed, such is their influence that athletes have been reported as having greater sway over their fans' behaviours (i.e., for product endorsements) than other well-known individuals such as musicians and actors (Carlson & Donavan, 2008). However, this view of athletes being society's best examples of health and prosperity may actually be somewhat erroneous, or even a myth, given the recent numbers of athletes speaking about their susceptibility to, and experiences of, mental illness (Gleeson & Brady, 2017). Indeed, a common message promoted by many mental health advocates using some online media campaigns (see Table 10.1 in Chapter 10), is that participating in sport, while often regarded as having many positive mental health and well-being benefits (Stanton & Reaburn, 2014), does not provide immunity to those participating in these activities against all mental and physical health risks and illnesses (Sebbens, Hassmen, Crisp, & Wensley, 2016; see Chapter 10 for more discussions regarding this important issue). Despite this, for some individuals, athletes' status may trigger an envy response and be part of the reason why they engage in negative bullying and harassing behaviour of such sport individuals.

Regarding the *lack of physical presence* of the athlete and the *affordances* the online world offers, these are both plausible reasons also proposed for why the bullying of athletes is more prevalent now than it was before the digital age. In the past, athletes, given their often intimidating stature, size, strength, agility and speed, and indeed their popularity among their peers too, perhaps would not have been regarded as the typical targets for bullying behaviour from others. However, the Internet now provides individuals who are not strong or fast, successful or popular by comparison to such athletes, to target these individuals because all that is required to initiate such an attack on an athlete is an Internet-enabled mobile phone or computer, so such behaviours may be *perceived as easy* then also (Notar, Padgett, & Roden, 2013; Poland, 2010). The bully does not need to face the targeted victim in real life and often the bully can remain anonymous, although this is not always the case given that some individuals may be identified using tracking data by law enforcement agencies now (as in the case of Tom Daley's aggressor).

Another noteworthy reason posed for these negative behaviours directed at some athletes is, as cited earlier in this chapter, that the bullying behaviour may be related to other online behaviours of the individual perpetrators, namely their online gambling behaviours and the losses they incur when athletes' performances do not match favourably with what they predicted and bet upon. Such situations may evoke feelings of anger in the bullies and a desire to lash out at the individuals deemed at fault for their financial losses (Rossingh, 2017). But while this, and the other previously cited reasons, may all be plausible explanations for why such harassment and bullying behaviour occurs against athletes, the impact of the behaviour on the athlete victims can be just as serious with regard to their mental health and well-being as it is for other cyberbullied individuals, as cited earlier in this chapter (Corcoran, Connolly, & O'Moore, 2012).

9.8 Consequences of online bullying and harassment for athletes

Victims of cyberbullying have reported psychological symptoms including stress, anxiety, depression, loss of appetite and sleep disturbances, decreases in confidence and self-esteem levels, as well as an increased feelings of anger, along with frustrated outbursts of negative behaviour themselves, and even substance abuse and self-harm (see Connolly, 2016, for a review of the research in this area). In the case of athletes specifically, such responses to online bullying also occur, as anecdotal evidence indicates (and as was illustrated in earlier athlete quotations in this chapter), as well as another important negative impact related to their environment – that of their inability to perform well within their sport.

Having detailed: (i) some samples cases of athlete bullying and harassment online, (ii) some of the methods used to cyberbully and harass athletes, (iii) why athletes are the potential targets of such online attacks and (iv) some of the potential consequences of these behaviours on the athletes' psychological states, the next logical question is: What strategies have been proposed and implemented to date to help combat these attacks on athletes?

9.9 Current strategies for combating online bullying and harassment of athletes

9.9.1 Education partnerships

Some sport organisations have engaged their athletes in educational programmes focused on their use of the online world as a communication device and especially their use of social media (as indicated in Chapter 7). They have also been a part of public-partnership campaigns to promote the intolerance of bullying in its many forms and to encourage an atmosphere of mutual respect within sport environments. For example, the New York Jets were part of such an anti-bullying campaign in 2017 (Lange, 2017). These initiatives could help to bridge the 'disconnect' between the potential athlete victims of online bullying and their aggressors, by making the victims 'real' for the bullies (Kwak et al., 2015).

9.9.2 Team policies

Many teams have also made some decisions to ban the use of social media by their athletes at certain times, such as during training sessions or games (Hambrick et al., 2010). The goal of these policies is often to prevent athletes from engaging in online commentary that is not in keeping with their teams' or organisations' overall ethos or objectives. However, it can also act as a way to protect athletes from viewing any negative messages written about them during important times when they are attempting to perform to their best standard within their sport.

Some famous names from within the world of sport have openly commented on what they consider to be the bizarre nature of, and attraction to, today's online world. Some older managers from the English Premiership Soccer League, for example, have admitted they do not understand the appeal of social media for young players today. One such individual is Sir Alex Ferguson, the former manager of MUFC who, following a number of unpleasant incidents involving interactions between soccer players and members of the public on Twitter (i.e., Wayne Rooney and Darren Gibson), openly commented on his disapproval of the use of the social media platform, Twitter, by his players. Ferguson remarked in 2011 that he could not see why players "would be bothered with it" and that they should "get (themselves) down to the library and read a book" (Stone, 2011). So, only a few years ago, MUFC, based on such comments, did not appear to encourage the use of Twitter by its players (contrary to their new stance of supporting their players, if they wish to use social media platforms – see Chapters 7 and 8 for details on this). It was suggested to Sir Alex Ferguson in 2011 that players' interactions on social media could allow them to "keep in touch" with their fans (The Telegraph, 2011, p. 1). However, Ferguson replied the players could probably achieve that if they "just play well on the pitch" (The Telegraph, 2011, p. 1). Of course, if athletes are not engaging with the online world, one might think this protects them from online bullying, but this is not the case. They may still be the subject of online negative commentary in the same way they can be exposed to it in the offline world. And while the preceding comments of Sir Alex Ferguson, to a generation that grew up and performed within their sport before the digital age, may seem logical and sensible, the world is now, in so many ways, reliant upon technology. The return to a time without the Internet, Google, smartphones and apps is not likely to happen. Therefore, sport psychologists and cyber psychologists should aim to advance their research work on cyberbullying within sport populations in order to be well positioned to advise and assist the new generation of coaches, as well as their athletes, in coping with these new challenges in their world as a result of technology.

According to Notar et al. (2013), "cyberbullying, like traditional bullying, is about power" (p. 6). Individuals who engage in bullying and harassing behaviour may be attempting to gain some kind of social status, using bullying behaviour as a means to achieve this (Bauman, cited in Holloday, 2011). Sanctions for such negative bullying behaviours, including disciplinary measures, litigation and criminal prosecution (Beale & Hall, 2007), may result in bullies re-thinking their cyber 'power plays', to use a sport analogy. But these are only some of the measures used to redress such problems. Other suggestions for tackling online bullying within school and workplace settings could be effective for sport settings too. For example, many workplaces have a zero tolerance policy regarding cyberbullying and clearly state their companies' positions and consequences for individuals who engage in such behaviour within their environments (Synman & Loh, 2015). Sport organisations could also implement such policies to deal with incidences of cyberbullying and harassment within their own settings. However, this may not be effective in the case of athletes if they are being victimised by 'outsider' individuals. What could be useful for the athletes is to remind them of the transferable nature of the coping skills they use for their sport to help them cope with these other stressors. Their resilience training techniques could be effective in protecting them from the negative mental consequences of the cyberbullying behaviour of others also (Snyman & Loh, 2015; and as highlighted in earlier chapters of this text).

9.10 Conclusion, including some directions for future research

To recap, the aims of this chapter were to outline some methods commonly used to cyberbully, harass, troll and stalk athletes, to present some reasons why athletes may often be the targets of such negative online behaviours and to highlight some current strategies employed by sport teams, sport organisations and lawmakers to counteract the negative online behaviours athletes appear to be frequently subjected to.

As commented in this chapter, empirical research on the prevalence of online victimisation of athletes in the form of cyberbullying and cyber harassment within sport-specific environments is lacking, as was evident when researching this topic. Therefore, more empirical research examining the impact such negative experiences could have on the physical and mental well-being of such athlete victims, as well as on their sport performances, would be beneficial in order to understand the nature of this problem for these victims.

As athletic performances are completed in public arenas, they will inevitability continue to attract attention from large numbers of the public. It is perhaps inevitable too that, at times, such attention will be unfavourable, unwanted and/or unwarranted, especially if it occurs outside the context or relevance of the athletes' sport and public lives. For example, athletes' personal lives, as well as their sport lives, can be the target of unpleasant commentary from members of the general public (ABC News, 2016) and this too could also then have a negative, distracting impact on the athletes' ability to perform well within their sport.

Policing bodies and legislators, as well as some sport organisations themselves, are beginning to take a stricter stance regarding this problematic issue in order to protect the athletes, in the same way that members of the general public are entitled to be protected from such threatening and negative behaviour (Australian Institute of Sport, 2016).

In the future, it is suggested that sport cyber psychologists look to bridge the gap in the current psychological literature on cyberbullying and cyber harassment of athletes by not only carrying out studies that examine these issues in a sport context, but also by evaluating some of the current safeguards put in place by various sport and non-sport policing bodies to protect their athletes from such negative cyber experiences, often elicited by individuals positioned outside of the athletes' sport world.

9.11 Open-ended discussion questions

1   What possible psychological impact could cyberbullying specifically have on the mental health and well-being of athletes?
2   How can athletes be protected from such cyber harassment and bullying? For example, can the same principles and guidelines issued in education and workplace settings be effectively applied to combat cyberbullying in sport settings also?
3   Could the cultures that already exist within some sports be a reason why anti-bullying policies may not be successful and, if so, how might this be changed?

9.12 Practical exercise

Devise an anti-bullying policy for application within a chosen sport-specific environment. Suggest some strategies that could be effectively used to evaluate the success, or not, of such a policy.

References

ABC News. (2016). *Rio 2016: Gymnast Gabby Douglas heartbroken by social media trolls.* Retrieved from www.abc.net.au/news/2016-08-16/rio-2016-gabby-douglas-heartbroken-by-social-media-tro/7746526

Australian Institute of Sport. (2016). *AIS helping protect athletes from cybercrime.* Retrieved from www.ausport.gov.au/news/asc_news/story_650613_ais_helping_protect_athletes_from_cybercrime

Baruch, Y. (2005). Bullying on the net: Adverse behaviour on email and its impact. *Information & Management, 42,* 361–371.

Bauman, S. (2010). Cyberbullying in a rural intermediate school: An exploratory study. *Journal of Early Adolescence, 41,* 191–201.

BBC. (2011). *Gay sports stars in No. 10 to back anti-homophobia plan.* Retrieved from www.bbc. com/news/uk-politics-13878271

BBC. (2012). *Tom Daley Twitter abuse: Boy arrested in Weymouth.* Retrieved from www.bbc. co.uk/news/uk-england-19059127

Beale, A.V., & Hall, K.R. (2007). Cyberbullying: What schools administrators (and parents) can do. *The Clearing House, 81,* 8–12.

Boardley, I.D., & Kavussanu, M. (2011). Moral disengagement in sport. *International Review of Sport and Exercise Psychology, 4,* 93–108.

Carbone-Lopez, K., Esbensen, F.A., & Brick, B.T. (2010). Correlates and consequences of peer victimization: Gender differences in direct and indirect forms of bullying. *Youth Violence and Juvenile Justice, 8,* 332–350.

Carlson, B.D., & Donavan, D.T. (2008). Concerning the effect of athlete endorsements on brand and team-related intentions. *Sport Marketing Quarterly, 17,* 154–162.

Cassidy, W., Faucher, C., & Jackson, M. (2013). Cyberbullying among youth: A comprehensive review of current international research and its implications and application to policy and practice. *School Psychology International: Special Issue on Cyberbullying, 34,* 575–612.

Connolly, I. (2016). Young people and the Internet. In I. Connolly, M. Palmer, H. Barton, & G. Kirwan (Eds.), *An introduction to cyberpsychology* (pp. 224–238). London, UK: Routledge-Taylor and Francis Group.

Corcoran, L., Connolly, I., & O'Moore, M. (2012). Cyberbullying in Irish schools: An investigation of personality and self-concept. *Irish Journal of Psychology, 33,* 153–165.

Coyne, I., Axtell, C., Sprigg, C.A., Farley, S., Best, L., & Kwok, O. (2015). Understanding the relationship between experiencing workplace cyberbullying, employee mental strain and job satisfaction: A disempowerment approach. *The International Journal of Human Resource Management, 28,* 945–972.

Ellison, N.B., Steinfield, C., & Lampe, C. (2007). The benefits of Facebook 'friends': Social capital and college students' use of online social network sites. *Journal of Computer-Mediated Communication, 12,* 1143–1168.

Farberov, S. (2017). *Heartbreak as middle school cheerleader 12, dies in a suspected suicide, on the same day her mother complained to her school that she was being bullied on social media.* Retrieved from www.dailymail.co.uk/news/article-4621936/Cheerleader-12-dies-possible-suicide-bullying.html

Gleeson, S., & Brady, E. (2017). *When athletes share their battles with mental illness.* Retrieved from www.usatoday.com/story/sports/2017/08/30/michael-phelps-brandon-marshall-mental-health-battles-royce-white-jerry-west/596857001/

Hambrick, M.E., Simmons, J.M., Greenhalgh, G.P., & Greenwell, C.T. (2010). Understanding professional athletes' use of Twitter: A content analysis of athlete tweets. *International Journal of Sport Communication, 3,* 454–471.

Hattenstone, S. (2012). *Racism in football: Putting the boot in.* Retrieved from https://www. theguardian.com/football/2012/jul/13/racism-football-premier-league-campbell

Higgins, A. (2017). *Principals ban SimiSimi-App banned in Irish Schools due to cyberbullying and sexually explicit language.* Retrieved from www.thesun.ie/news/790109/app-banned-in-irish-schools-due-to-cyberbullying-and-sexually-explicit-language/

Hinduja, S., & Patchin, J. (2010). Bullying, cyberbullying and suicide. *Archives of Suicide Research, 14,* 206–210.

Holloday, J. (2011). Cyberbullying. *Education Digest, 76,* 4–9.

Irish Independent. (2017). *Non-league player sacked for sending 'disgraceful' tweets to Ireland's Harry Arter over his stillborn child.* Retrieved from www.independent.ie/sport/soccer/nonleague-player-sacked-for-sending-disgraceful-tweets-to-irelands-harry-arter-over-his-stillborn-daughter-35340732.html

Juvonen, J., & Gross, E.F. (2008). Extending the school grounds? Bullying experiences in cyberspace. *Journal of School Health, 78,* 496–505.

Kahneman, D. (2011). *Thinking fast and slow.* London: Penguin.

Katzer, C., & Fetchenhauer, D. (2007). Aggression and sexuelle Vikimisierung in Chatrooms. In M. Gollwitzer, V. Schnedier, C. Ulrick, T. Steffke, A. Schulz, & J. Pfetsch (Eds.), *Gewalt-praevention bei Kindern und Jugendlichen. Aktuelle Erkenntnisse aus Forschung and Praxis.* Goettingen: Hogrefe.

Katzer, C., Fetchenhauer, D., & Belschak, F. (2009). Cyberbullying: Who are the victims? *Journal of Media Psychology: Theories, Methods and Applications, 21,* 25–36.

Kavanagh, E.J., & Jones, I. (2014). #cyberviolence: Developing a typology for understanding virtual maltreatment in sport. In D. Rhind & C. Brackenridge (Eds.), *Researching and enhancing athlete welfare* (pp. 34–43). London: Brunel University Press.

Kwak, H., Blackburn, J., & Hun, S. (2015). *Exploring cyberbullying and other toxic behaviour in team competition online games.* CHI Conference on Human Factors in Computing Systems. Seoul, Republic of Korea, April 18–23, 2015.

Lange, R. (2017). *Jets host anti bullying symposium.* Retrieved from www.newyorkjets.com/news/article-randylangefb/Jets-Host-Anti-Bullying-Symposium-/ca418ce3-a629-4b6c-b031-ed7a7425b193

Mishna, F., Cook, C., Gadalla, T., Daciuk, J., & Solomon, S. (2010). Cyberbullying behaviours among middle and high school students. *American Journal of Orthopsychiatry, 80,* 362–374.

Morse, F. (2016). *Renaud Lavillenie: Crowds booing him to tears 'shocking' says IOC chief.* Retrieved from https://inews.co.uk/essentials/sport/olympics/renaud-lavillenie-crowds-booing-tears-shocking-says-ioc-chief/

Notar, C.E., Padgett, S., & Roden, J. (2013). Cyberbullying: A review of the literature. *Universal Journal of Educational Research, 1,* 1–9.

Olweus, D. (1993). *Bullying at school: What we know and what we can do.* Cambridge, MA: Blackwell.

O'Moore, M. (2012). Cyberbullying: The situation in Ireland: Pastoral care in education. *An International Journal of Personal, Social and Emotional Development, 30,* 209–223.

Poland, S. (2010). Cyberbullying continues to challenge educators. *District Administration, 46,* 55.

Pornari, C.D., & Wood, J. (2010). Peer and cyber aggression in secondary school students: The role of moral disengagement, hostile attributional bias, and outcome expectancies. *Aggressive Behaviour, 36,* 81–94.

Raacke, J., & Bonds-Raacke, J. (2008). MySpace and Facebook: Applying the uses and gratifications theory to exploring friend-networking sites. *Cyberpsychology & Behaviour, 11,* 169–174.

Rooney, B., Connolly, I., Hurley, O., Kirwan, G., & Power, A. (2015). Social media and networking behaviour. In A. Attrill (Ed.), *Cyberpsychology* (pp. 88–102). Oxford, UK: Oxford University Press.

Rossingh, D. (2017). *Australian open: 'Hope you die slowly – tennis star trolled'.* Retrieved from http://edition.cnn.com/2017/01/18/tennis/australian-open-tennis-trolls-social-media-hate-epidemic/index.html

Rothon, C., Head, J., Klineberg, E., & Stansfield, S. (2011). Can social support protect bullied adolescents from adverse outcomes? A prospective study on the effects of bullying on the educational achievements and mental health of adolescents at secondary schools in east London. *Journal of Adolescents, 34,* 576–588.

Runions, K.C., & Bak, M. (2015). Online moral disengagement, cyberbullying and cyber-aggression. *Cyberpsychology, Behaviour and Social Networking, 18,* 400–405.

Runions, K.C., Shapka, J.D., Dooley, J., & Modecki, K. (2013). Cyber-aggression and victimisation and social information processing: Integrating the medium of and the message. *Psychology of Violence*, *3*, 9–26.

Sebbens, J., Hassmen, P., Crisp, D., & Wensley, K. (2016). Mental Health in Sport (MHS): Improving the early intervention knowledge and confidence of elite sport staff. *Frontiers in Psychology*, *7*, 911. Retrieved from http://dx.doi.org/10.3389/fpsyg.2016.00911

Stanton, R., & Reaburn, P. (2014). Exercise and the treatment of depression: A review of the exercise program variables. *Journal of Science and Medicine in Sport*, *17*, 177–182. doi: 10.1016/j.jsams.2013.03.010

Steinfeldt, J.A., Vaughan, E.L., LaFollette, J.R., & Steinfeldt, M.C. (2011). Bullying among adolescent football players: Role of masculinity and moral atmosphere. *Psychology of Men & Masculinity*, *13*, 340–353.

Steinberg, L. (2012). *A social neuroscience perspective on adolescent risk taking*. Retrieved from www.youtube.com/watch?v=LrVPKYsRxMw

Stone, S. (2011). *Alex Ferguson slams Twitter and considers banning Manchester United players*. Retrieved from www.independent.co.uk/sport/football/premier-league/alex-ferguson-slams-twitter-and-considers-banning-manchester-united-players-2286889.html

Suler, J. (2004). The online disinhibition effect. *Cyberpsychology and Behaviour*, *7*, 321–326. doi: 10.1089/1094931041291295

Synman, R., & Loh, J. (2015). Cyberbullying at work: The mediating role of optimism between cyberbullying and job outcomes. *Computers in Human Behaviour*, *53*, 161–168.

The Telegraph. (2011). *Twitter is 'a waste of time', says Manchester United manager Sir Alex Ferguson*. Retrieved from http://www.telegraph.co.uk/sport/football/teams/manchester-united/8525859/Twitter-is-a-waste-of-time-says-Manchester-United-manager-Sir-Alex-Ferguson.html

The Telegraph. (2015). *Online trick 'led to teen boy's suicide'*. Retrieved from www.telegraph.co.uk/news/uknews/law-and-order/11661272/Online-trick-led-to-teenage-boys-suicide.html

White-Ajmani, M.L., & Bursik, K. (2014). Situational context moderates the relationship between moral disengagement and aggression. *Psychology of Violence*, *4*, 90–100.

Wolke, D., Lee, K., & Guy, A. (2017). Cyberbullying: A storm in a teacup? *European Journal of Child & Adolescent Psychiatry*, *26*, 899–908.

Ybarra, M.L., Diener-West, M., & Leaf, P.J. (2007). Examining the overlap in Internet harassment and school bullying: Implications for school intervention. *Journal of Adolescent Health*, *41*, S42–S50.

Yuvonen, J., & Gross, E.F. (2008). Extending the school grounds? – Bullying experiences in cyberspace. *Journal of School Health*, *78*, 496–505.

10

ATHLETES' MENTAL HEALTH AND PROBLEMATIC ONLINE BEHAVIOURS

CASE STUDY 10

John is a 22-year-old Gaelic football player from a well-known Irish county team. He is also an active user of a well-known online gambling website. John's family and teammates are unaware that he has accumulated debts from his gambling habit of over 50,000 euros. John is experiencing symptoms of severe anxiety and a decrease in his sport performances as a result of his online gambling behaviour.

(i) How has the online world facilitated John's problematic online behaviours?
(ii) How might John's relationships with his family members, friends and teammates be affected upon learning of John's behaviour?
(iii) What general lessons can be learned from this case study (i.e., what advice should be given to young athletes, like John, who wish to use online gambling platforms for social and entertainment purposes)?

10.1 Overview

Finally, here in Chapter 10, some specific technology-related mental health issues for athletes are discussed. Problematic Internet-based behaviours that athletes may display when interacting with the online world can include excessive online gambling, problematic gaming, the overuse/misuse of social networking platforms, problematic online purchasing (i.e., buying supplements containing banned ingredients) as well as negative information seeking (i.e., related to restrictive dieting, self-harm and suicide, for example). Some of these issues are discussed in light of various cognitive-behavioural frameworks that psychology researchers have applied to explain these behaviours. The consequences of such negative behaviours, specifically for athletes, are also addressed in this chapter. Some strategies aimed at protecting and helping athletes in these situations to overcome their technology-assisted problems within their lives are also presented.

10.2 Learning objectives

1   To introduce the reader to some of the problematic Internet-based behaviours displayed by athletes and to provide some explanations for why these behaviours are sometimes a problem for sportspeople
2   To highlight the cognitive processes that may influence athletes' decisions to engage in such behaviours
3   To provide some solutions for how such individuals who seek out treatment for such behaviours may be assisted
4   To make some suggestions for how these problematic, technology-facilitated, behaviours might be studied in more depth among athlete populations in the future

10.3 Definitions of relevant terms

Addiction

The term used to describe behaviours in which an individual feels compelled to engage, without a sense of feeling in control of the behaviours; being a 'slave' to the behaviour. A behaviour is regarded as addictive for a person if it possesses these six components: salience, mood alteration, tolerance, withdrawal symptoms, relapse and conflict.

Conflict

This refers to a clash or struggle a person experiences with another person or with a behaviour.

Cybertherapy

Therapy that is instigated using Internet-based tools or approaches.

Escapism

A behaviour that provides individuals with a way to forget about their real-life situations for a period of time.

eSports

This term is used to describe electronic sports. Electronic sports are defined by Hamari and Sjöblom (2017, p. 211) as "a form of sports where the primary aspects of the sport are facilitated by electronic systems; the input of players and teams as well as the output of the eSport system are mediated by human–computer inter-faces". Other phrases synonymous with the term eSports include cybersports, gam-ing, competitive computer games and virtual sports.

Mental toughness

An agreed definition of this concept is lacking, with some researchers regarding it as trait-like (Clough, Earle, & Sewell, 2002), while others have referred to it in a more process-focused way (Coulter, Mallett, & Gucciardi, 2010). It has been considered an ability to overcome and cope with pressure, stress and various life challenges in order to achieve goals (similar in ways to the term resilience, defined futher on; see Cowden, Meyer-Weitz, & Oppong Asante, 2016, for a review of this construct).

Mood modification

A behaviour that has the power to change the mood state of the individual who engages in that behaviour (e.g., the 'buzz' individuals may report experiencing from engaging in certain behaviours).

Relapse

This term refers to a return to a previously ceased behaviour, such as the taking of drugs or consuming alcohol. People who have addictive conditions may suffer one or more relapses of their behaviours before they successfully cease the negative behaviour indefinitely.

Resilience

This is described as a dynamic process that involves some positive adaptation by an individual when faced with adverse situations (Luthar, Cicchetti, & Becker, 2000).

Salience

This word describes the way in which a behaviour becomes the most important thing in an individual's life and dominates his/her thought process.

Tolerance

This refers to the situation in which an individual needs larger amounts of a substance, or increased time engaging in a behaviour, in order to experience the same 'high', or 'buzz', similar to the preceding description for a person addicted to a drug, who reports needing to consume larger amounts of the substance in order to experience the same high from the compound.

Virtual athletes

These 'athletes' are electronically represented individuals who perform or compete in a virtually represented sport world. As the term virtual means 'not being real', or artificial in nature, these skilled performances are, likewise, not performed in a real capacity, but rather only take place in a digital, computer-based setting.

Withdrawal symptoms

These symptoms refer to the unpleasant feelings a person often experiences when prevented from partaking in a behaviour. Commonly reported psychological symptoms of withdrawal or being prevented from engaging in a certain behaviour include irritability, a negative mood or feelings of moodiness, confusion and a lack of ability to concentrate.

10.4 Introduction

Until recently, much of the sport and performance psychology research, and applied consultancy work, focused on performance enhancement–related issues. However, sport psychologists, as well as mental health professionals, have now begun to emphasise the importance of athletes' mental health and well-being also. Contrary to public opinion that elite athletes are somehow 'super human' (Lebrun & Collins, 2017), they are, in fact, not immune to mental health problems, with some research studies placing them at an equivalent risk to that of the general population (Gulliver, Griffiths, Mackinnon, Batterham, & Stanimirovic, 2015; Rice et al., 2016). Indeed, other studies have put athletes at a higher risk of certain mental health issues, such as depression (Hughes & Leavey, 2012) and eating disorders (Thompson & Sherman, 2014). They have also been shown to experience other mental health problems such as anxiety and substance abuse (Gouttebarge, Backx, Aoki, & Kerkhoffs, 2015). Cases of athletes across many sports not adapting well to the pressures of life as athletes, or indeed as former professional athletes when they have retired from their sport careers have been noted, such as this quote from retired Irish 400 m track and field athlete, David Gillick (2017), illustrates: "I wasn't happy with my day-to-day life and found it hard to get stimulated by anything. Nothing really 'excited' me and I was constantly in a negative mood" (speaking about the impact of his retirement from athletics on his mental health). Indeed, tragic outcomes in news bulletins in recent years have highlighted cases of high-profile former athletes taking their own lives, such has been their state of mental distress post-retirement from professional sport (Williams, 2017).

While such tragic cases are a reminder of the high levels of stress athletes often face in their chosen careers (MacNamara & Collins, 2015), a more positive consequence to emerge from such sad cases has been the initiation of conversations within the sport domain about the importance of equipping athletes with the necessary skills and supports in order for them to cope not only with the pressures and challenges presented to them in their lives as athletes, but also those presented to them in their lives after retirement. Many sport organisations have launched mental health campaigns to promote the importance of athletes seeking out social and professional support when they think they are not coping with the challenges life is presenting to them. See Table 10.1 for examples of recent mental health–focused campaigns in some sport settings.

Along with this somewhat change in focus, away from the solely dominant issue of performance enhancement in elite sport, some terminology used within sport

TABLE 10.1 Examples of some sport-linked, mental health, social media campaigns

Organisation and Country	Twitter Hashtag for the Campaign	Weblink Resource
Gaelic Players Association (GPA; Ireland)	#itsthelittlethings	www.gaa.ie/my-gaa/community-and-health/mental-fitness/little-things
National Football League Players Association (NFLPA; USA)	#MentalHealth	www.nflpa.com/
Rugby Players Ireland (Ireland)	#TackleYourFeelings	www.tackleyourfeelings.com/
Rugby league & rugby union (UK, Ireland and Australia)	#StateofMind	www.stateofmindsport.org/
The Rugby Players' Association (UK)	#LiftTheWeight	https://therpa.co.uk/lifttheweight/
Multi-sports (UK)	#HeadsTogether	www.headstogether.org.uk/
Guernsey Mind (UK)	#TeamTalk	www.guernseymind.org.gg/about-guernsey-mind/team-talk-campaign/

psychology has also begun to change in relation to mental health constructs, with phrases such as 'mental toughness' being replaced by 'resilience', for example (see the work of Sarkar & Fletcher, 2013, 2017, on this topic). However, some have commented that resilience may just be a component of mental toughness (Cowden et al., 2016). But the replacement of terms such as mental toughness with resilience is, perhaps, more in harmony with communicating the message that athletes are not super human, rather, they too, IF in need of help and support, should be encouraged to seek it out. They should also be encouraged to speak about their weaknesses or failures, to cry and feel comfortable expressing their emotions. Thankfully, things are beginning to change, with many famous elite athletes, across a range of sports, speaking out publically about their mental health struggles (Gleeson & Brady, 2017). Global forms of communication using the Internet and social media networks, as detailed in prior chapters in this text, has helped to shape this transformation and spread this positive message of mental health awareness in elite sport. The use of the online environment has enabled many athlete-focused mental health and well-being campaigns to be shared and promoted on a scale that could never have happened before the age of the Internet. However, the online world has also provided athletes with the tools to engage in problematic behaviours that could damage their mental and physical health as well. These issues are the focus of the content for the remainder of this chapter.

10.5 Problematic Internet behaviours displayed by athletes

So, while mental health issues among athletes are now being spoken about in many positive ways using the online world, this world has also provided athletes with a tool for engaging in problematic behaviours, that can be hidden more from others than would perhaps have been the case in the past, before the existence of the Internet or advanced smart technologies. The ease with which athletes, and others, can now use their mobile phones to: (i) engage in online gambling, (ii) order products online and (iii) search for negative forms of information, is startling. Some professionals working in addiction services with athletes have reported increased numbers of their clients presenting with such disordered behaviours (Harris, 2014; The Irish Times, 2012), and their impact on such athletes' lives are often immense. Retired Armagh Gaelic football player, Oisin McConville, speaking about his gambling addiction, for example, stated: "I felt as if the walls were closing in on me. I couldn't sleep, and I became suicidal" (cited in Orpen, 2015). Athletes speaking out in this way about their problems should be considered as very brave, and their honesty is commendable. Their actions help to heighten public awareness of these issues and bring them out into the public domain for discussion.

But what are these common problematic Internet-facilitated behaviours and how are various technologies implicated in their prevalence in today's society? Some of the research findings available to illustrate the extent of these issues within sport settings, as well as some solutions for how such behaviours are currently, and may in the future be treated are discussed. Suggestions for how individuals working with such athletes (e.g., their psychologists, coaches, and support networks) might help to educate and protect athletes from engaging in such problematic behaviours, are also presented. Some Internet behaviours that have the potential to lead to serious mental and physical health problems for athletes include: (i) excessive general Internet use, as well as, more specifically, (ii) excessive social networking, (iii) problematic online gambling, (iv) problematic information seeking and (v) excessive gaming. Some of these issues, considering athlete populations, are explored in the following sections.

10.5.1 Excessive general Internet use

Excessive Internet use is considered to be linked to impulse-control disorder (Young, 1998). It does not involve the ingestion of potentially toxic substances, for example alcohol, tobacco or illegal drugs such as cocaine, heroin or methamphetamines. However, it may be considered a disorder that shares similar characteristics of dependence or addiction in the way such substances do, namely those of mood disturbances, salience, tolerance, withdrawal symptoms, relapse and conflict (Block, 2008).

Caplan (2007, 2010) devised a theory to explain Internet misuse, stating that it provided a type of communication that helped some individuals to avoid feelings of loneliness and anxiety. However, the use of the term 'Internet addiction' remains a somewhat controversial discussion point among academics and practitioners specifically regarding whether or not such a mental disorder actually does exist (Flood, 2016; Kirwan & Power, 2014).

While the debate around Internet addiction or dependence continues, some screening tools have been devised to test for excessive Internet use. One such example is the 20-item Internet Addiction Test (IAT; Young, 1998). This tool allows Internet use to be categorised in four ways (1 – no addictive behaviour is evident, 2 – mild, 3 – moderate or 4 – excessive). Some studies have attempted to link excessive Internet use to personality traits. For example, traits such as extroversion, socialisation, awareness, neuroticism and openness to experimentation have been linked to the risk of addiction to social networking sites and susceptibility to excessive Internet use (Griffiths, 2013; Griffiths, Kuss, & Demetrovics, 2014). Sensation seeking has also been positively associated with Internet addiction, especially among young adolescents (Li, Zhang, Zhen, & Wnag, 2010, 2016; Bitton & Medina, 2015). Sensation seeking, as a personality trait, is typified by a willingness to engage in often risky behaviours that could potentially result in harm to the individual. These behaviours are engaged in, in the pursuit of a more stimulating and enjoyable affective experience (often referred to as a 'buzz' or a high, in everyday language). Interestingly, athletes often refer to such intense feelings when engaged in their sport endeavours. Perhaps this is one explanation for why they may be at risk of some of the types of excessive online activity to be discussed next, especially when they retire from their sport or are injured? Their online behaviour may be motivated by a desire to seek out experiences that mimic their 'sport high'. Anecdotal evidence supports this assertion. Indeed the quote from athlete David Gillick at the start of this chapter alludes to this 'difficulty in getting stimulated' and that 'nothing excited me' (upon retiring from athletics in David's case).

However, more research to date appears to be focused on the specific Internet-facilitated behaviours individuals actually engage in (rather than on their general Internet excessive use), behaviours such as excessive social networking, excessive online gambling and problematic information seeking. These activities, and how they relate to athlete populations, are the focus of the following sections of this chapter.

10.5.2 Excessive social networking

Like many individuals within the general population, elite athletes are keen users of social media (discussed in Chapter 7). As such, they are also susceptible to the problematic behaviours associated with the overuse of such networking platforms. But what is considered excessive or problematic social networking? As mentioned previously in the definition of addiction, Griffiths (2005, 2013) described a behaviour as an addiction if it possesses six key components, namely: (i) salience, (ii) mood modification, (iii) tolerance, (iv) withdrawal symptoms, (v) relapse and (vi) conflict. However, a key problem with the research in this particular area is the lack of a clear model or description of what actually constitutes 'excessive' social networking or an 'addiction to social networking'. Despite this, some authors have spoken about it and used terms such as Facebook Addiction Disorder or SNS Addiction Disorder, if the behaviours exhibited by individuals lead to the following situations for these individuals within their lives: (i) a neglect of their personal lives, (ii) mental preoccupation with the activity, (iii) the activity provides escapism for them, (iv) they experience mood modification, (v) tolerance to the activity occurs (they engage in the activity for longer periods of time before reporting the 'high' from it) and finally (vi) concealment of the behaviour.

Problems with the methodologies used to investigate such SNS addiction issues have also been highlighted (Griffiths, 2015). For example, many of the studies examining such issues have focused on young, female, convenient and small participant groups (Cam & Isbulan, 2012; Koc & Gulyagci, 2013). Also of note is the bias in favour of examining the SNS of Facebook alone (Griffiths, 2012), without considering other SNS platforms highlighted in other chapters of this text, such as Twitter, Instagram and Snapchat. With these notes of caution in mind, it could, perhaps, be regarded as 'problematic social networking behaviour' if the behaviour begins to negatively affect the personal, family and/or working life of the individual engaged in that SNS behaviour. Indeed, the same criteria could be applied to any other problematic behaviour that occurs, either online or offline. However, athlete-focused research regarding their specific potential for excessive SNS use is needed, as findings in this area appear to be extremely lacking and yet the implications of such use for athletes' mental health and well-being could be significant, based on the findings of research in this area among other populations with shared demographics (Griffiths, 2015). However, an area where athlete populations have been the focus of more empirical research is in the area of problematic online gambling. This issue in the context of athlete groups is explored next.

10.5.3 Problematic online gambling

One recognised addiction where technology has increasingly been accused of playing a significant facilitative role is in the area of online gambling. Before the technology era, gamblers had to travel to a betting premises in order to place wagers on events (Orpen, 2015). However, now nearly all such betting companies have an online presence. This makes it much easier for individuals, such as professional athletes, who often have an inherent interest in sport performances and outcomes (and given their areas of performance expertise, may be more likely to predict a sport performance outcome correctly; The Irish Times, 2012), to engage in such activities. Professional athletes may also have surplus income and extensive periods of leisure time in which to place bets. The ease with which, in the click of a button on their laptops or smart devices once they have Internet connections, they can engage in such activities is perhaps one of the attractive features of the activity, along with the secrecy such an activity provides (unlike other excessive behaviours such as alcohol or drug consumption). The dangers of such recreational behaviours then leading to excessive practices and having negative consequences for athletes' lives have been extensively documented in the media (Harris, 2014; The Irish Times, 2012).

The increasing numbers of individuals engaging in online gambling has prompted concerns over these consequences of such behaviours for many at-risk individuals. Gambling, while a pleasant form of entertainment for some individuals, has the potential to be mentally, physically, socially and economically damaging for individuals who are unable to control the behaviour. Similar to research findings on negative psychological associations with excessive Internet use (see Caplan, 2002; Jang, Hwang, & Chio, 2008; Jenero, Flores, Gomez-Vela, Gonzalez-Gill, & Caballo, 2007), problematic gambling, both on and offline in general has been associate with psychological conditions such as depression, anxiety and increased stress (see the case study of John at the beginning of this chapter as an example of this), as well as having social consequences for the individuals, such as loneliness and isolation, as reported in both adolescent and adult populations (Gupta & Derevensky, 1998; Kessler et al., 2008; Porter, Ungar, Frisch, & Chorpra, 2004; Ste-Marie, Gupta, & Derevensky, 2002). There is, however, also evidence to suggest that some psychological conditions precede the emergence of problematic gambling behaviour (see Kessler et al., 2008, for details on such conditions).

Researchers interested in this specific area of gambling have focused on the *characteristics, prevalence and associated risk factors* for individuals who have become problem gamblers (Gainsbury, Russell, Hing, & Blaszczynski, 2013; Hing, Russell, Gainbury, & Blaszczynski, 2014). When compared to offline gamblers, online gamblers are more often males, who gamble on a greater range of activities and spend more on their gambling behaviour (Gainsbury, Russell, Wood, Hing, & Blaszczynski, 2015; Wood & Williams, 2007, 2009). Often lacking in the research on online gambling to date has been the type of online gambling considered most problematic for at-risk individuals. Recently, Hing, Russell, and Browne (2017) did specifically identify different problematic forms of gambling (i.e., online or offline), as well as the specific forms of gambling engaged in by problem gamblers (i.e., land-based, Electronic Gambling Machines (EGMs), race betting and sport betting). Hing et al. (2017) did not, however, identify the specific risk factors that could lead a non-problematic offline gambler to become a problematic online gambler. This is an area where future research would be most welcome among athlete and non-athlete populations alike, if effective solutions to this issue are to be devised.

As mentioned earlier, the increased use of online platforms on which to place wagers on all kinds of sport events is thought to have considerably facilitated the rise in problematic online gambling among the general population and, especially of interest here, among often young, elite athlete populations. Reasons why such online, problematic gambling may be more of an issue for these successful young, mainly male, athletes have been proposed. They include (as was alluded to earlier): (i) *more disposable incomes* among such groups, due to their higher comparable salaries from their sport careers, when compared to the earnings of their non-elite, athlete peers and (ii) *more extensive downtime/free time* that such successful young athletes have scheduled into their work day due to the differences in the physical demands placed upon their bodies to enable them to do their jobs in the best possible state. For example, comparing a male athlete's training day with that of a typical eight-hour working day for most young males, only a small part of any one day for elite professional athletes is devoted to actually engaging in their training and competing activities. Other long periods of their time are then devoted to resting/recovery from training loads, eating (often referred to as 'refuelling' within sport environments) and physiotherapy sessions to assist in the physical recovery of muscles from extensive use, as well as video analysis sessions and team meetings. It is not surprising then that boredom (mentioned as a feature of sport life for some athletes in previous chapters also) may be experienced by these young elite athletes and that they then may seek out other activities, such as online gambling to engage in, in order to fill in these gaps in their free time. A third possible reason why online gambling behaviours may be a problem for elite athletes is that the *emotional feedback* or 'buzz' that such risk-taking behaviour may provide for these individuals (as mentioned earlier) may put retiring athletes at a higher risk for such activities too (also mentioned earlier).

Interestingly, new research on problematic online gambling has examined this specific 'buzz' issue in the context of the flow state (also referred to as a peak performance state; Moran & Toner, 2017). Research by Csikszentmihalyi (1975) set in motion the extensive interest in this area within the psychological literature, and sport environments have provided interesting settings in which to study this phenomenon (Schuler & Brunner, 2009; Swann, Piggott, Crust, Keegan, & Hemmings, 2015). Typically, the flow state is considered to be a positive state with nine characteristics, including a sense of focus, a sense of control, transformation of time and loss of self-consciousness (Martin & Jackson, 2008). *Immersion* in the activity is also one of the key features of the flow state, which can be described as a feeling of total involvement in the activity being carried out. Given the often pleasant and desirable nature of such a feeling, the pursuit of this feeling through greater involvement in the activity can, however, lead to problems, such as addictive behaviours emerging. Indeed, Csikszentmihalyi (1975) referred to the potential addictive properties of the flow state in his early research on the phenomenon. However, research specifically linking the flow state with addictive online behaviours has resulted in inconclusive and contradictory findings (see Chou & Ting, 2003; Wan & Chiou, 2006; Wu, Scott, & Yang, 2013, for examples of such research studies). These contradictory research findings prompted Trivedi and Teichert (2017) to examine the potential relationship between the positive mental states of flow experiences and the negative consequences of addiction. Trivedi and Teichert chose online gambling as their activity of choice because some of its features are thought to support the flow experience in those that engage in the activity. These features of online gambling include its accessibility, convenience, disinhibition and anonymity features and instant reinforcement potential for players (Griffiths & Barnes, 2008; Griffiths, Davies, & Chappell, 2004; Scholes-Balog & Hemphill, 2012). The addictive nature of online gambling (Griffiths & Barnes, 2008) is said to be enhanced by the instant reinforcement the behaviour provides. Due to its easy accessibility, it also results in short time intervals between the gambling behaviours, which is thought to facilitate the increase in the frequency and time spent engaging in the behaviour online, compared to that engaged by offline gamblers, in casinos for example (Gainsbury et al., 2015;

King & Barak, 1999). Trivedi and Teichert (2017) reported that a sense of control, which is thought to typify the flow state, was negatively associated with online problematic gambling, while the behaviour was positively enhanced by the two flow state features of transformation of time and the behaviour being a means-to-an-end in itself (also referred to as an autotelic experience). The findings of this study provide some valuable empirical support for the anecdotal accounts of athletes (and others with such online gambling problems), who often report a feeling of not being in control of their behaviour, but also of the activity being absorbing in terms of the passage of time (The Irish Times, 2012). So, having detailed some of the characteristics identified for online gambling behaviour, what are the specific risk factors and prevalence rates of the behaviour, again considering athlete populations?

Athletes do possess some of the risk factors associated with problematic gambling behaviour, in general, namely, their typically young age and their sensation seeking tendencies (Grall-Bronnec et al., 2016; Hu, Zhen, Yu, Zhang, & Zhang, 2017). Gambling as an issue for athletes is not a new phenomenon. For example, Ellenbogen, Jacobs, Derevensky, Gupta, and Paskus (2008) reported, in a study of nearly 21,000 student athletes, that 62.4% of males and 43% of females reported gambling, although only small percentages of these individuals considered themselves to be engaged in problematic gambling behaviours (4.3% of males and only 0.4% of females). Within general populations, across many countries, the majority of individuals who gamble online are reported to be male (Hing et al., 2017). Unsurprisingly, the number of individuals who present as having problematic online gambling behaviours are also typically male (although more females may be presenting with such behaviours in more recent times; The Irish Times, 2017). Perhaps then it is unsurprising that young male athletes are regarded as being at a higher risk of displaying such problematic online gambling behaviours.

Sport type may also be a risk factor in determining whether or not problematic gambling behaviour is likely to occur. For example, young male collegiate athletes in high-profile sports in the United States, such as American football and baseball, reported higher levels of problematic gambling than athletes from lower-profile sports such as volleyball and athletics (Ellenbogen et al., 2008). These percentages in 2008 were higher than the general population, where rates of excessive gambling behaviours had been reported as ranging only between 0.15% and 6.6%.

Five years on from Ellenbogen et al.'s (2008) study, in 2013, St-Pierre, Temcheff, Gupta, Deverensky and Paskus also published findings of their research study on the gambling behaviours of 7,517 US NCAA student athletes. Interestingly, their findings indicated that the fun, or enjoyment, element often thought to be associated with such gambling behaviour (Nower & Blaszczynski, 2010) was not evident in their participants who displayed problematic gambling behaviours. Such individuals did, however, indicate expectations of financial gains from the behaviour, more so than their non-problematic gambling peers. However, such student athletes would not typically have the same amount of surplus income as their professional athlete comparisons. It would be interesting to see if such motivations existed for professional groups.

In 2016, Grall-Bronnec et al. were among the first to study the gambling behaviours of (1,236) European professional athletes. Their participants included athletes from a diverse number of individual and team sports such as professional ice hockey, rugby, handball, basketball, football, volleyball, and cricket, from countries such as Spain, France, Greece, Ireland, Italy, Sweden, and the United Kingdom. Grall-Bronnec et al. (2016) cited prevalence of what was considered problematic gambling at 8.2%. They also reported that problem gambling professional athletes were more likely to gamble online, citing the attractiveness of such technology for their young adult sample as a reason for this preference, along with the more addictive characteristics of online gambling, when compared to offline gambling (Griffiths, Wardle, Orford, Sproston, & Erens, 2009), as well as to alleviate boredom when such athletes were travelling and waiting around between training sessions (reasons already mentioned for such behaviours). However, online gambling is only one way such athletes may choose to spend such downtime. Other behaviours that could become problematic for them include excessive online gaming, which is addressed next.

10.5.4 Excessive online gaming

Online gaming has become popular within the last two decades as a form of entertainment (Yani-de-Soriano, Javed, & Yousafzai, 2012). This trend has been facilitated by greater access to high-speed Internet, especially among younger generations (Hu et al., 2017). The revenue such online gaming activities generate is extensive, with growth in the past five years, from 2012 to 2017, estimated at over 20 billion dollars (from 28.32 billion dollars to 49.64 billion dollars, reported by the Global Betting and Gaming Consultancy; GBGC, 2013).

The use of the term 'Internet gaming addiction' has sparked much debate within the cyberpsychology research community in recent times, with some questioning the legitimacy of such a disorder. As a result, the term 'problematic gaming' has been offered as a more helpful term (Errity, Rooney, & Tunney, 2016). Given this apparent lack of agreement among researchers regarding this issue, more research to identify if online gaming can actually be addictive in nature, in the same way that other activities, such as gambling have been considered, is warranted.

But this position aside, online gaming has definite attractions for athletes, especially when one considers the reasons why individuals report gaming in the first incidence. For example, in 2006, Wan and Chiou asked ten Taiwanese teens, considered to be 'addicted to gaming', why they engaged in the activity. The four main reasons these teens reported for gaming were: (i) the challenge it provided, (ii) the excitement it generated, (iii) the emotional coping it afforded them and (iv) the escape from reality it provided them with from their daily lives. Interestingly, culture and societal differences have also been reported with regard to what is considered excessive gaming behaviour. For example, Kuss (2013) reported that, in Korea, the rates of 'addiction to gaming' could be as high as 50%, while in Germany the rates could be as low as 0.2% of their online game playing population. Why should such wide ranging differences exist in some countries for what is considered problematic online game playing? Such cultural differences need to be explored in more depth. However, recall in Chapter 3 how some online gaming was reported as helpful within some athletic settings, especially with regard to mental skills training (Ramsey, Tangermann, Haufe, & Blankertz, 2009; Spence & Feng, 2010). When is such an activity considered to have turned pathological? Some have suggested that sensation seeking, often linked to athlete populations (Hu et al., 2017), could play a key role in the development of problematic online gaming behaviour.

Hu et al. (2017) examined if such a link between sensation seeking and online gaming behaviours did indeed exist. They recruited young male Chinese adolescents and their study was considered one of the first studies to apply the dual systems model to online gaming behaviours in young adolescents. The dual systems model was proposed to explain the problematic behaviours often seen in young adolescents (Steinberg, 2010). Such behaviours are considered to be a function of an immature limbic system seen in such populations. Hu et al. (2017) reported that "high sensation seeking was associated with high levels of positive affective (emotional) associations with online games, which subsequently was associated with a high likelihood of online gaming addiction" (p. 4). However, Hu et al. emphasised the need for further study in this area, as causal conclusions between sensation seeking and problematic online gaming have not been definitely established. They also encouraged others to expand their participant groups to include females and other nationalities beyond the Chinese population they sampled from (for a more detailed review of problematic online gaming, see Griffiths, 2015). A similar study to Hu et al.'s, using athletes as the participant group, has not been reported to date. However, such a study would be welcomed if it could help to identify at-risk groups within such specific populations also. Another interesting point in relation to such online gaming behaviour could centre round the arguments surfacing for the recognition of virtual athletes who play *e-sports* and, therefore, are required to spend a lot of their time gaming online (Jenny, Manning, Keiper, & Olrich, 2016). There have even been calls for the inclusion of s-sports in global sport events such as the Olympic Games (Armen Graham, 2017; see Hamari & Sjöblom, 2017, and Jenny et al., 2016, for a review of this new type of virtual sport and virtual athlete).

10.6 Current strategies employed to help athletes overcome problematic online behaviours

As mentioned previously, one of the reasons all of the preceding problematic behaviours may occur for athletes is because of the difference in their work-day schedules. One way to combat the issue of *boredom*, discussed previously for such athletes, is perhaps for sport clubs and organisations to insist their athletes engage in some after-training educational programmes or work placements in order to prevent large time gaps within their daily schedules. If such times are not filled with productive worthwhile activities, athletes may fill their leisure or travel times with some of the problematic online behaviours discussed previously (Grall-Bronnec et al., 2016).

Other problematic behaviours also exist in the online world for athletes, such as problematic information seeking by athletes regarding banned supplements (referred to in Chapter 6) and restrictive dieting. Detailed discussions of such issues are beyond the scope of this edition of *Sport Cyberpsychology*, unfortunately. However, other researchers interested in this newly proposed area of sport cyberpsychology study are very much encouraged to carry out research in these areas with athlete populations in order to support vulnerable athletes at risk of such practices, which the cyber world has been shown to sometimes facilitate (Kirwan, 2015).

More education for athletes, regarding the risks and observable signs associated with the problematic online behaviours discussed in this chapter, is also called for so that these athletes can recognise the symptoms in their teammates and also in themselves, and then seek out the appropriate help and support which their organisations should make them aware of. Athletes' support personnel (e.g., coaches, parents and medical staff) should also be trained to recognise such problematic behaviours early on so that they too can refer the athletes for appropriate professional help when needed (Figure 10.1). Cognitive behavioural therapy and some cybertherapy, such as online counselling, may also be considered and offered to athletes who experience difficulties with their mental health and/or their problematic online behaviours (Flood, 2016; Young, 2011).

10.7 Conclusion, including future directions for research

Some of the interesting topics for future research in this area of problematic online behaviour for athletes could include more empirical research to determine the extent of the problems highlighted in this chapter specifically, among athlete populations, across different sports and cultures. Online gambling as a specific problem for athletes has been the focus of much discussion in recent times due to the increased interest in the impact of the transition period for elite athletes from their sport careers into other second careers, as well as the increased interest in the general mental health and well-being of athletes globally. Athletes, especially males, are starting to speak out about such problems they have experienced (Gleeson & Brady, 2017; Orpen, 2015). However, with increased professional opportunities for elite female athletes, is it possible that these more typical 'male' problems, such as online gambling, could become risk factors for female athlete groups too (The Irish Times, 2012). Research in this area would be most welcome. Such is the potential seriousness and risk of developing online gambling addiction, some researchers have called for it to be banned (Smith & Rupp, 2005), while others have suggested more legislation to limit its potential reach (Smeaton & Griffiths, 2004). While the banning of such activities is unlikely, given the revenue they generate as well as the positive outcomes with regard to entertainment they provide in healthy doses, awareness, education and treatment options would appear to remain the best ways to manage such problems in vulnerable athletic groups.

FIGURE 10.1 Former professional rugby player, Niall Breslin, being awarded an Honorary Fellowship for his work as a mental health advocate (pictured with film director, Lenny Abrahamson, who was also honoured) by the Institute of Art, Design + Technology (IADT), Dún Laoghaire in November 2016

Source: Courtesy of the Institute of Art, Design + Technology (IADT), Dún Laoghaire, with thanks to Niall Breslin and Lenny Abrahamson.

However, the online world has provided so many positive opportunities for athletes across their sport lives, as well as their everyday lives, and their post-sport careers too, that perhaps it is appropriate to return to the opening quote of this text where Wiederhold (cited in Connolly, Palmer, Barton, & Kirwan, 2016, p. xix) commented on the words of Carl Jung: "Technology . . . is neutral. It is how we use that technology that determines whether it will be positive or negative".

10.8 Open-ended discussion questions

1   How has online gambling facilitated the problematic behaviours of gambling addiction, especially among successful young male athletes?
2   How can technology and cybertherapy be best utilised to support and treat athletes who present with problematic online behaviours, such as excessive gambling and excessive gaming behaviours?

10.9 Practical exercise

Have your students consider the case of John presented at the start of this chapter again. How has the content of this chapter helped them to understand John's situation?

What approach might they now take to help one of their friends or teammates they suspect is also having such a difficulty with some problematic online activities?

References

Armen Graham, B. (2017). *eSports could be medal event at 2024 Olympics, Paris bid team says.* The Guardian. Retrieved from https://www.theguardian.com/sport/2017/aug/09/esports-2024-olympics-medal-event-paris-bid-committee

Bitton, M.S., & Medina, H.C. (2015). Problematic Internet use and sensation seeking: Differences between teens who live at home and in residential care. *Child Youth Service? Review?, 58,* 35–40. doi: 10.1016/j.childyouth2015.09.004

Block, J.J. (2008). Issues for DSM-V: Internet addiction. *American Journal of Psychiatry, 165,* 306–307.

Cam, E., & Isbulan, O. (2012). A new addiction for teacher candidates: Social networks. *Turkish Online Journal of Educational Technology, 11,* 14–19.

Caplan, S.E. (2002). Problematic Internet use and psychosocial well-being: Development of a theory-based cognitive-behavioural measurement instrument. *Computers in Human Behaviour, 18,* 553–575.

Caplan, S.E. (2007). Relations among loneliness, social anxiety, and problematic Internet use. *Cyberpsychology and Behaviour, 10,* 234–242. doi: 10.1089/cpb.2006.9963

Caplan, S.E. (2010). Theory and measurement of generalized problematic Internet use: A two-step approach. *Computer and Human Behaviour, 26,* 1089–1097. doi: 10.1016/j.chb.2010.03.012

Chou, T.J., & Ting, C.C. (2003). The role of flow experience in cyber-game addiction. *Cyberpsychology and Behaviour, 6,* 663–675.

Clough, P., Earle, K., & Sewell, D. (2002). Mental toughness: The concept and its measurements. In I. Cockerill (ed.), *Solutions in sport psychology* (pp. 32–45). London: Thomson.

Connolly, I., Palmer, M., Barton, B., & Kirwan, G. (Eds.). (2016). *An introduction to cyberpsychology.* London: Routledge.

Coulter, T., Mallett, C., & Gucciardi, D. (2010). Understanding mental toughness in Australian soccer: Perceptions of players, parents, and coaches. *Journal of Sports Sciences, 28,* 699–716. doi: 10.1080/02640411003734085

Cowden, R.G., Meyer-Weitz, A., & Oppong Asante, K. (2016). Mental toughness in competitive tennis: Relationships with resilience and stress. *Frontiers in Psychology, 7,* 320. doi: 10.3389/fpsyg.2016.00320

Csikszentmihalyi, M. (1975). Play and intrinsic rewards. *Journal of Humanistic Psychology, 15,* 41–63.

Ellenbogen, S., Jacobs, D., Derevensky, J., Gupta, R., & Paskus, T. (2008). Gambling behaviour among college student-athletes. *Journal of Applied Sport Psychology, 20,* 349–362.

Errity, A., Rooney, B., & Tunney, C. (2016). Gaming. In I. Connolly, M. Palmer, H. Barton, & G. Kirwan (Eds.), *An introduction to cyberpsychology* (pp. 257–270). London: Routledge.

Flood, C. (2016). Abnormal cyberpsychology and cybertherapy. In I. Connolly, M. Palmer, H. Barton, & G. Kirwan (Eds.), *An introduction to cyberpsychology* (pp. 153–166). London: Routledge.

Gainsbury, S.M., Russell, A., Hing, N., & Blaszczynski, A. (2013). How the Internet is changing gambling: Findings from an Australian prevalence survey. *Journal of Gambling Studies, 31,* 1–5.

Gainsbury, S.M., Russell, A., Wood, R., Hing, N., & Blaszczynski, A. (2015). How risky is Internet gambling? A comparison of subgroups of Internet gamblers based on problem gambling status. *New Media & Society, 17,* 861–879. doi: 10.1177/1461444813518185

Gillick, D. (2017). *When people said I should go talk to someone, I told them to shut up. I thought I was right, but I was weak and lost*. Retrieved from www.the42.ie/david-gillick-mental-health-interview-3350266-Apr2017/

Gleeson, S., & Brady, E. (2017). *When athletes share their battles with mental illness*. Retrieved from www.usatoday.com/story/sports/2017/08/30/michael-phelps-brandon-marshall-mental-health-battles-royce-white-jerry-west/596857001/

Global Betting and Gaming Consultancy (GBGC). (2013). *Interactive gambling report*. GBGC, Isle of Man.

Gouttebarge, V., Backx, F.J.G., Aoki, H., & Kerkhoffs, G.M.M.J. (2015). Symptoms of common mental disorders in professional football (soccer) across five European countries. *Journal of Sports Science & Medicine, 14*, 811–818.

Grall-Bronnec, M., Caillon, J., Humeau, E., Perrot, B., Remund, M., Guilleux, A., Rocher, B., Sauvaget, A., & Bouiu, G. (2016). Gambling among European professional athletes: Prevalence and associated factors. *Journal of Addictive Diseases, 35*, 278–290.

Griffiths, G. (2012). Facebook addiction: Concerns, criticisms and recommendations. *Psychological Reports, 110*, 518–520.

Griffiths, M., Wardle, H., Orford, J., Sproston, K., & Erens, B. (2009). Sociodemographic correlates of Internet gambling: Findings from the 2007 British gambling prevalence survey. *CyberPsychology & Behavior, 12*, 199–202. doi: 10.1089/cpb.2008.0196

Griffiths, M.D. (2005). A 'components' model of addiction within a biopsychosocial framework. *Journal of Substance Abuse, 10*, 191–197.

Griffiths, M.D. (2013). Social networking addiction: Emerging themes and issues. *Journal of Addiction Research and Therapy, 4*, e118. doi: 10.4172/2155–6105.1000e118

Griffiths, M.D. (2015). The psychology of online addictive behaviour. In A. Attrill (Ed.), *Cyberpsychology* (pp. 183–196). New York: Oxford University Press.

Griffiths, M.D., & Barnes, A. (2008). Internet gambling: An online empirical study among student gamblers. *International Journal of Mental Health and Addiction, 6*, 194–204.

Griffiths, M.D., Davies, M.N., & Chappell, D. (2004). Demographic factors and playing variables in online computer gaming. *Cyberpsychology and Behaviour, 7*, 479–487.

Griffiths, M.D., Kuss, D.J., & Demetrovics, Z. (2014). Social networking addiction: An overview of preliminary findings. In K. P. Rosenberg & C. Feder (Eds.), *Behavioral addictions: Criteria, evidence, and treatment* (pp. 119–141). London: Academic Press.

Gulliver, A., Griffiths, K.M., Mackinnon, A., Batterham, P.J., & Stanimirovic, R. (2015). The mental health of Australian elite athletes. *Journal of Science and Medicine in Sport, 18*, 255–261.

Gupta, R., & Derevensky, J. (1998). Adolescent gambling behaviour: A prevalence study and examination of the correlates associated with problem gambling. *Journal of Gambling Studies, 14*, 319–345.

Hamari, J., & Sjöblom, M. (2017). What is e-sports and why do people watch it? *Internet Research, 27*, 211–232. doi: 10.1108/IntR-04-2016-0085

Harris. (2014). *Gambling addiction a threat to for Premier League stars as new study shows professional sportsmen three times more likely to be 'problem gamblers'*. Retrieved from www.dailymail.co.uk/sport/football/article-2858934/Gambling-addiction-threat-Premier-League-stars-new-study-shows-professional-sportsmen-three-times-likely-problem-gamblers.html

Hing, N., Russell, A.M., & Browne, M. (2017). Risk factors for gambling problems on online electronic gaming machines, race betting and sports betting. *Frontiers in Psychology, 8*, 779. doi: 10.3389/fpyg.2017.00779

Hing, N., Russell, A.M.T., Gainbury, S.M., & Blaszczynski, A. (2014). Characteristics and help-seeking behaviours of Internet gamblers based on most problematic mode of gambling. *Journal of Medical Internet Research, 17*, e13. doi: 10.2196/jmir.3781

Hu, J., Zhen, S., Yu, C., Zhang, Q., & Zhang, W. (2017). Sensation seeking and online gaming addiction: A moderated mediation model of positive affective associations and impulsivity. *Frontiers in Psychology, 8,* 699. doi: 10.3389/psyg.2017.00699

Hughes, L., & Leavey, G. (2012). Setting the bar: Athletes and vulnerability to mental illness. *British Journal of Psychiatry, 200,* 95–96.

The Irish Times. (2012). *A silent addiction rife within sport.* Retrieved from www.irishtimes.com/news/a-silent-addiction-rife-within-sport-1.547130

Jang, K.S., Hwang, S.Y., & Chio, J.Y. (2008). Internet addiction and psychiatric symptoms among Korean adolescents. *Journal of School Health, 78,* 165, 171.

Jenero, C., Flores, N., Gomez-Vela, M., Gonzalez-Gill, F., & Caballo, C. (2007). Problematic Internet and cell-phone use: Psychological behavioural and health correlates. *Addiction Research & Theory, 15,* 309–320.

Jenny, S.E., Manning, D.R., Keiper, M.C., & Olrich, T.W. (2016). Virtual(ly) athletes: Where eSports fit within the definition of 'Sport'. *Quest.* Retrieved from http://dx.doi.org/10.1080/00336297.2016.114517

Kessler, R.C., Hwang, I., LaBrie, R., Petukhova, M., Sampson, N.A., Winters, K.C., & Schaffer, H.J. (2008). DSM-IV pathological gambling in the National Comorbidity Survey Replication. *Psychological Medicine, 38,* 1351–1360.

King, S.A., & Barak, A. (1999). Compulsive Internet gambling: A new form of an old clinical pathology. *Cyberpsychology and Behaviour, 2,* 441–456.

Kirwan, G. (2015). Health psychology online. In A. Attrill (ed.), *Cyberpsychology* (pp. 164–182). Oxford, UK: Oxford University Press.

Kirwan, G., & Power, A. (2014). What is cyberpsychology? In A. Power & G. Kirwan (Eds.), *Cyberpsychology and new media: A thematic reader* (pp. 3–14). London: Psychology Press: Taylor and Francis Group.

Koc, M., & Gulyagci, S. (2013). Facebook addiction among Turkish college students: The role of psychological health, demographic, and usage characteristics. *Cyberpsychology, Behaviour and Social Networking, 16,* 279–284.

Kuss, D.J. (2013). Internet gaming addiction: Current perspectives. *Psychology Research and Behaviour Management, 3,* 125–137.

Lebrun, F., & Collins, D. (2017). Is elite sport (really) bad for you? Can we answer the question? *Frontiers in Psychology, 8,* 324. doi: 10.3389/fpsyg2017.00324

Li, D., Zhang, W., Zhen, S., & Wnag, Y. (2010). Stressful life events and problematic Internet use by adolescent females and males: A mediated moderation model. *Computers in Human Behaviour, 26,* 1199–1207.

Li, W., O'Brien, J.E., Snyder, S.M., & Howard, M.O. (2015). Characteristics of Internet addiction/pathological Internet use in U.S. university students: A qualitative-method investigation. *PLoS One, 10*(2), e0117372. doi: 10.1371/journal.pone.0117372

Li, X., Newman, J., Li, D., & Zhang, H. (2016). Temperament and adolescent problematic Internet use: The mediating role of deviant peer affiliation. *Computers in Human Behaviour, 60,* 342–350. doi: 10.1016/j.chb.2016.02.075

Luthar, S., Cicchetti, D., & Becker, B. (2000). The construct of resilience: A critical evaluation and guidelines for future work. *Child Development, 71,* 543–562.

MacNamara, Á., & Collins, D. (2015). Profiling, exploiting, and countering psychological characteristics in talent identification and development. *Sport Psychology, 29,* 73–81. doi: 10.1123/tsp.2014–0021

Martin, A.J., & Jackson, S.A. (2008). Brief approaches to assessing task absorption and enhanced subjective experience: Examining 'short' and 'core' flow in diverse performance domains. *Motivation and Emotion, 32,* 141–157.

Moran, A., & Toner, J. (2017). *A critical introduction to sport psychology.* London: Routledge.

Nower, L., & Blaszczynski, A. (2010). Gambling motivations, money-limiting strategies, and precommitment preferences of problem versus non-problem gamblers. *Journal of Gambling Studies, 26*, 361–372. doi:10.1007/s10899-009-9170-8

Orpen, J. (2015). *Former GAA star Oisin McConville on his gambling addiction: 'I felt as if the walls were closing in on me and I became suicidal'*. Retrieved from www.independent. ie/life/health-wellbeing/health-features/former-gaa-star-oisin-mcconville-on-his-gam bling-addiction-i-felt-as-if-the-walls-were-closing-in-on-me-and-i-became-suicidal-30851965.html

Porter, J., Ungar, J., Frisch, R.G., & Chorpra, R. (2004). Loneliness and life dissatisfaction in gamblers. *Journal of Gambling Issues, 11*. doi: 10.4309/jgi.2004.11.13

Ramsey, L., Tangermann, M., Haufe, S., & Blankertz, B. (2009). *Practising fast decision BCI using a 'goalkeeper' paradigm*. Poster presentation at the Eighteenth Annual Computational Neuroscience Meeting, on 18–23 July, Berlin, Germany.

Rice, S.M., Purcell, R., De Silva, S., Mawren, D., McGorry, P.D., & Parker, A.G. (2016). The mental health of elite athletes: A narrative systematic review. *Sports Medicine, 46*, 1333–1353. doi: 10.1007/s40279-016-0492-2

Sarkar, M., & Fletcher, D. (2017). Adversity-related experiences are essential for Olympic success: Additional evidence and considerations. *Progress in Brain Research, 232*, 159–165.

Scholes-Balog, K.E., & Hemphill, S.A. (2012). Relationships between online gambling, mental health, and substance use: A review. *Cyberpsychology, Behaviour and Social Networking, 15*, 688–692.

Schuler, J., & Brunner, S. (2009). The rewarding effect of flow experience on performance in a marathon race. *Psychology of Sport & Exercise, 10*, 168–174.

Smeaton, M., & Griffiths, M. (2004). Internet gambling and social responsibility: An exploratory study. *Cyberpsychology and Behaviour, 7*, 49–57.

Smith, A.D., & Rupp, W.T. (2005). Service marketing aspects associated with the allure of e-gambling. *Service Marketing Quarterly, 26*, 83–103.

Somerville, L.H., Jones, R.M., & Casey, B. (2010). A rime of change: Behavioural and neural correlates of adolescent sensitivity to appetitive and aversive environmental cues. *Brain and Cognition, 72*, 124–133.

Spence, I., & Feng, J. (2010). Video games and spatial cognition. *Review of General Psychology, 14*, 92–104.

Steinberg, I. (2010). A dual systems model of adolescent risk-taking. *Developmental Psychobiology, 52*, 216–224.

Ste-Marie, C., Gupta, R., & Derevensky, J. (2002). Anxiety and social stress related to adolescent gambling behaviour. *International Gambling Studies, 2*, 123–141.

St-Pierre, R.A., Temcheff, C., Gupta, R., Deverensky, J.L., & Paskus, T.S. (2013). Predicting gambling problems from gambling outcome expectancies in college student-athletes. *Journal of Gambling Behaviour, 30*, 47–60.

Swann, C., Piggott, D., Crust, L., Keegan, R., & Hemmings, B. (2015). Exploring the interactions underlying flow states: A connecting analysis of flow occurrence in European Tour golfers. *Psychology of Sport & Exercise, 16*, 60–69.

Thompson, R.A., & Sherman, R. (2014). Reflections on athletes and eating disorders. *Psychology of Sport & Exercise, 15*, 729–734. doi: 10.1016/j.psychsport.2014. 06.005

Trivedi, R.H., & Teichert, T. (2017). The Janus-faced role of gambling flow in addiction issues. *Cyberpsychology, Behaviour and Social Networking, 20*, 180–186.

Wan, C.S., & Chiou, W.B. (2006). Why are adolescents addicted to online gaming? An interview study in Taiwan. *Cyberpsychology & Behaviour, 9*, 762–766.

Williams, M. (2017). *Matt Williams: Dan Vickerman's death highlights the dangers of silence*. Retrieved from www.irishtimes.com/sport/rugby/international/matt-williams-dan-vickerman-s-death-highlights-dangers-of-silence-1.2987793

Wood, R.T., & Williams, R.J. (2007). Problem gambling on the Internet: Implications for Internet gambling policy in North America. *New Media & Society, 9*, 520–542.

Wood, R.T., & Williams, R.J. (2009). *Internet gambling: Prevalence, patterns, problems, and policy options.* Final report prepared for the Ontario Problem Gambling Research Centre, Guelph, ON.

Wu, T.C., Scott, D., & Yang, C.C. (2013). Advanced or addicted? Exploring the relationship of recreation specialization to flow experiences and online game addiction. *Leisure Sciences, 35*, 203–217.

Yani-de-Soriano, M., Javed, U., & Yousafzai, S. (2012). Can an industry be socially responsible if its products harm consumers? The case of online gambling. *Journal of Business Ethics, 110*, 481–497.

Young, K.S. (1998). Internet addiction: The emergence of a new clinical disorder. *Cyberpsychology & Behaviour, 1*, 237–244. doi: 10.1089/cpb.1998.1.237

Young, K.S. (2011). CBT-IA: The first treatment model for Internet addiction. *Journal of Cognitive Psychotherapy, 25*, 304–312.

INDEX

Note: Page numbers in italics indicate figures and page numbers in bold indicate tables.